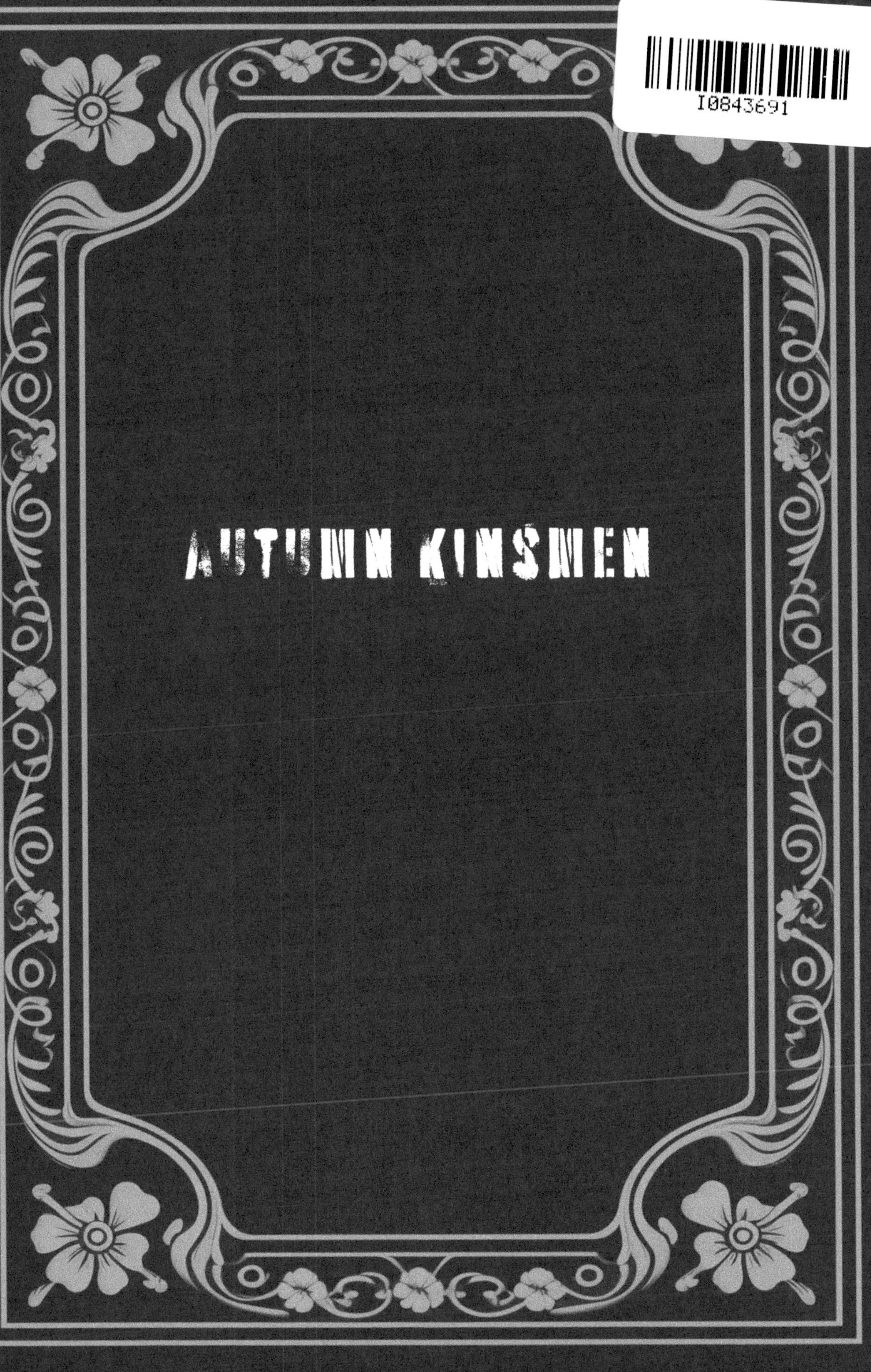

AUTUMN KINSMEN

And thou art dead, as young and fair
As aught of mortal birth;
And form so soft, and and charms so rare,
Too soon return'd to Earth!

Lord Byron

Contents

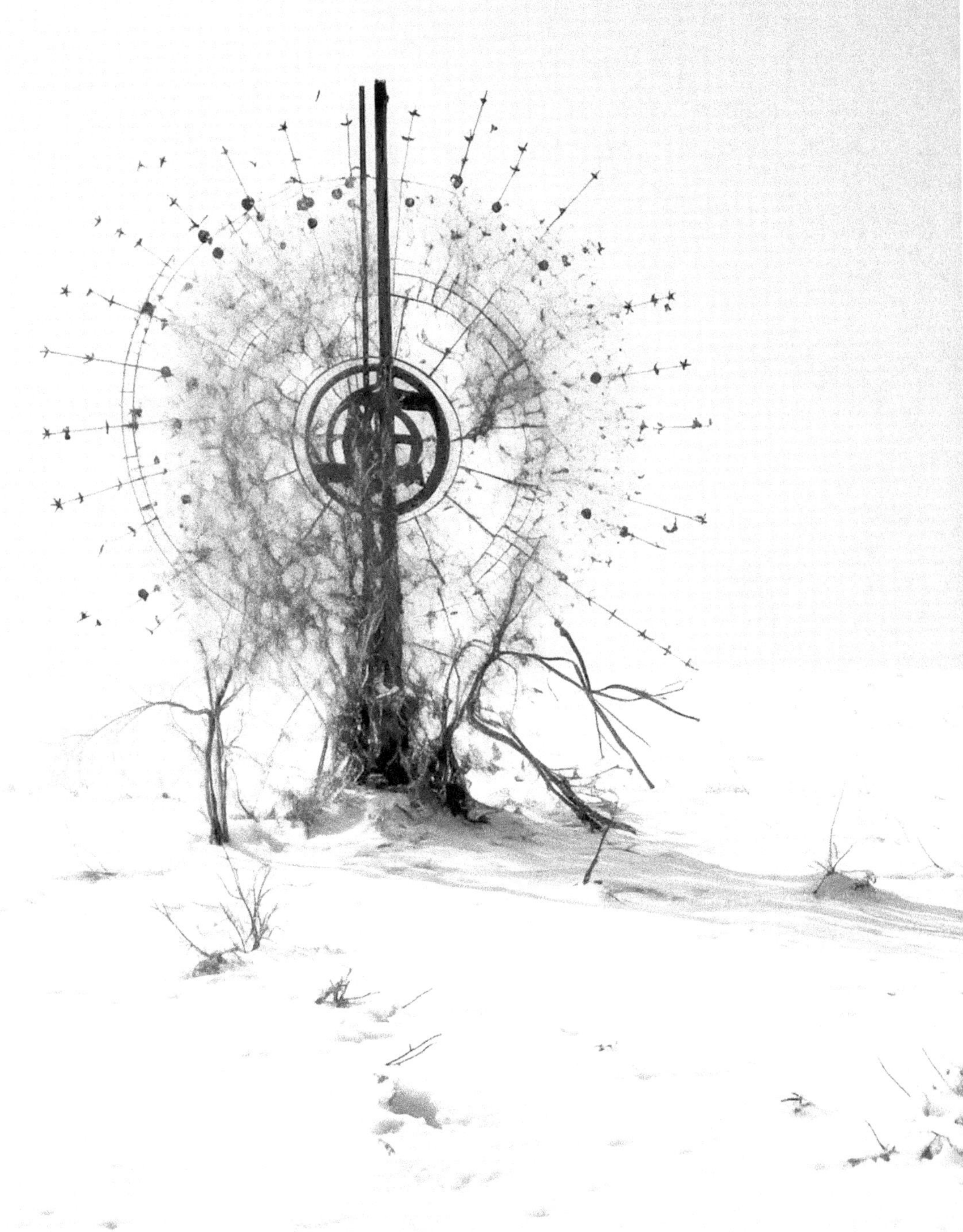

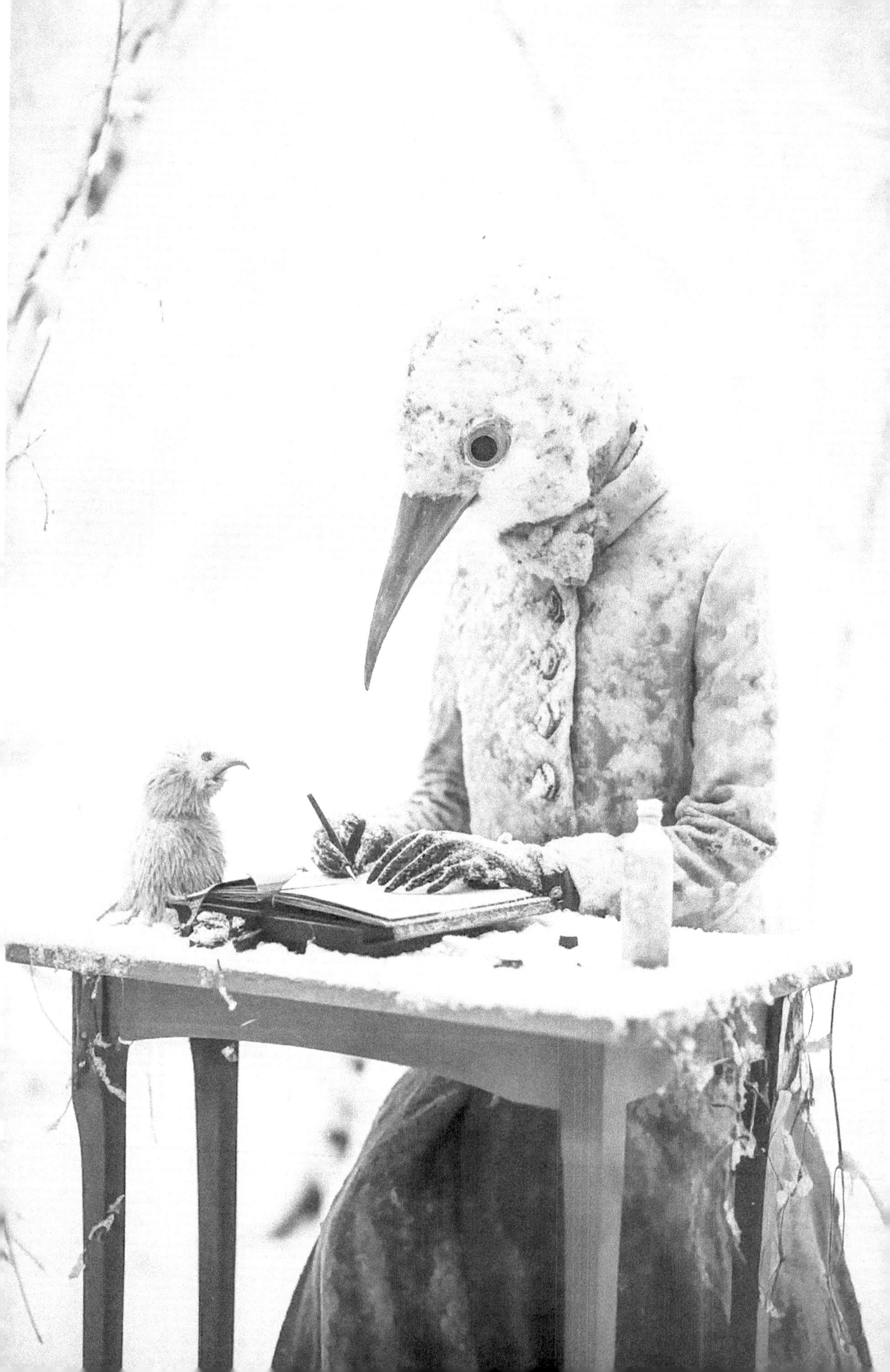

IN THE FADING
DAYLIGHT,
THE CONTOURS
OF REFLECTION
BECOME
SHARPER.

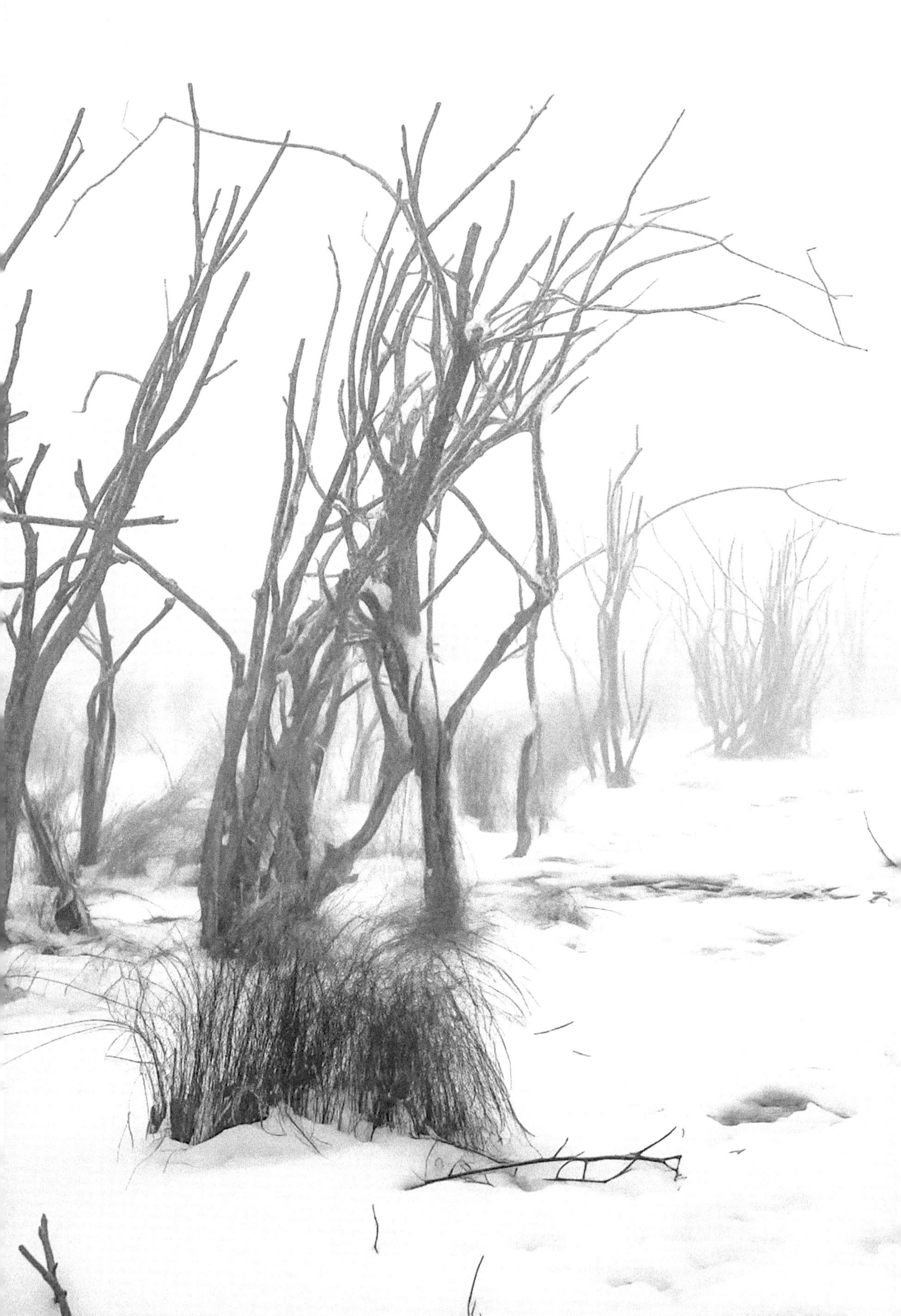

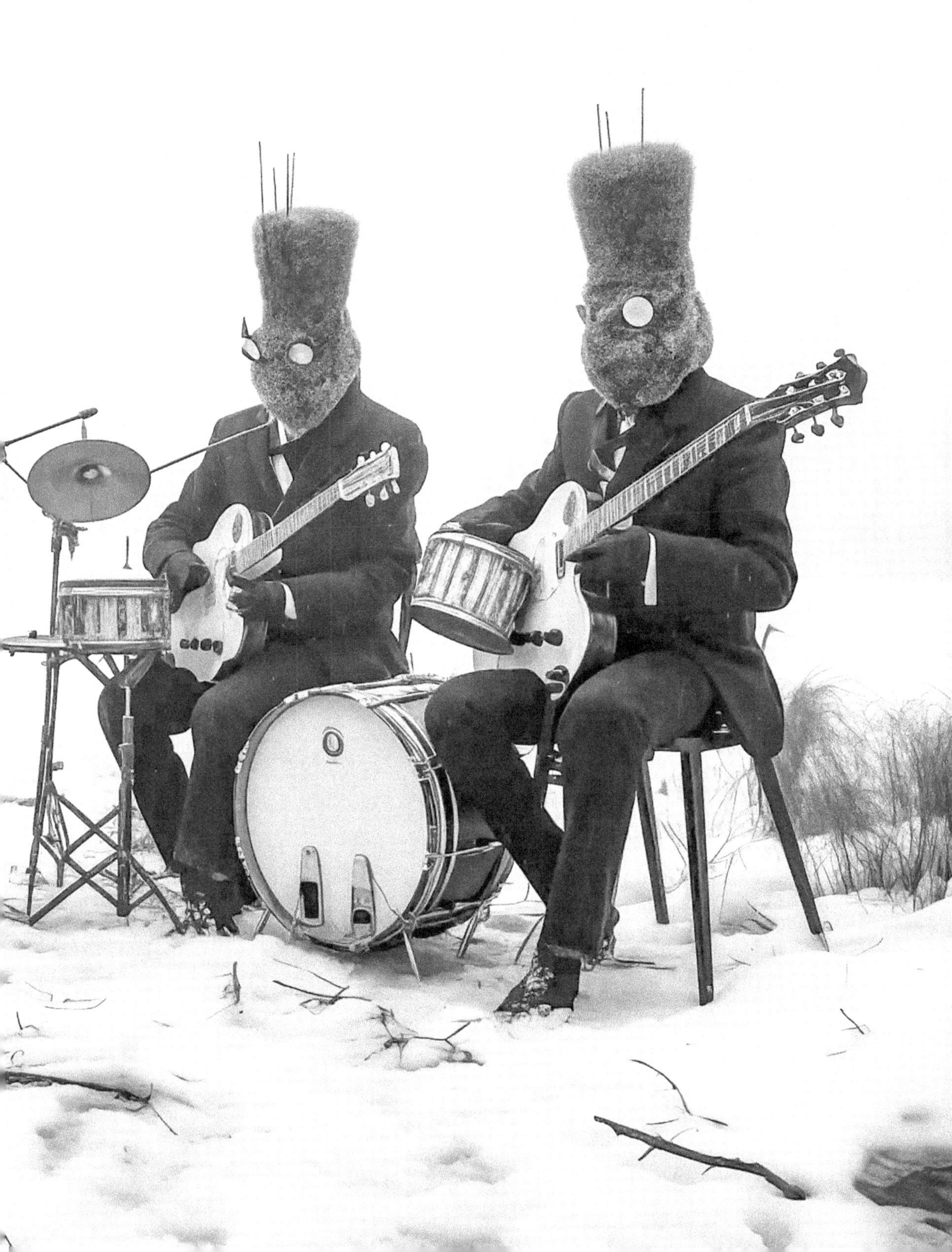

ip the
bright nectar
of winter.

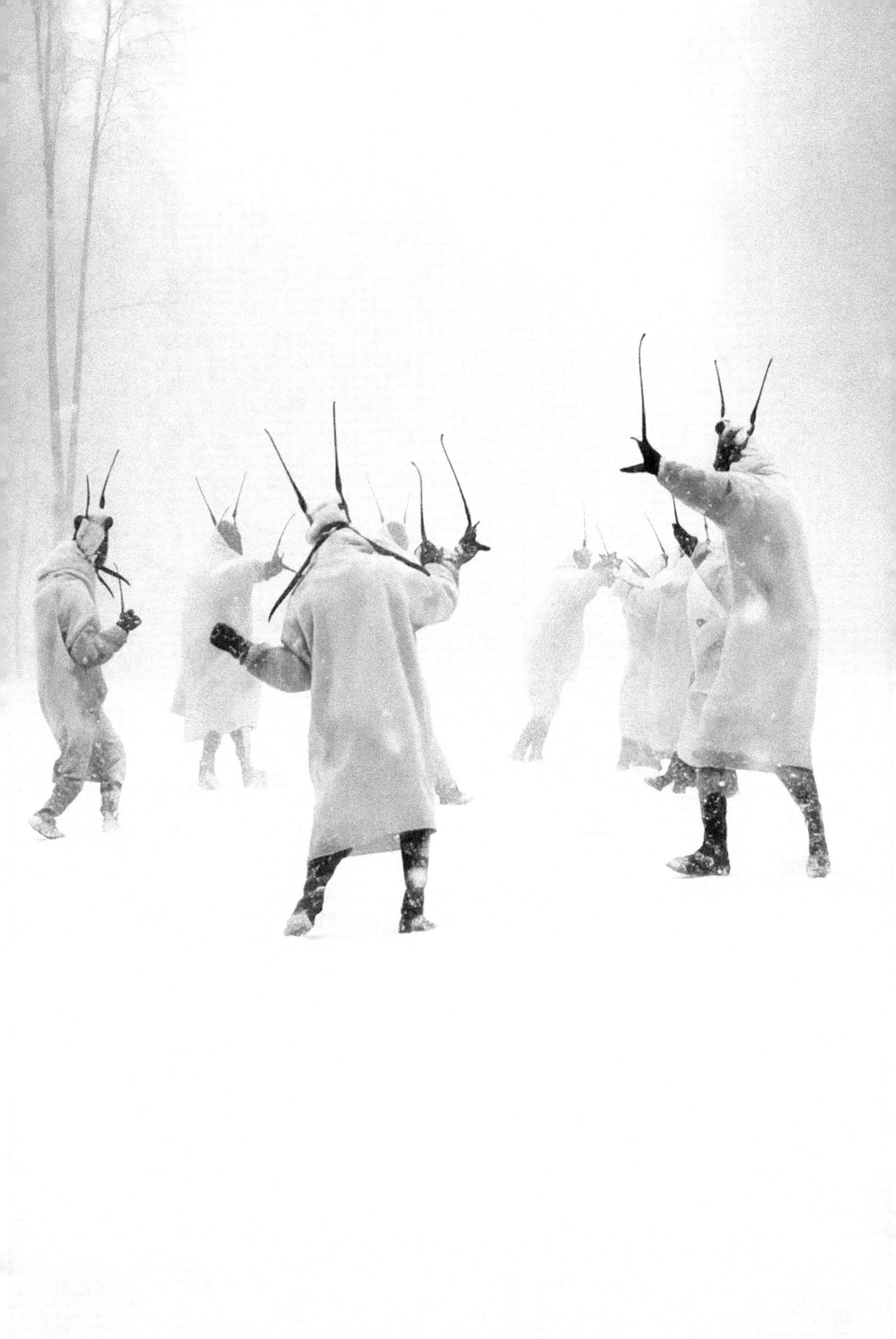

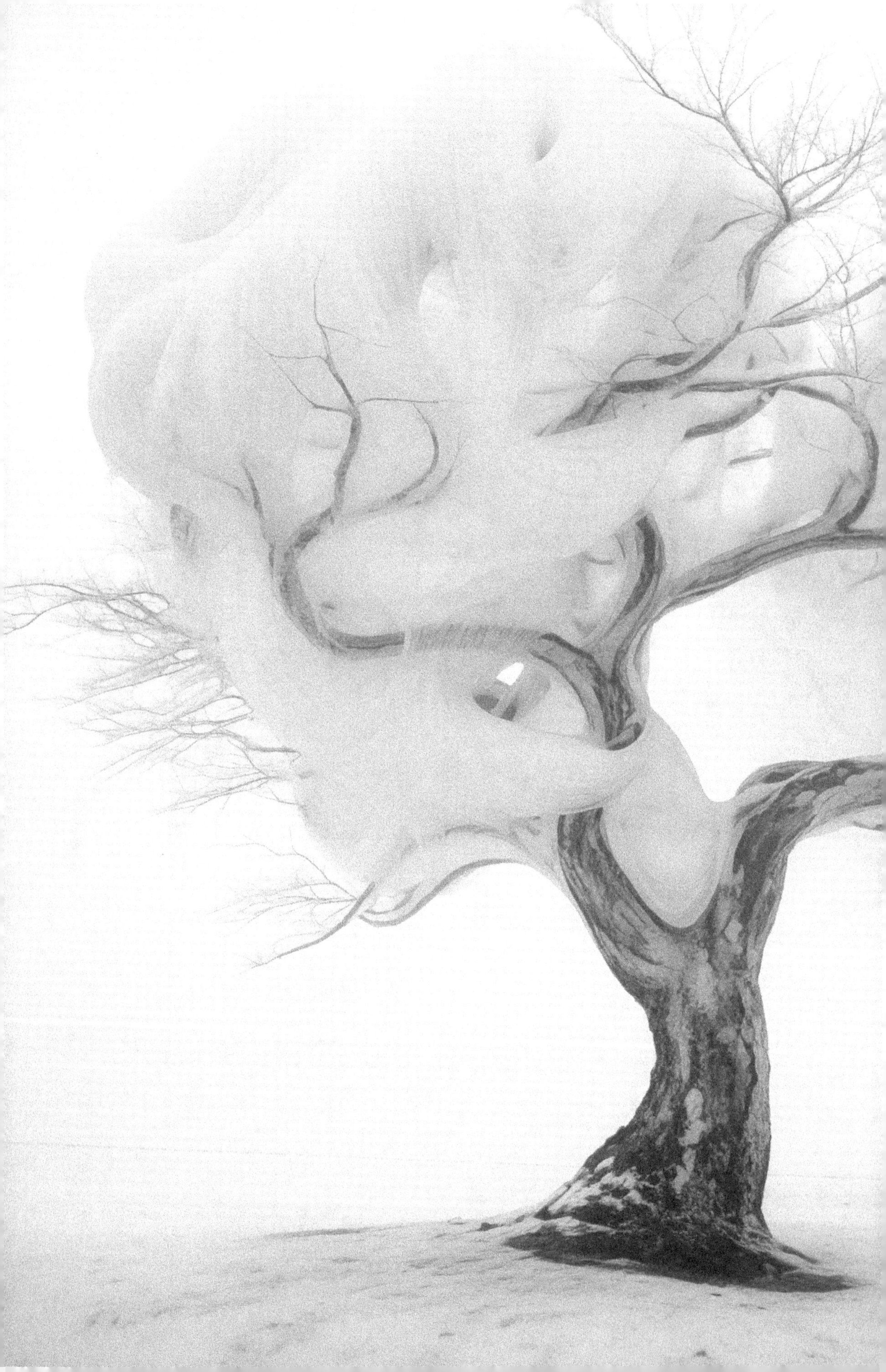

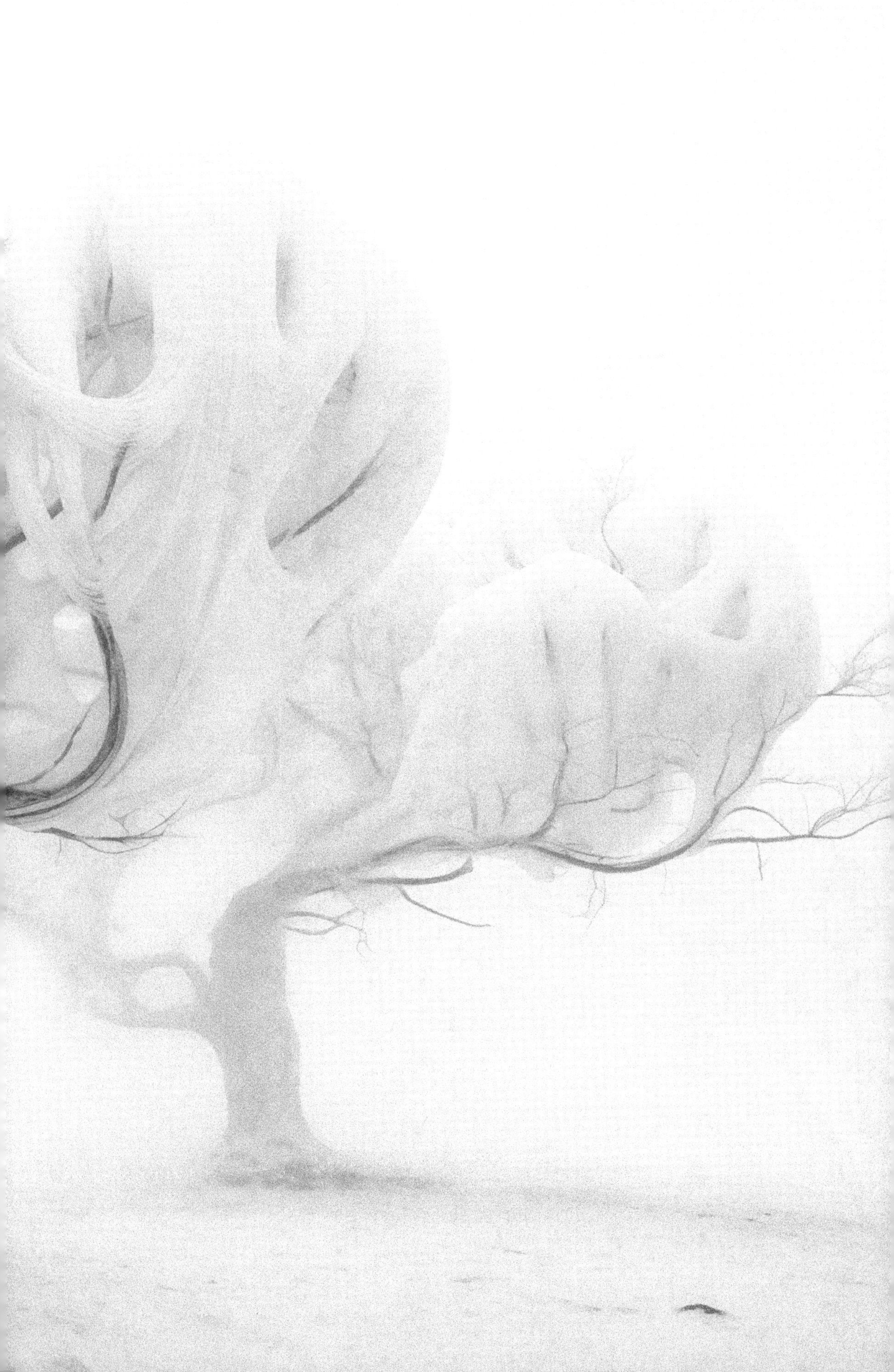

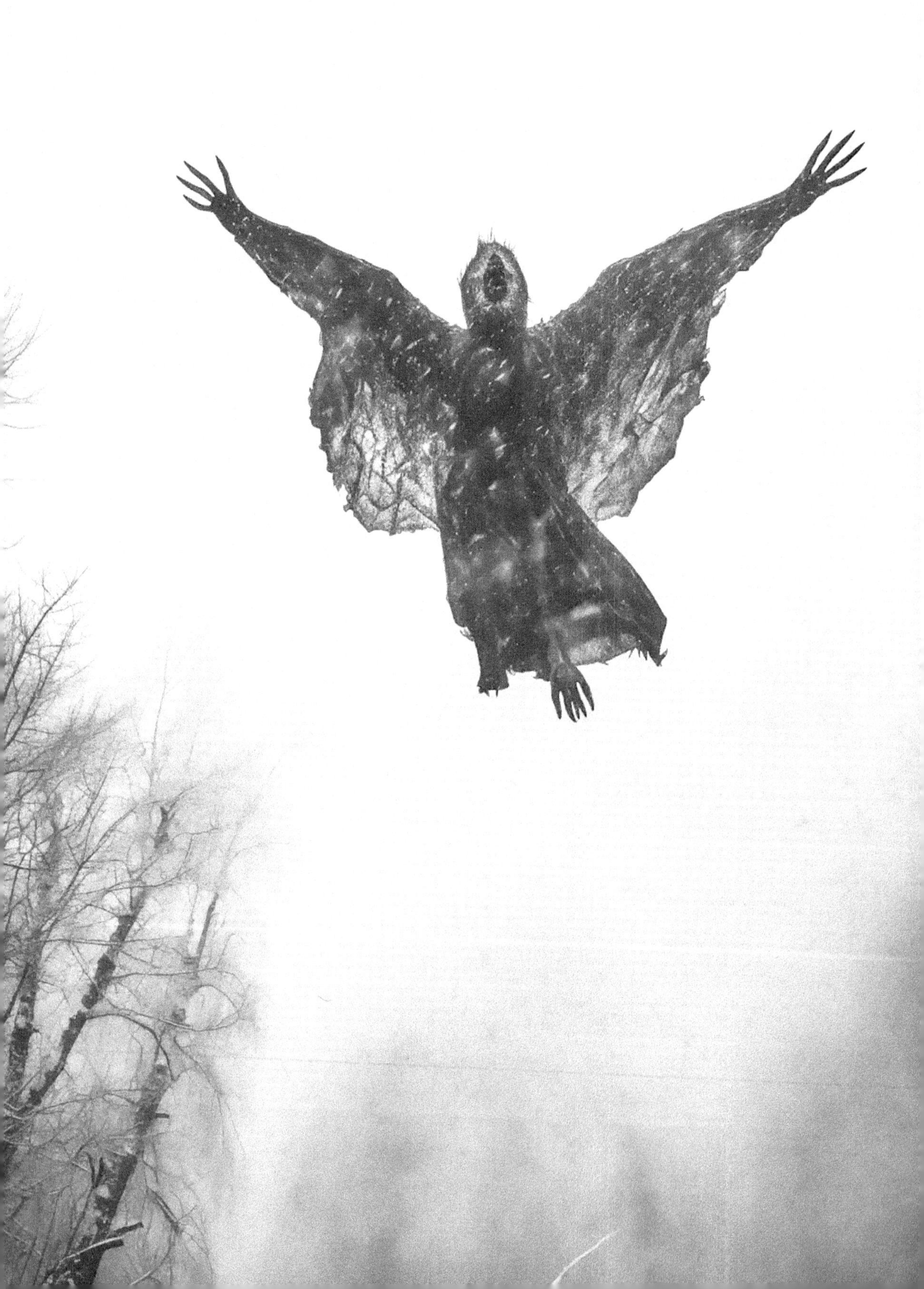

DREAM

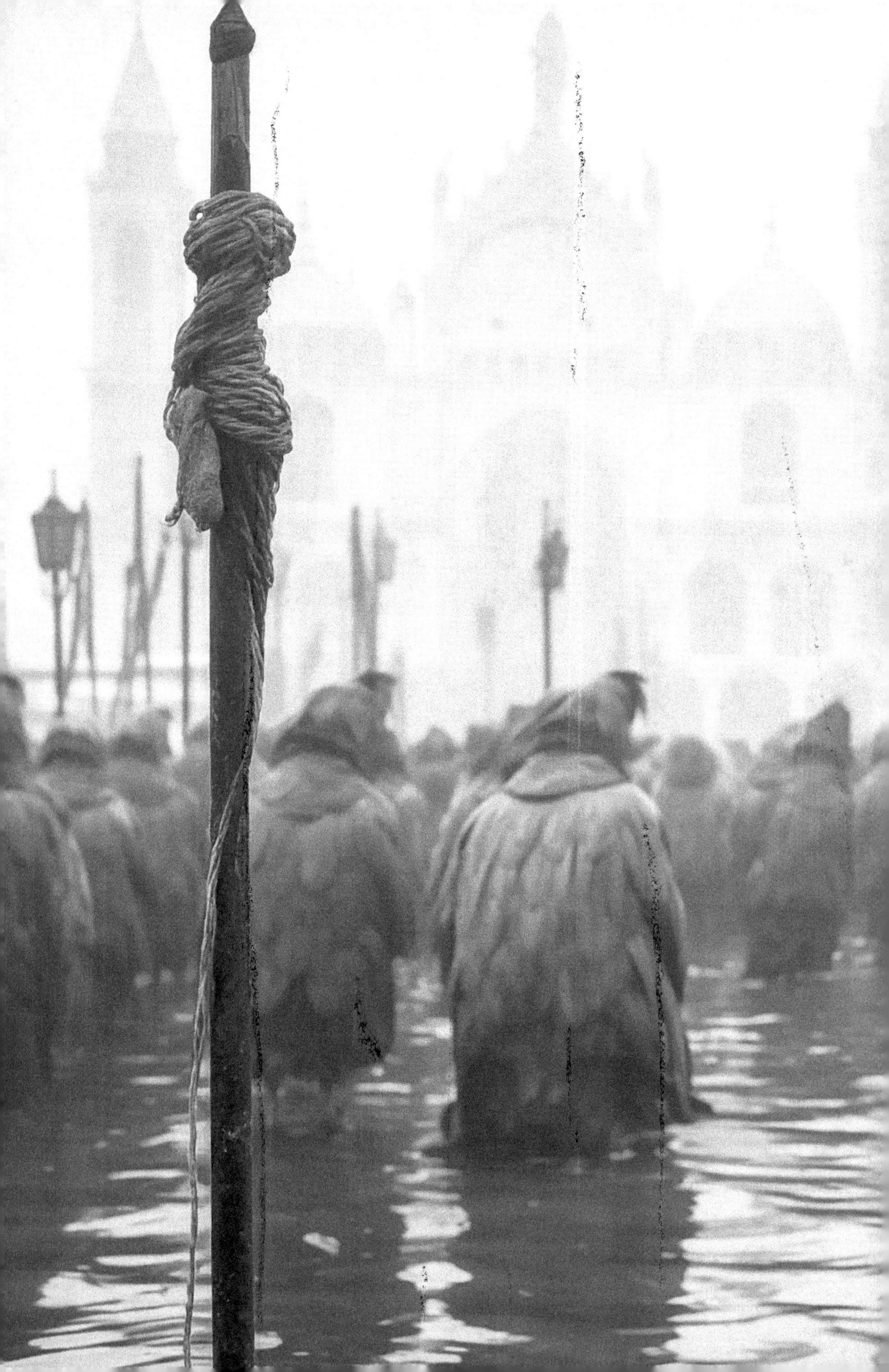

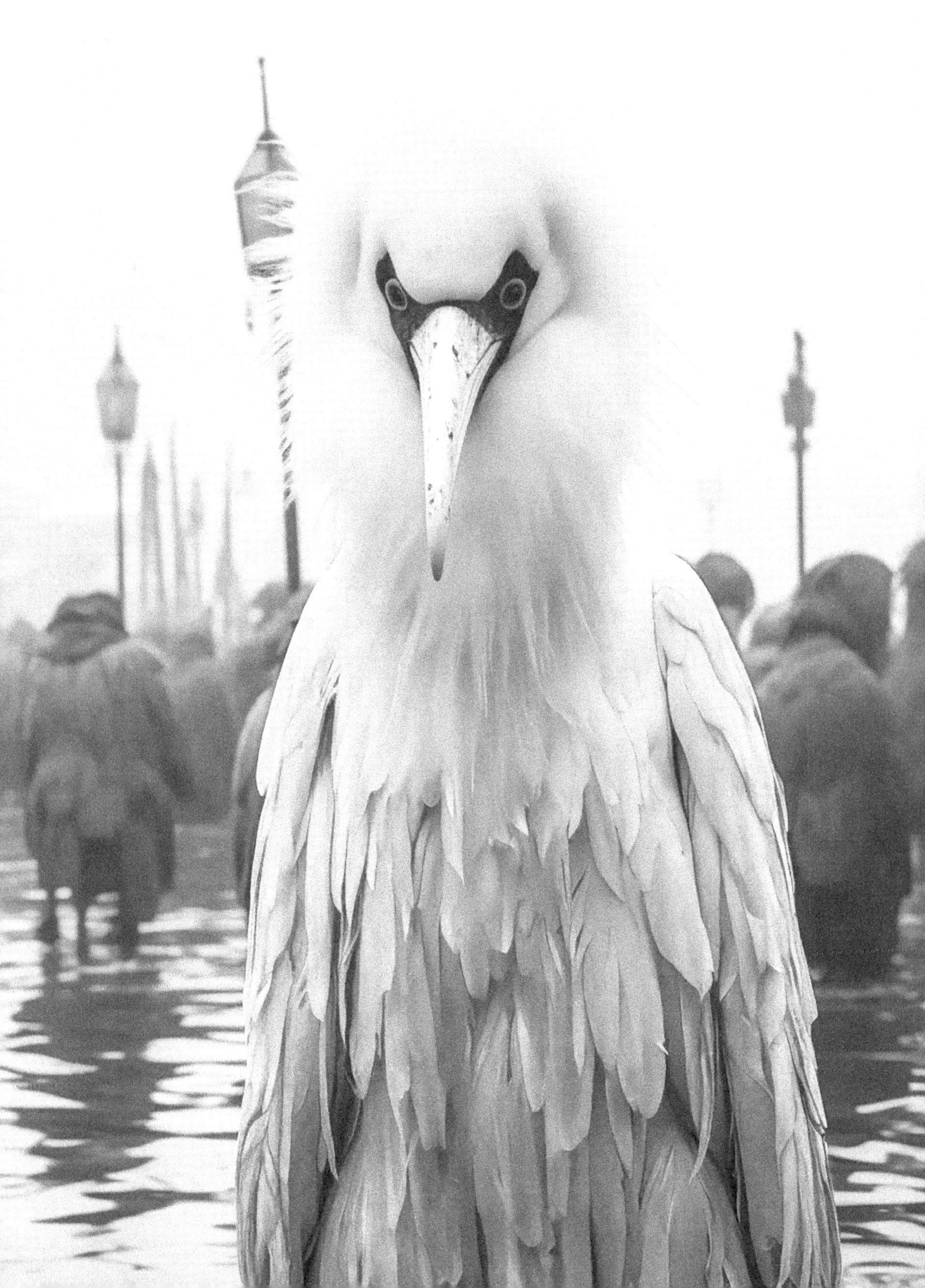

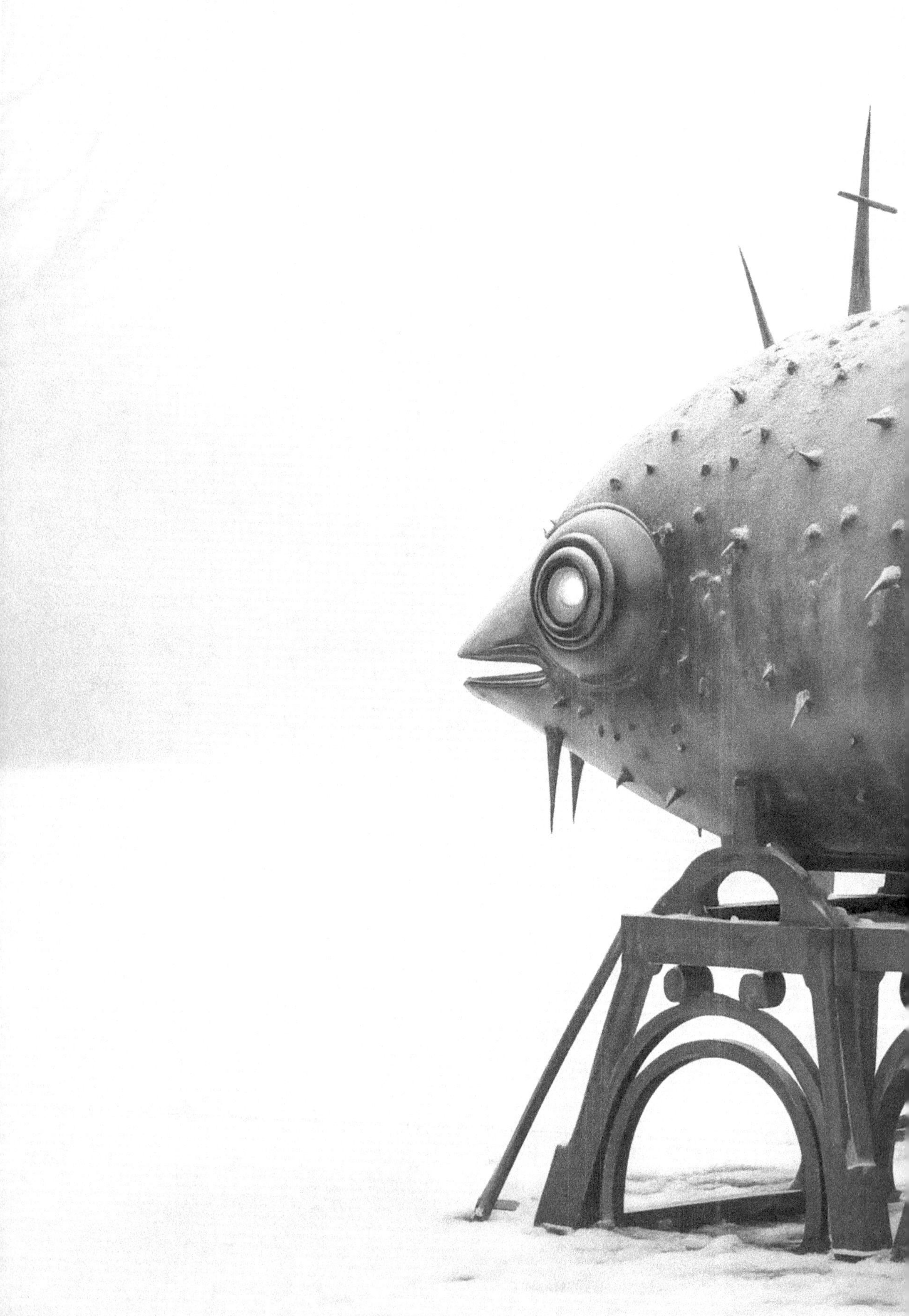

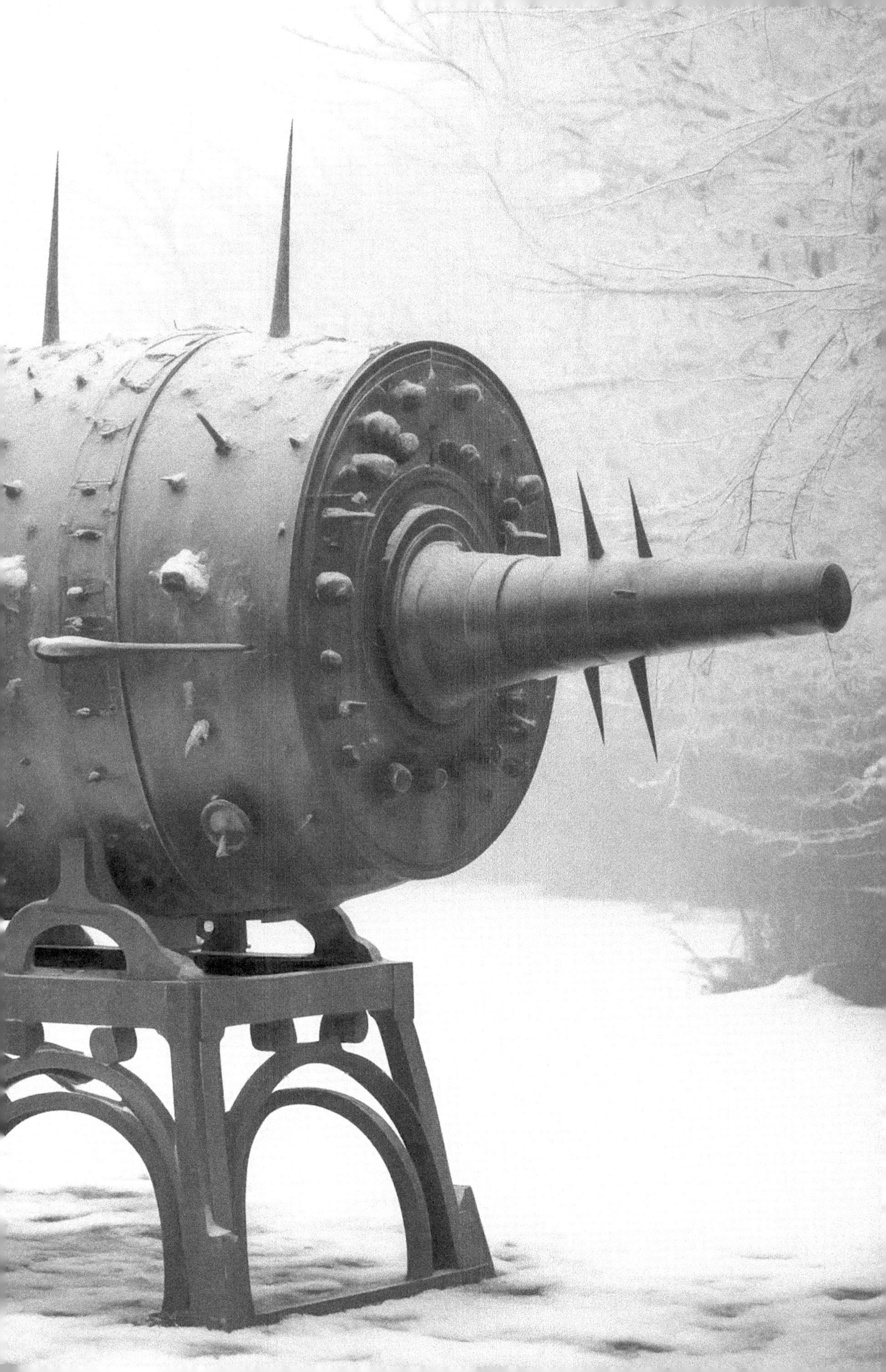

The measurability
of things lessens
our fear.

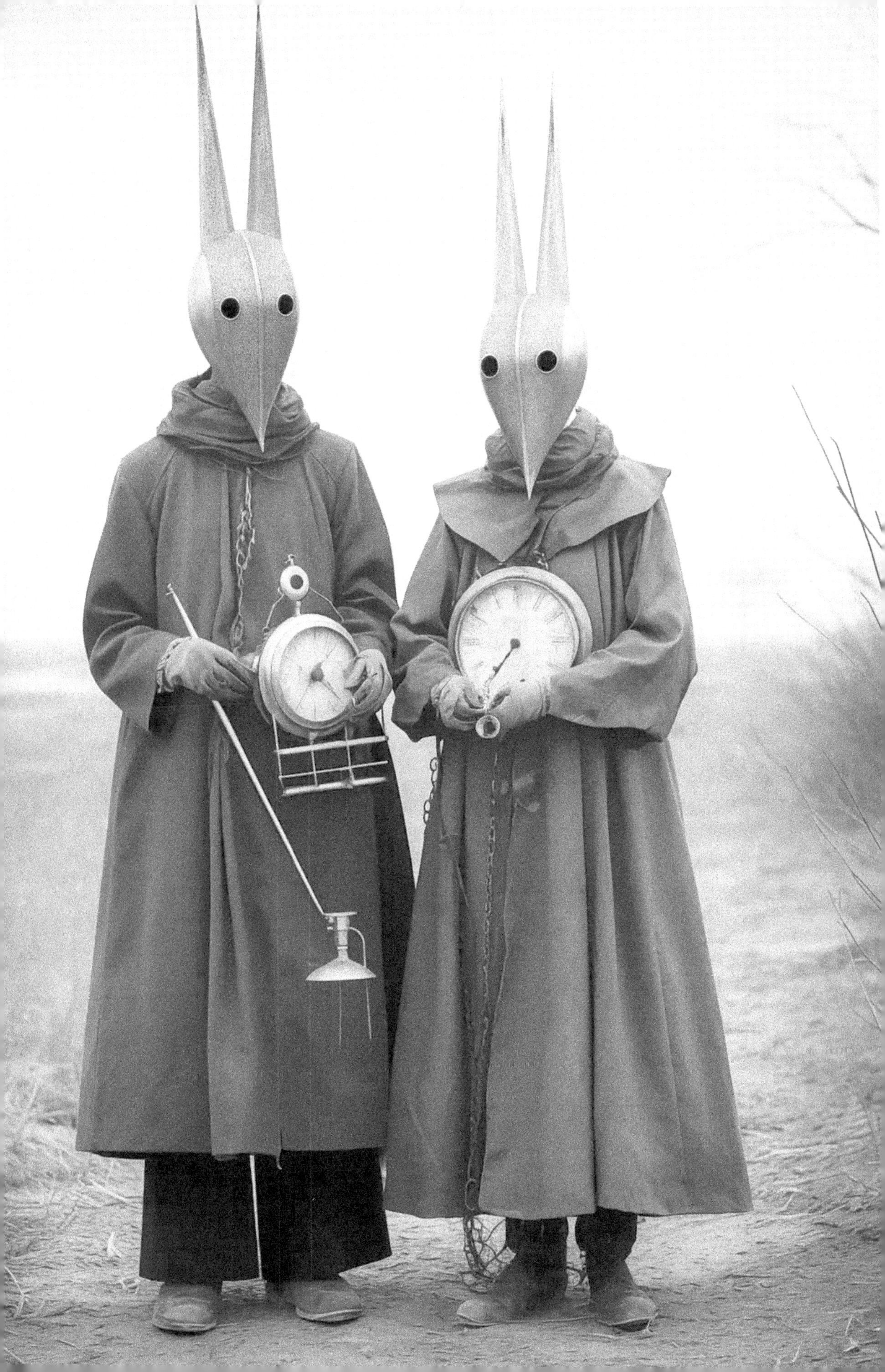

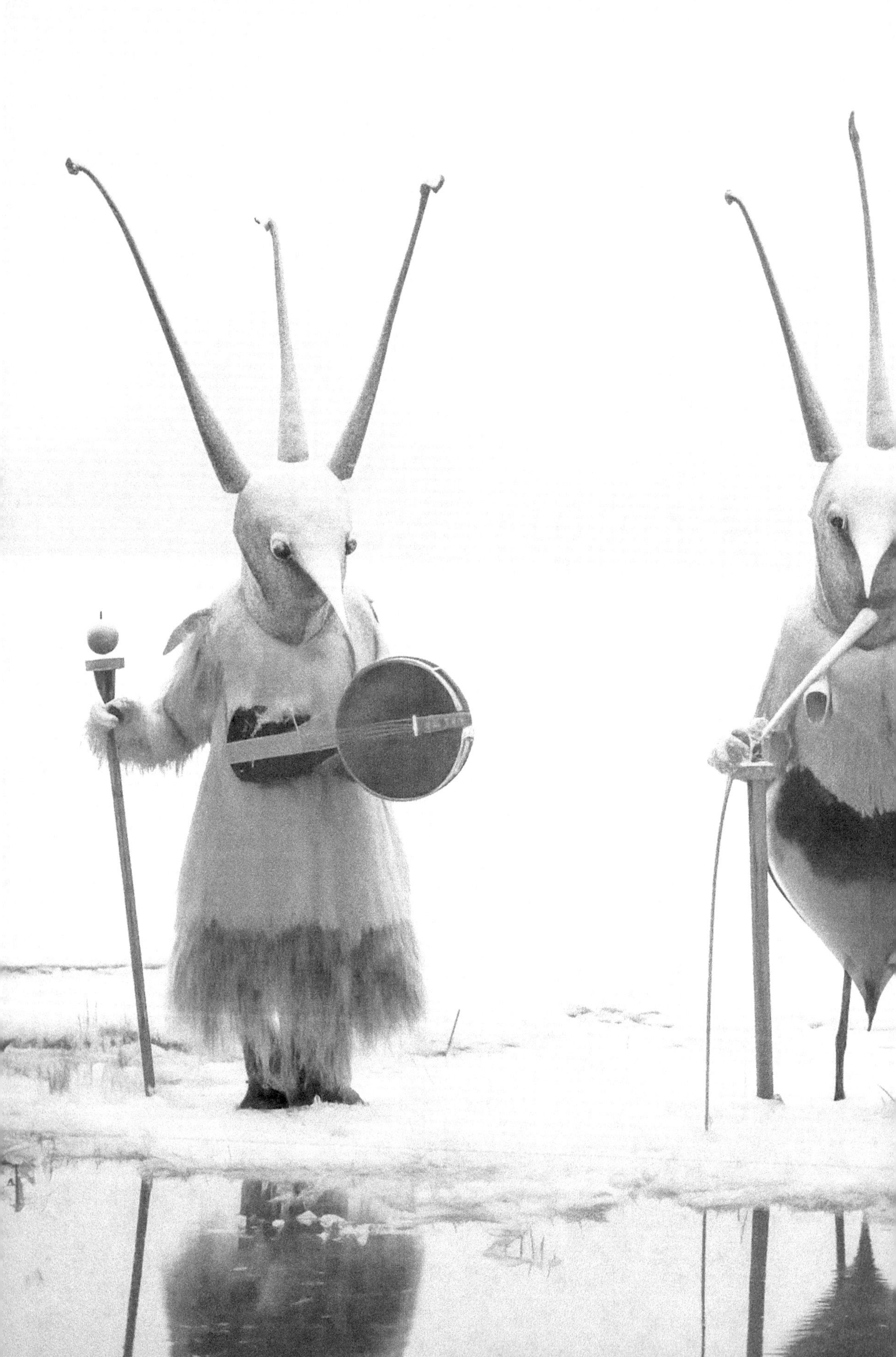

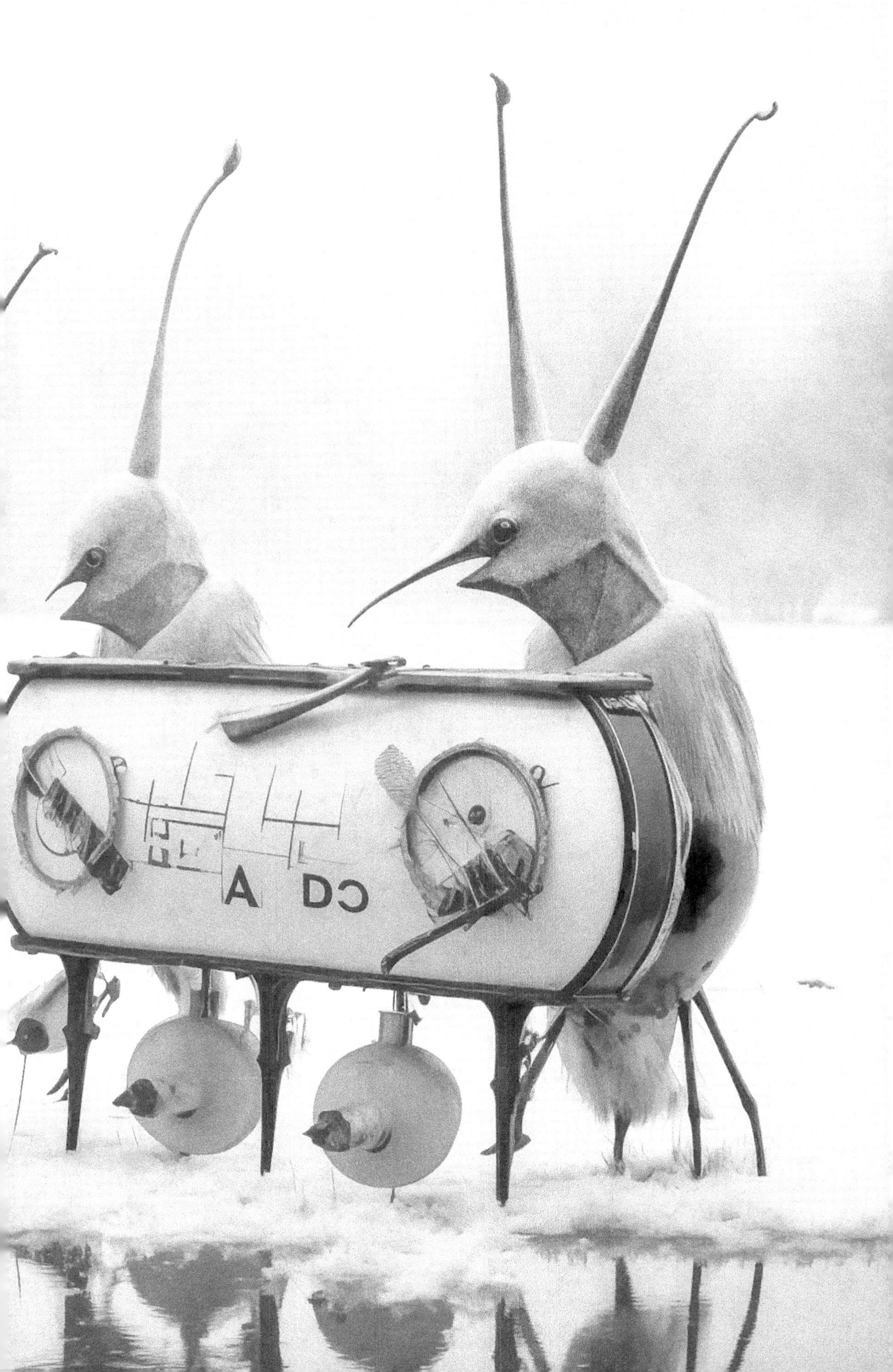

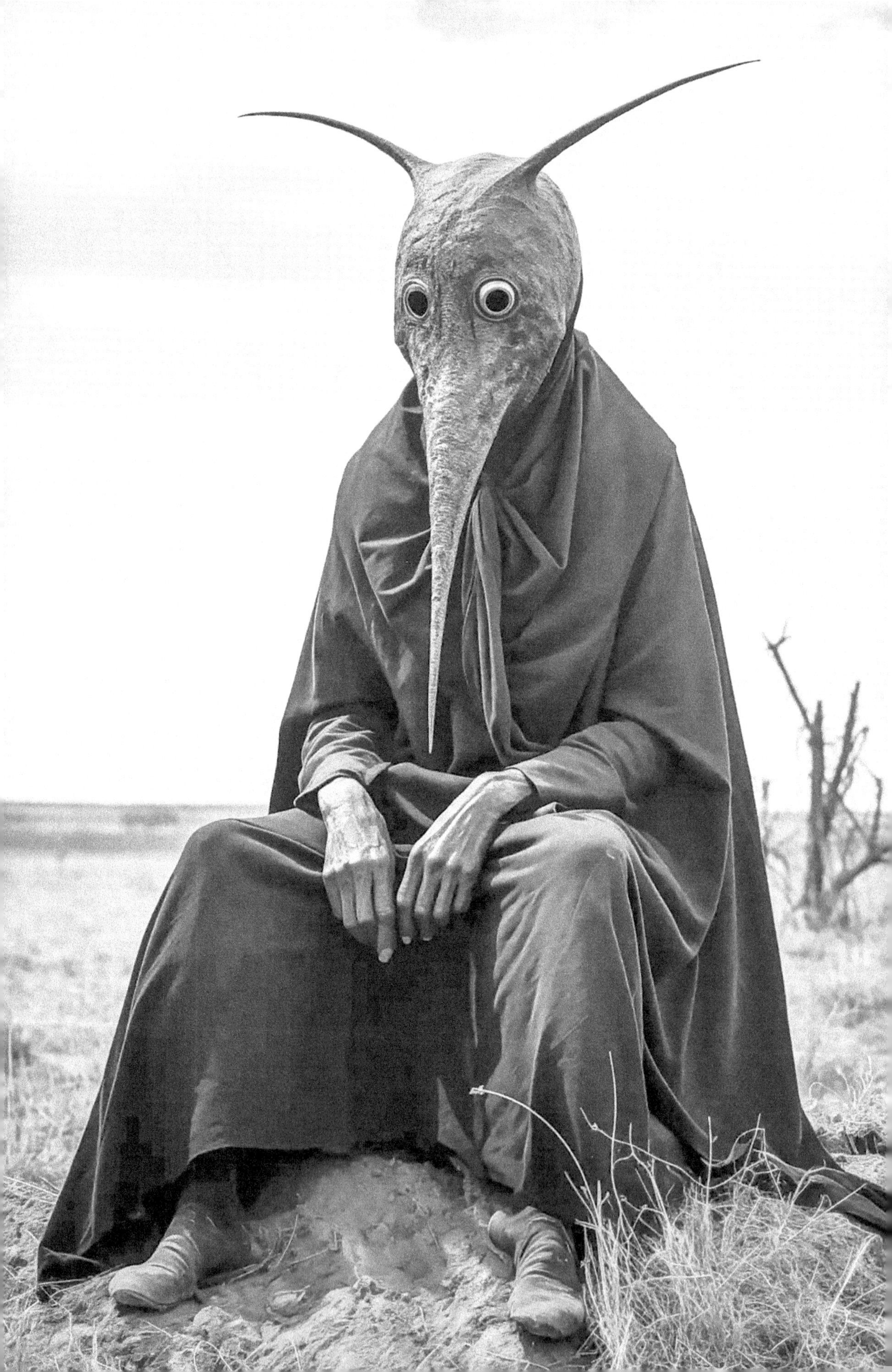

On the
suffering
of waiting.

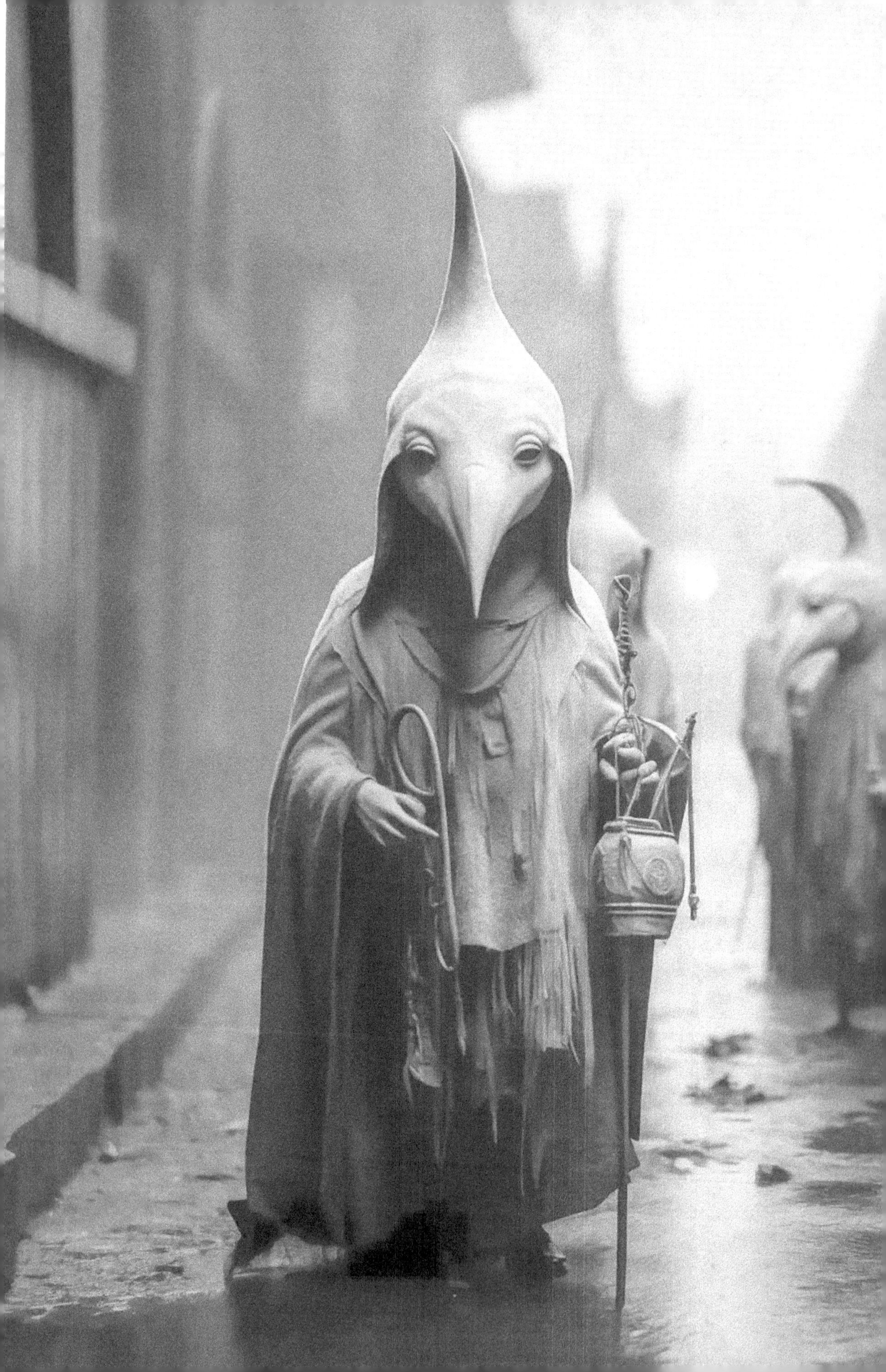

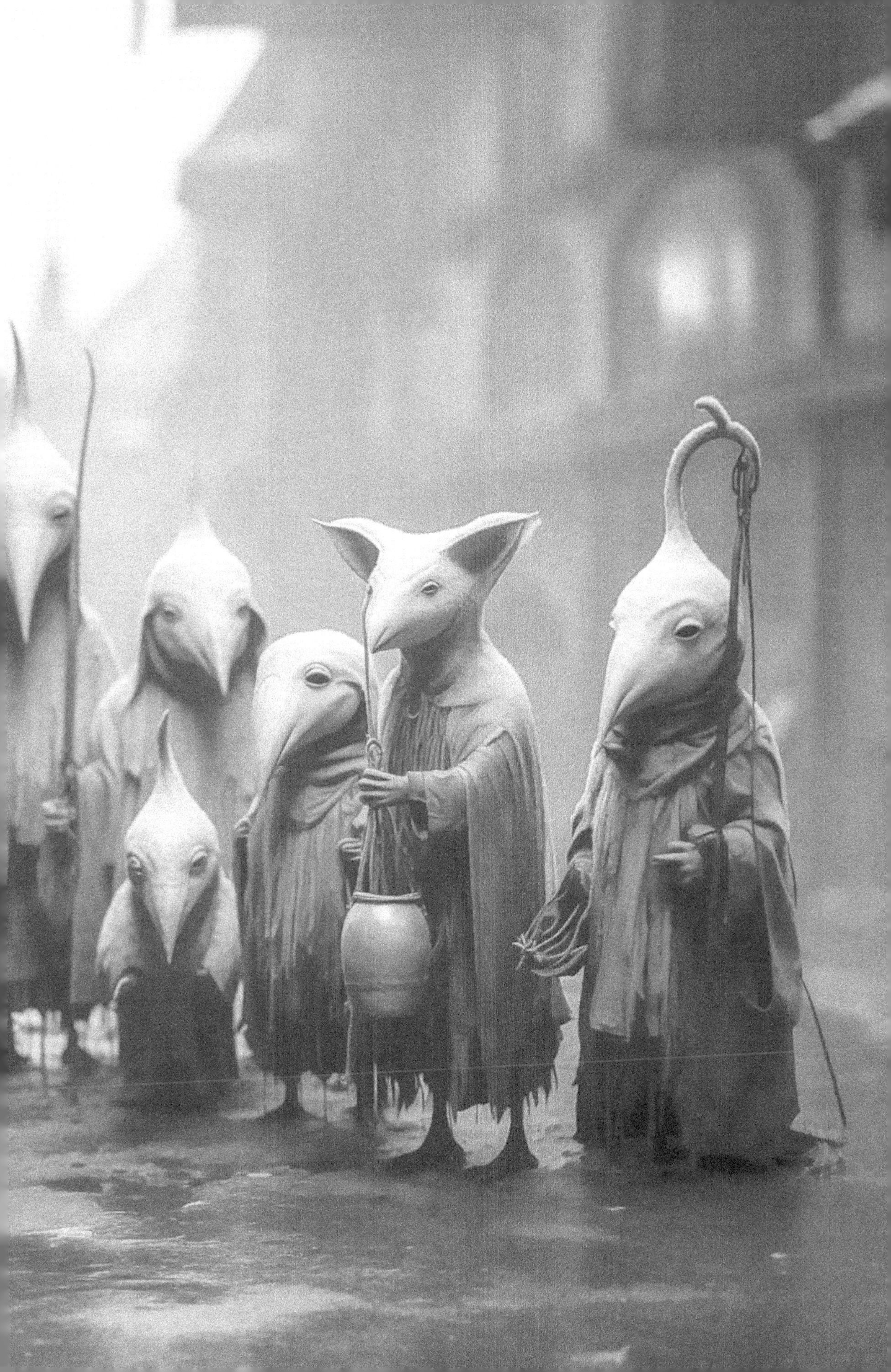

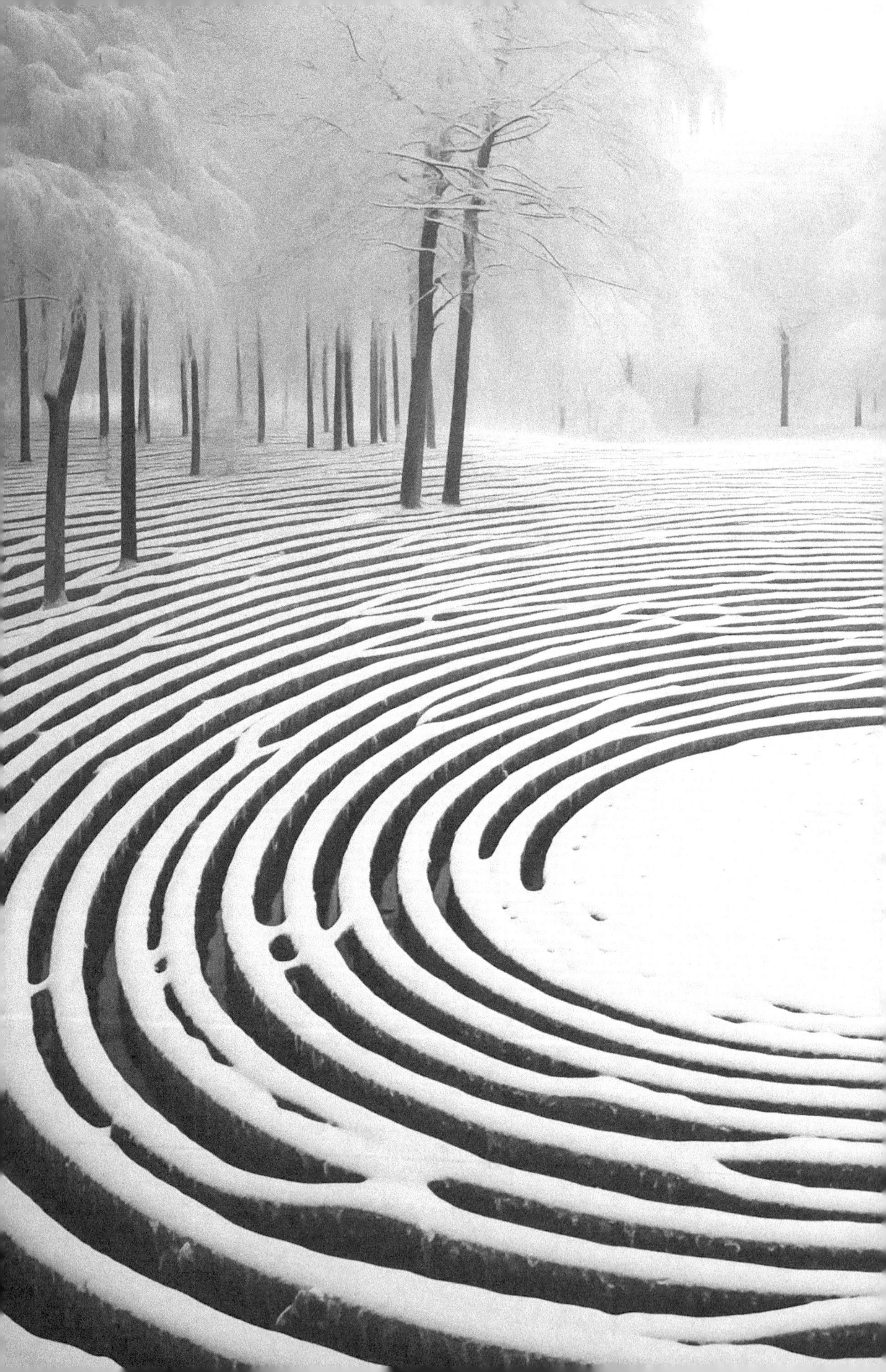

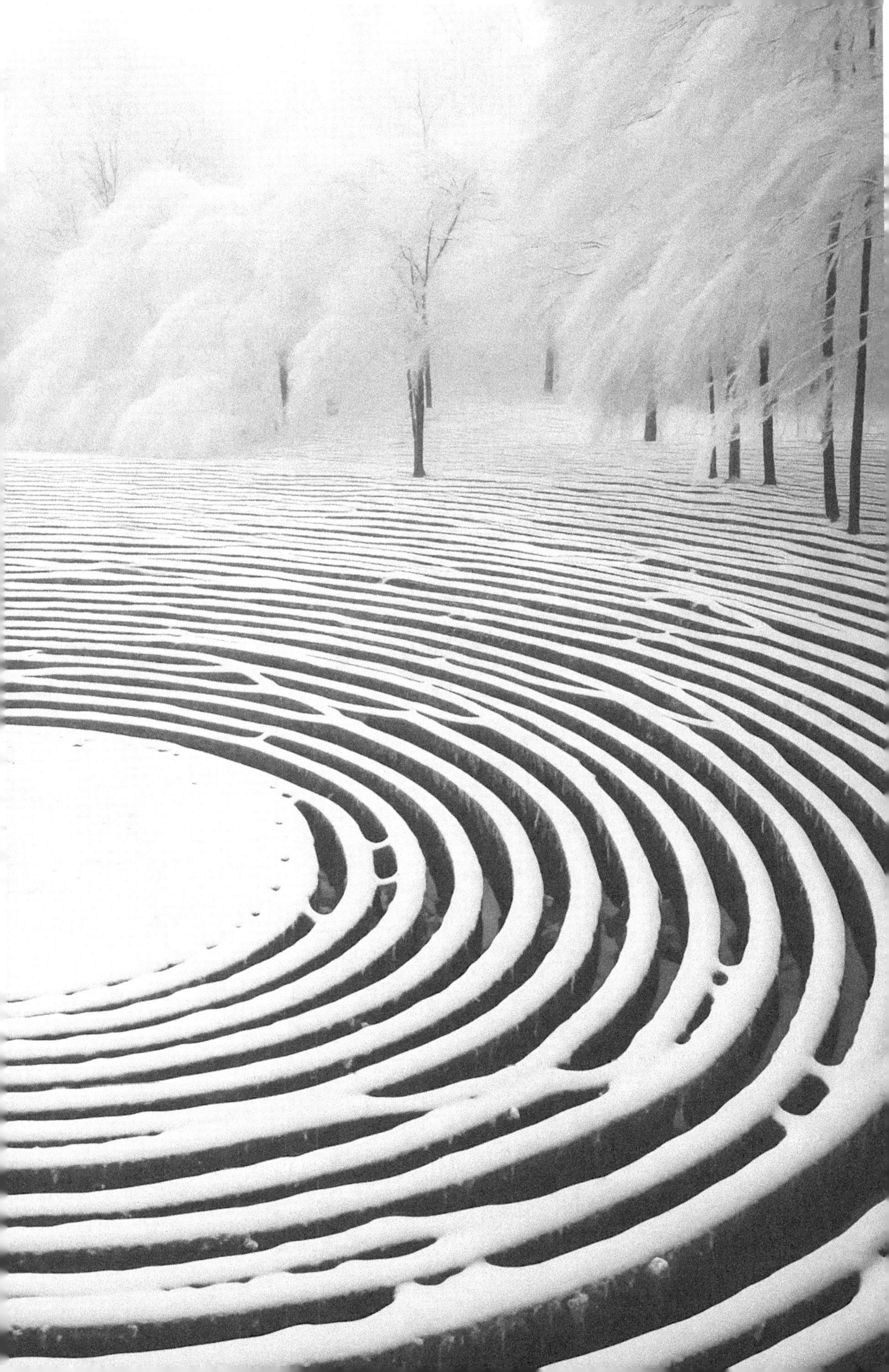

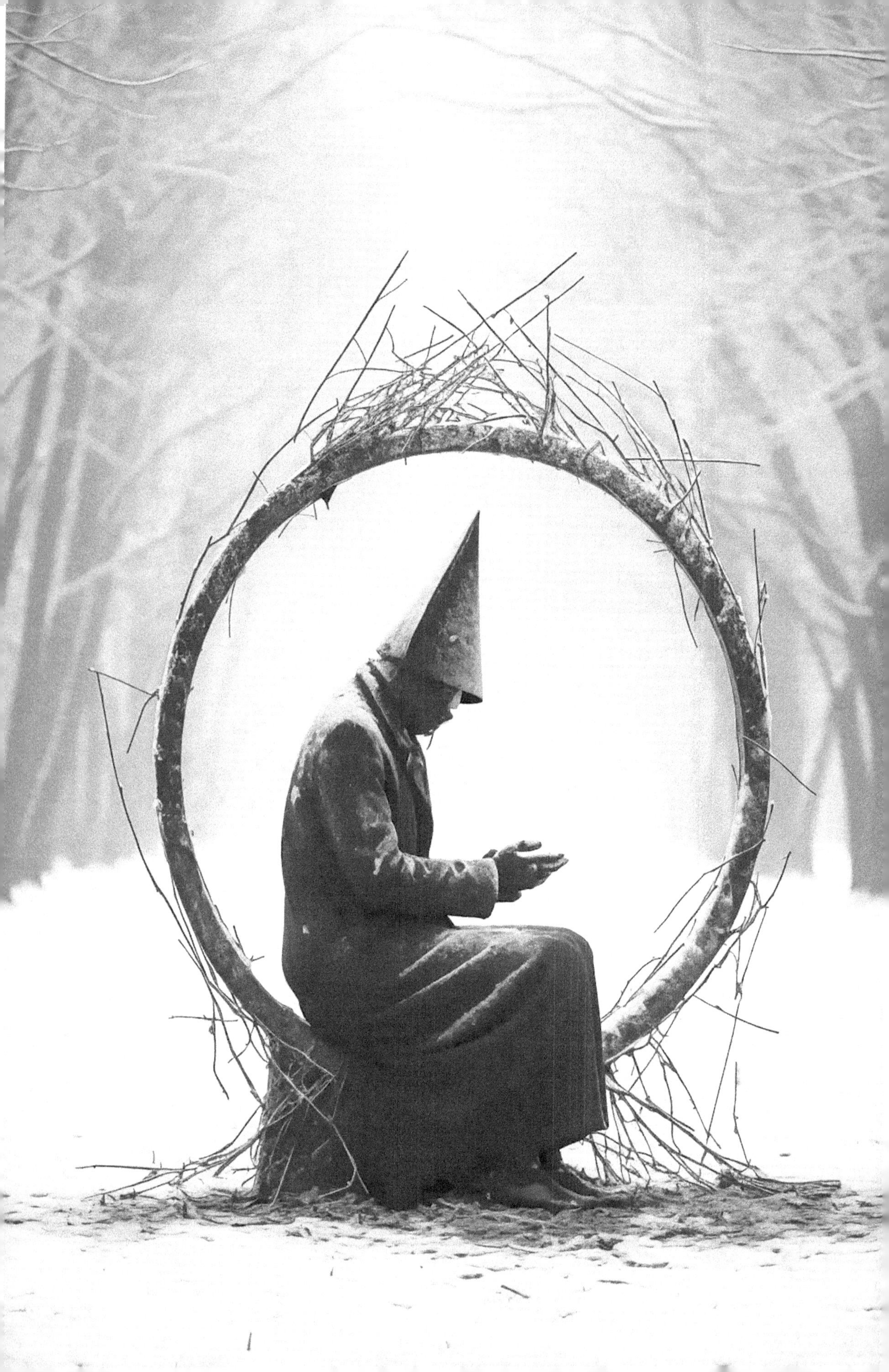

After

months of contemplation in solitude, he realized that he had wasted his life.

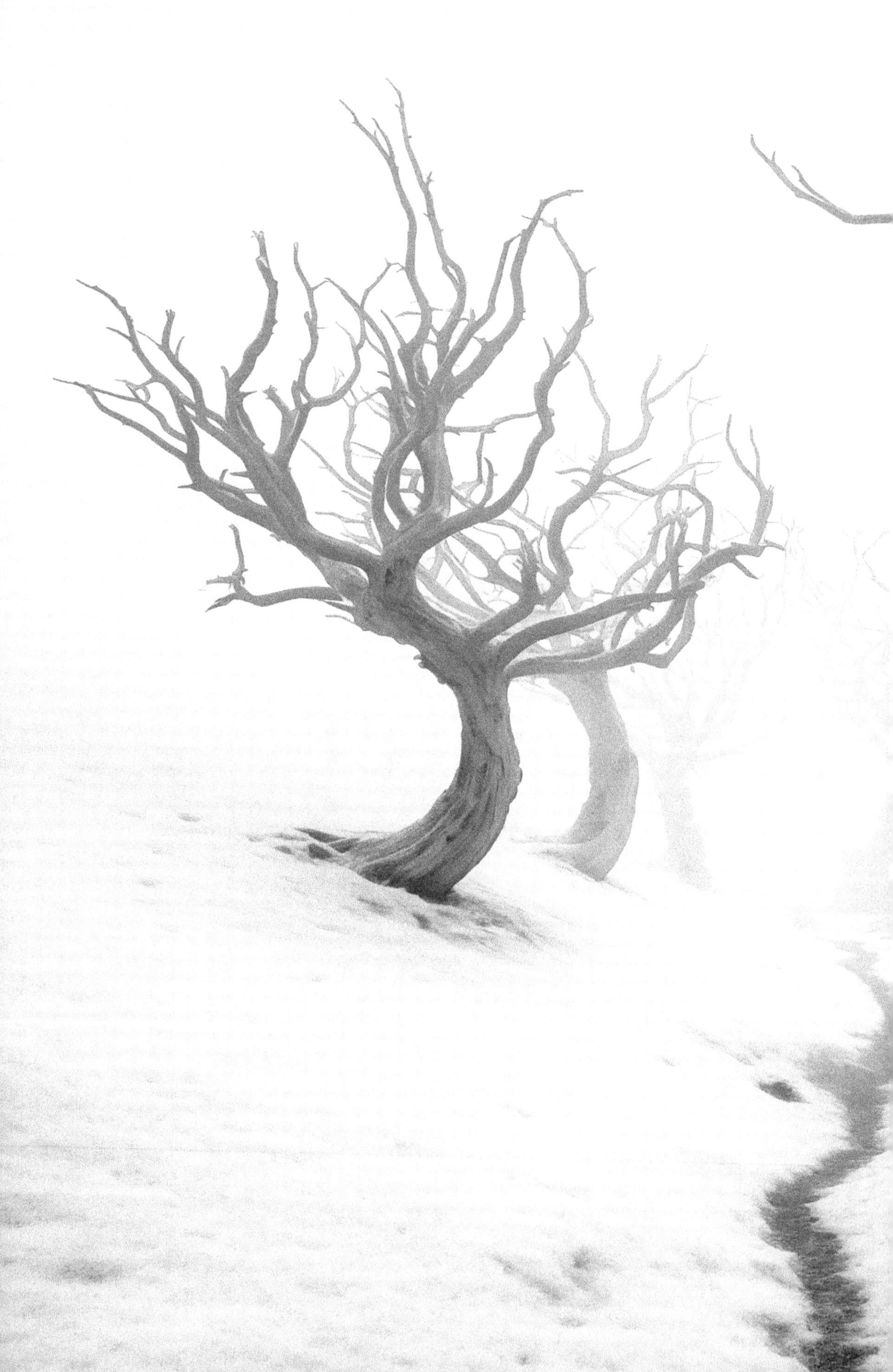

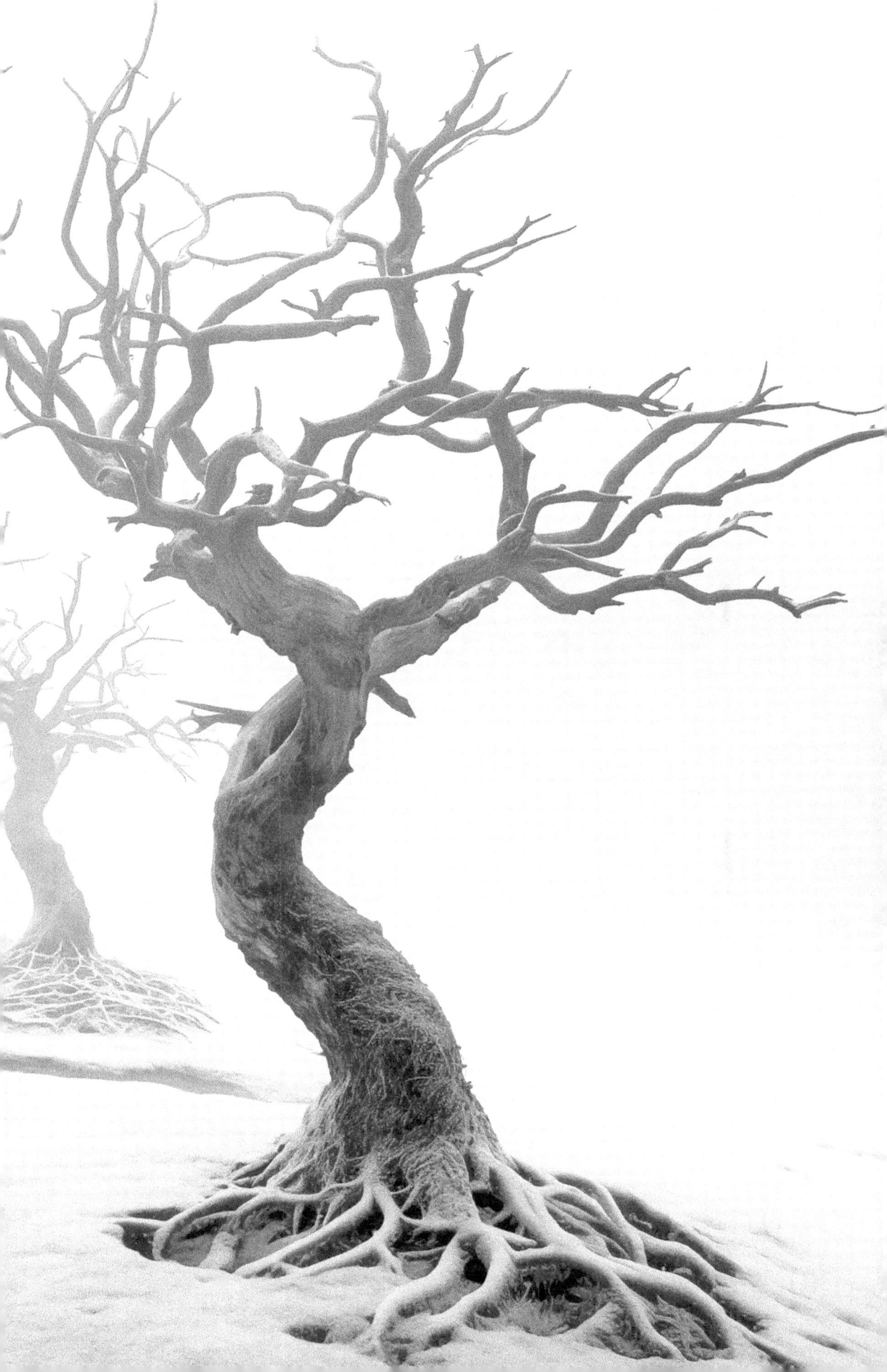

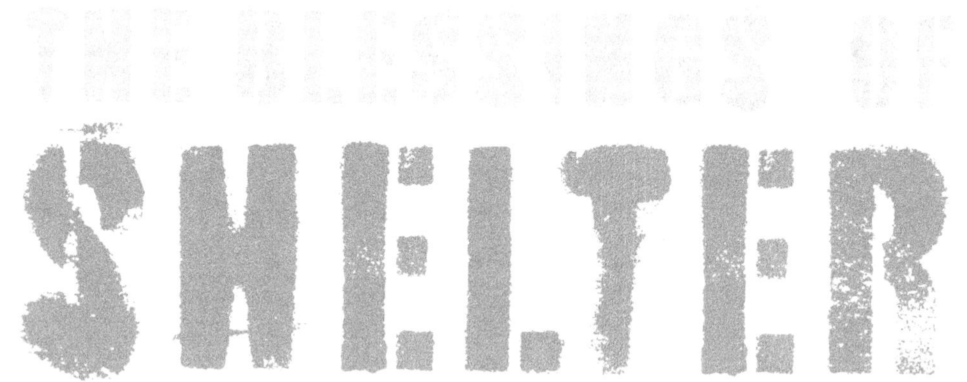
THE BLESSINGS OF
SHELTER

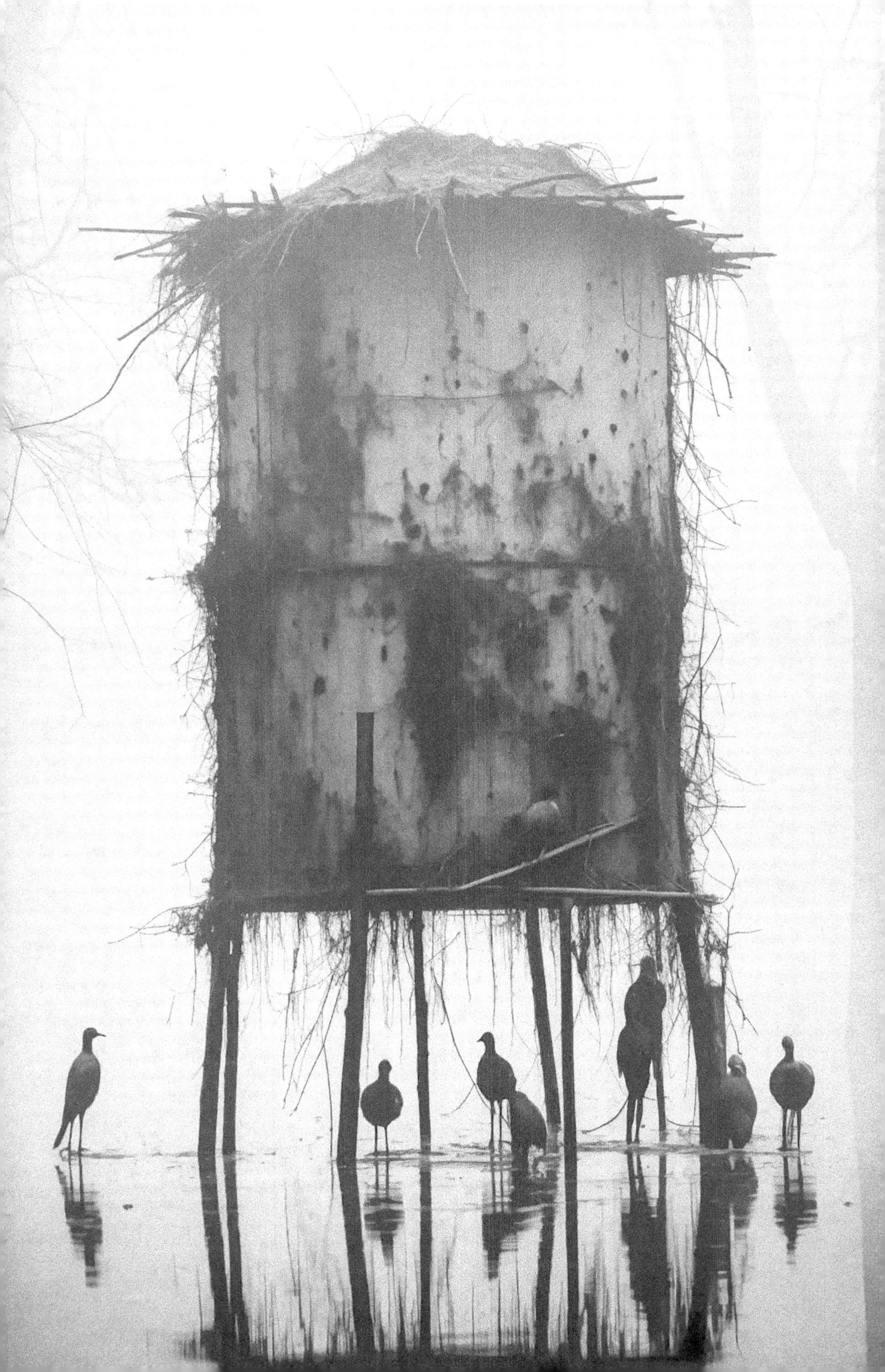

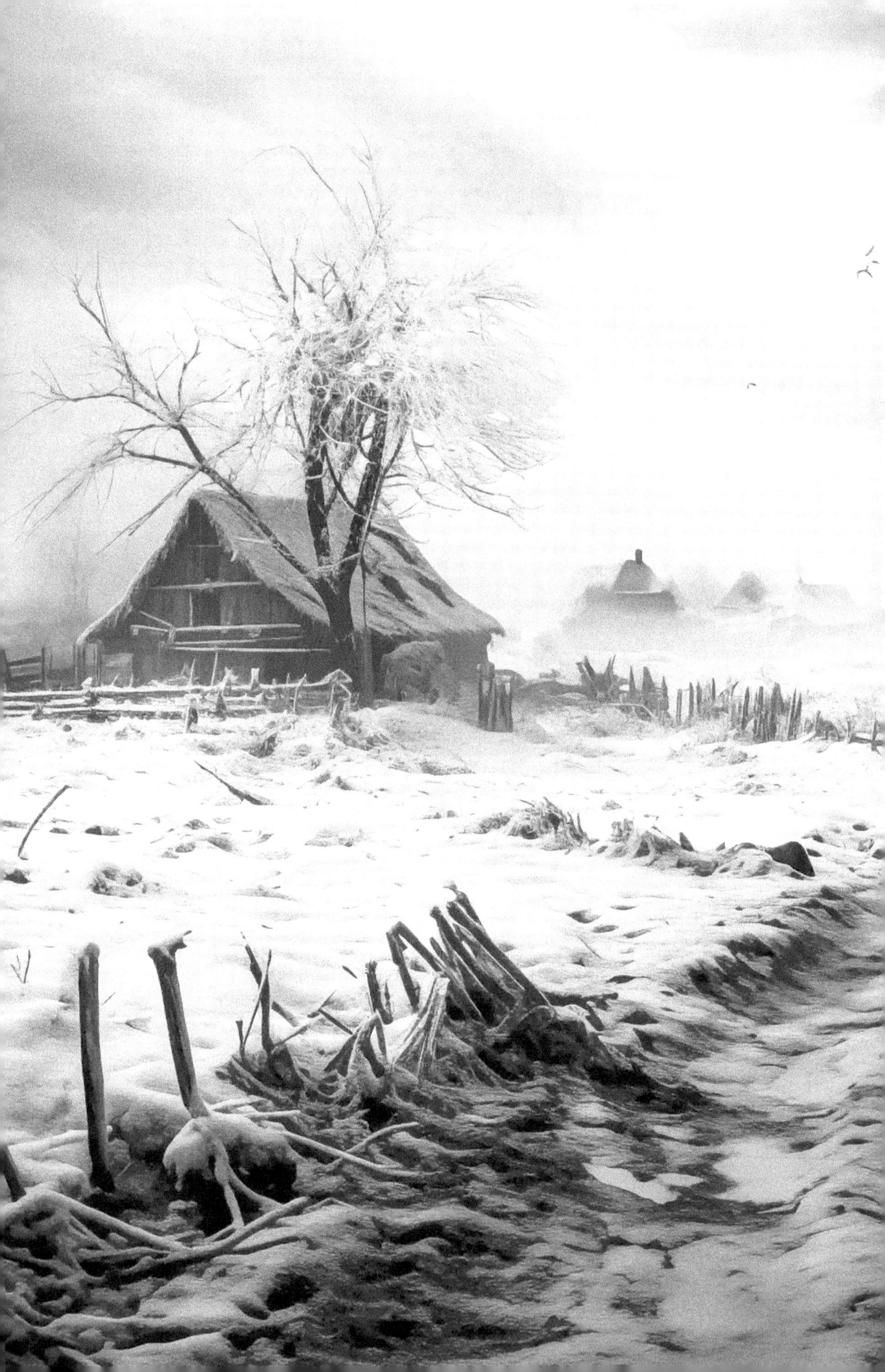

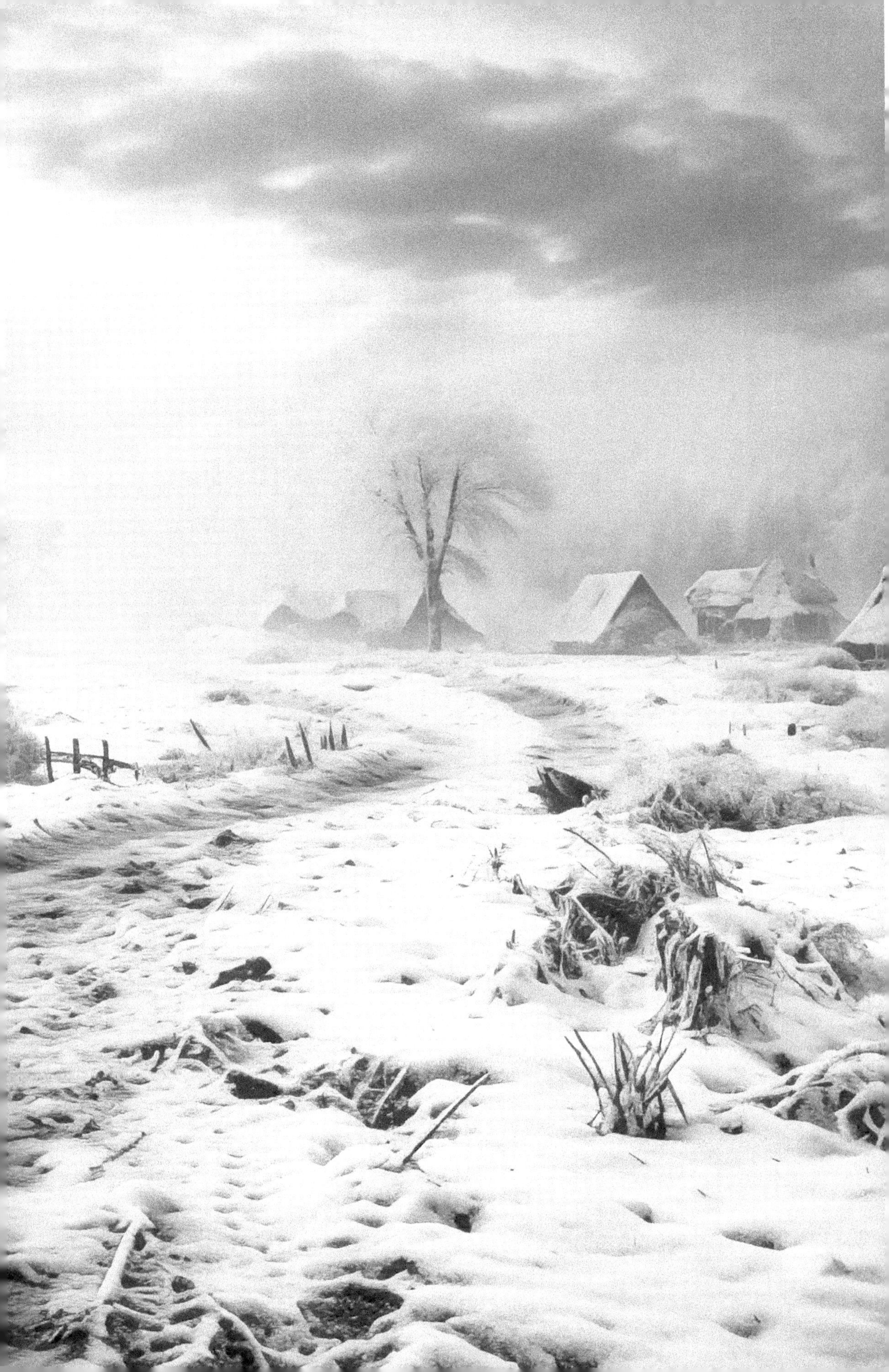

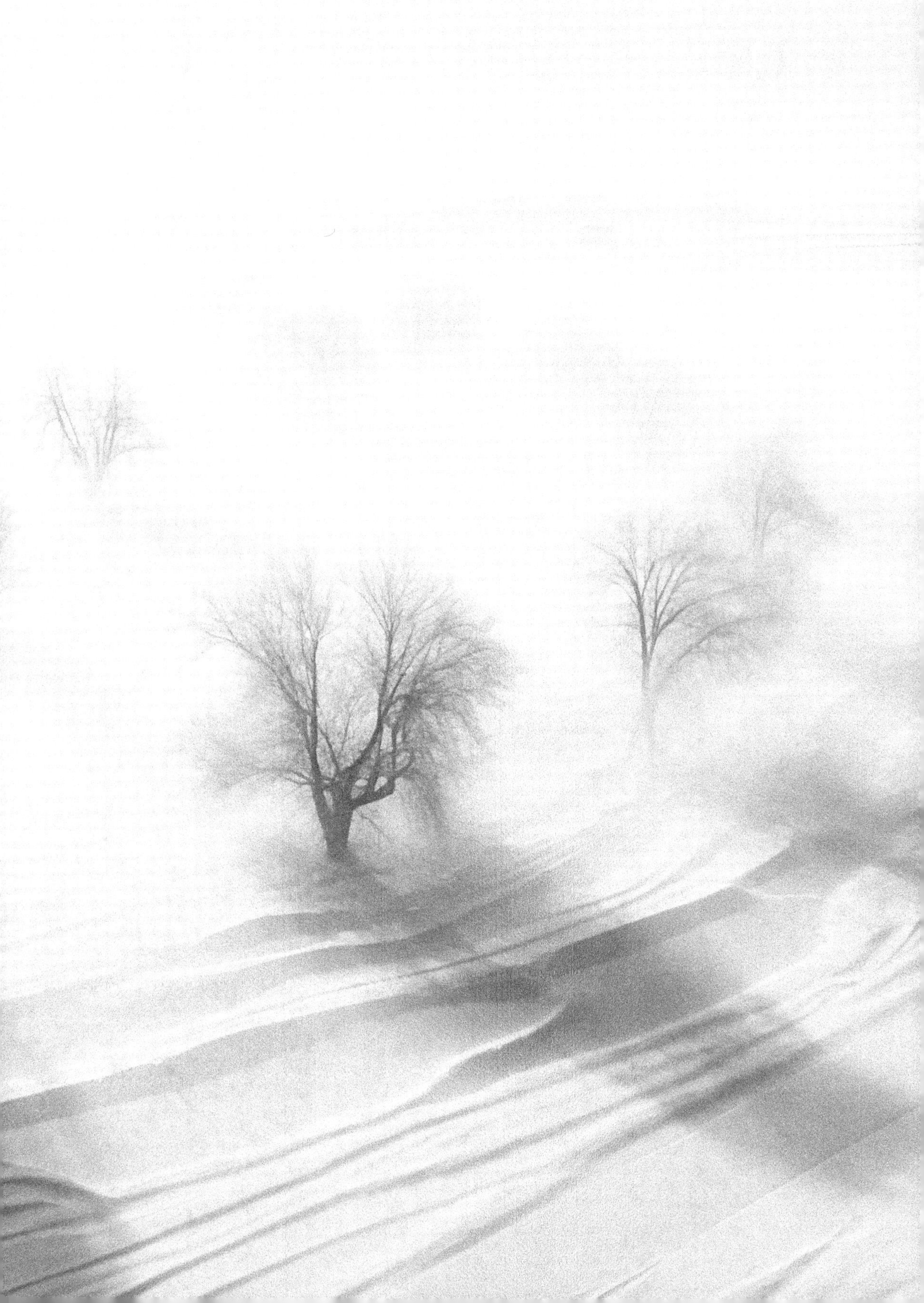

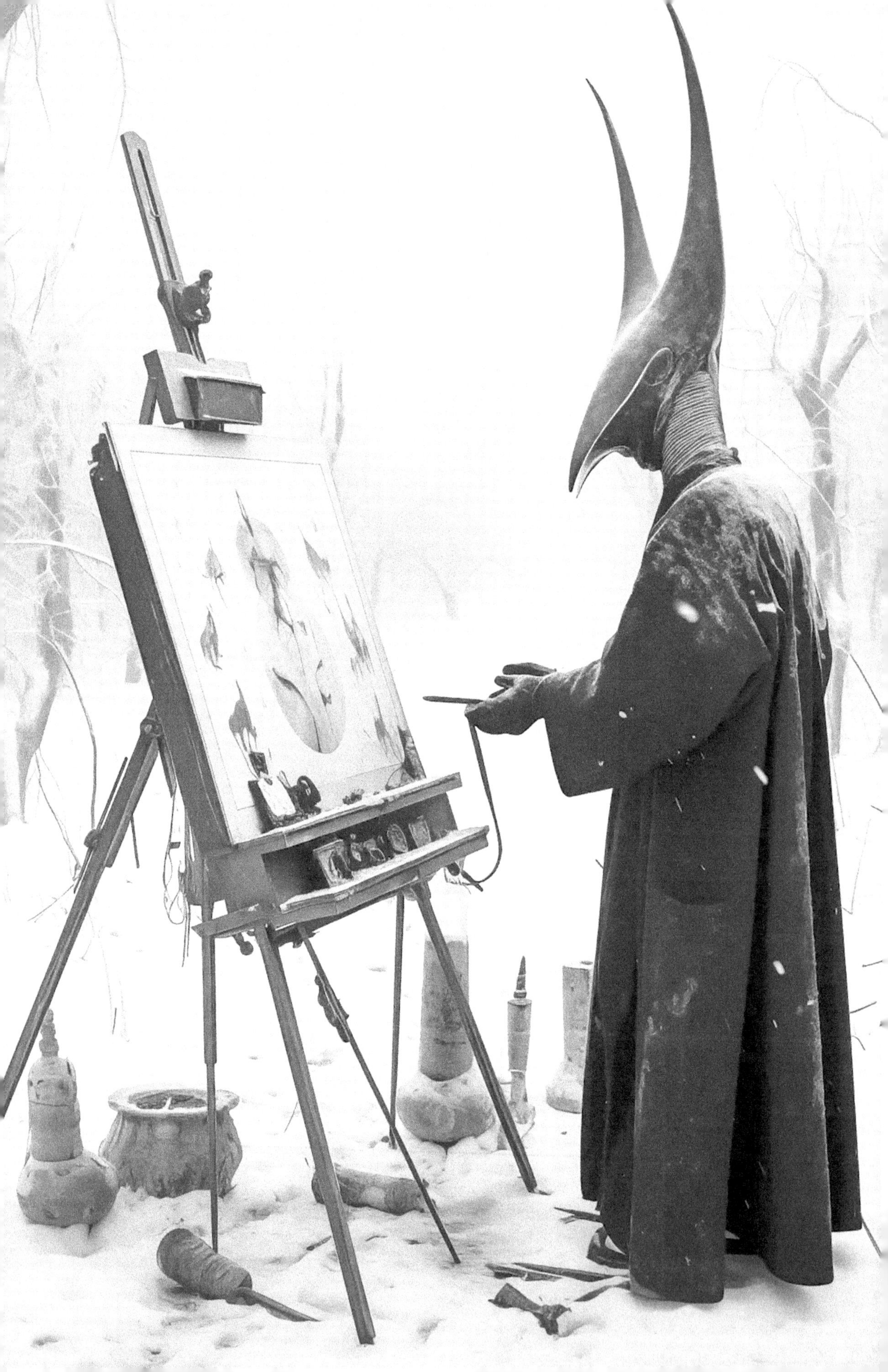

rtists do not explain, they raise questions.

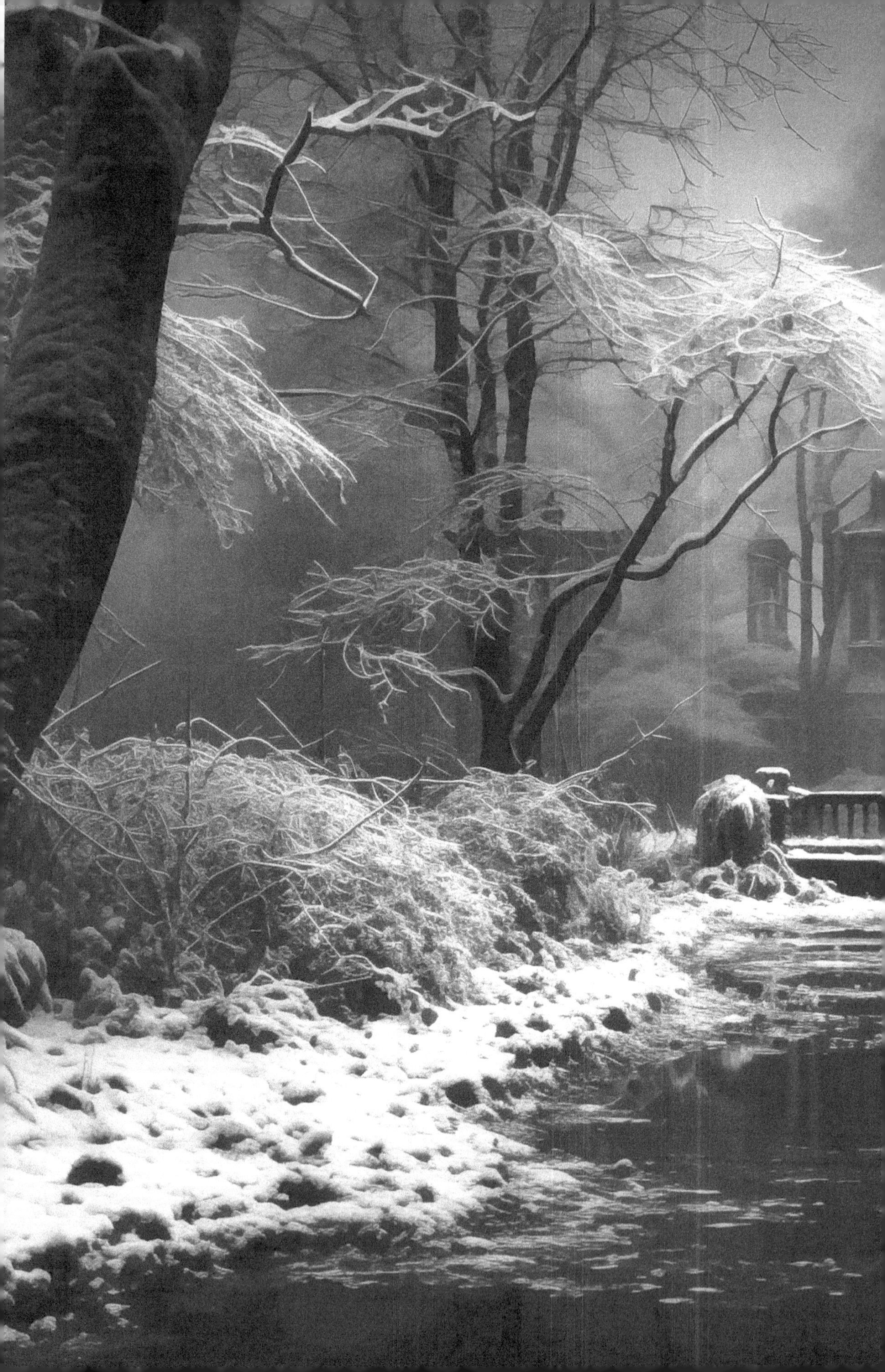

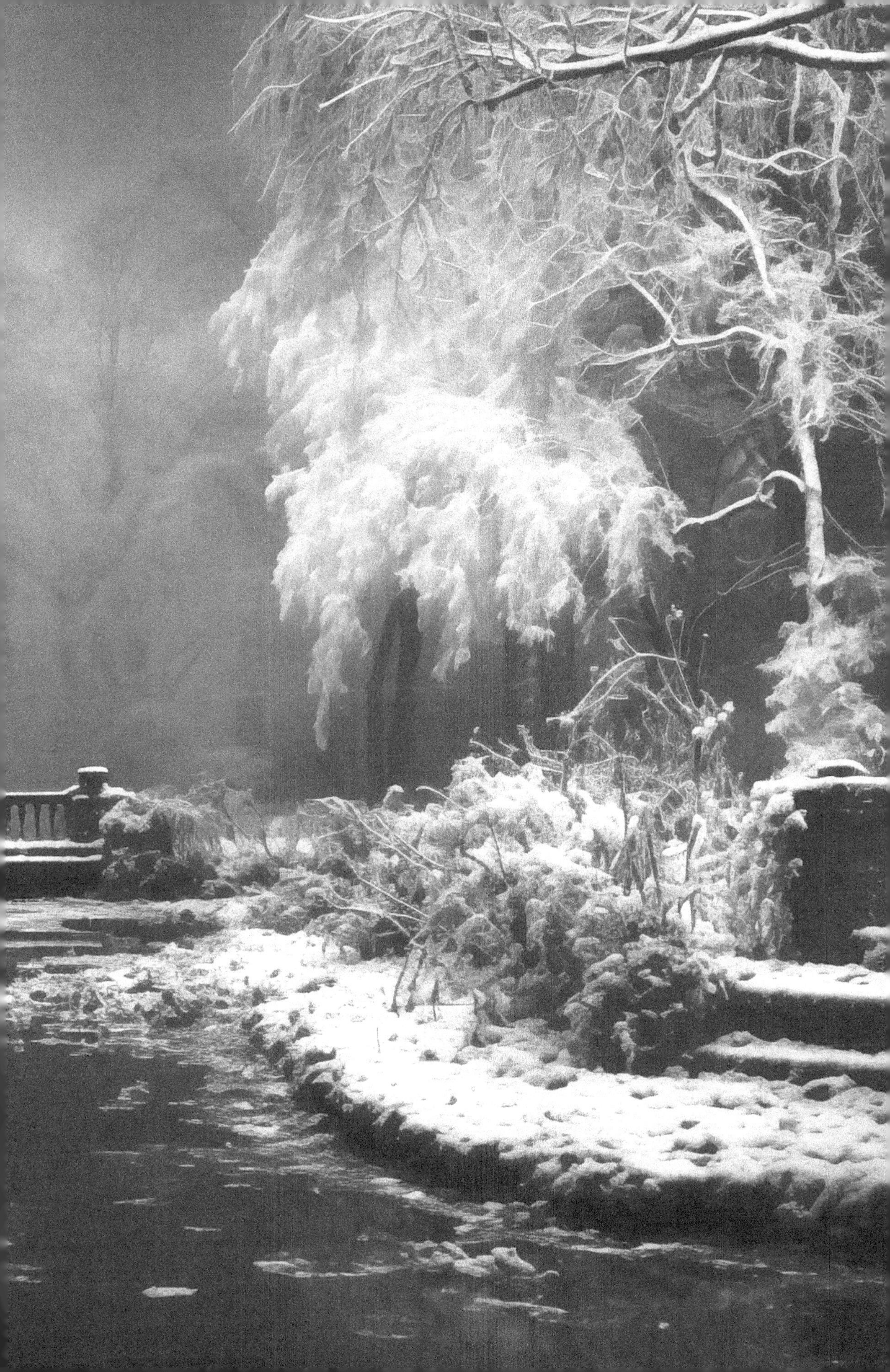

FADE

INTO

DARKNESS

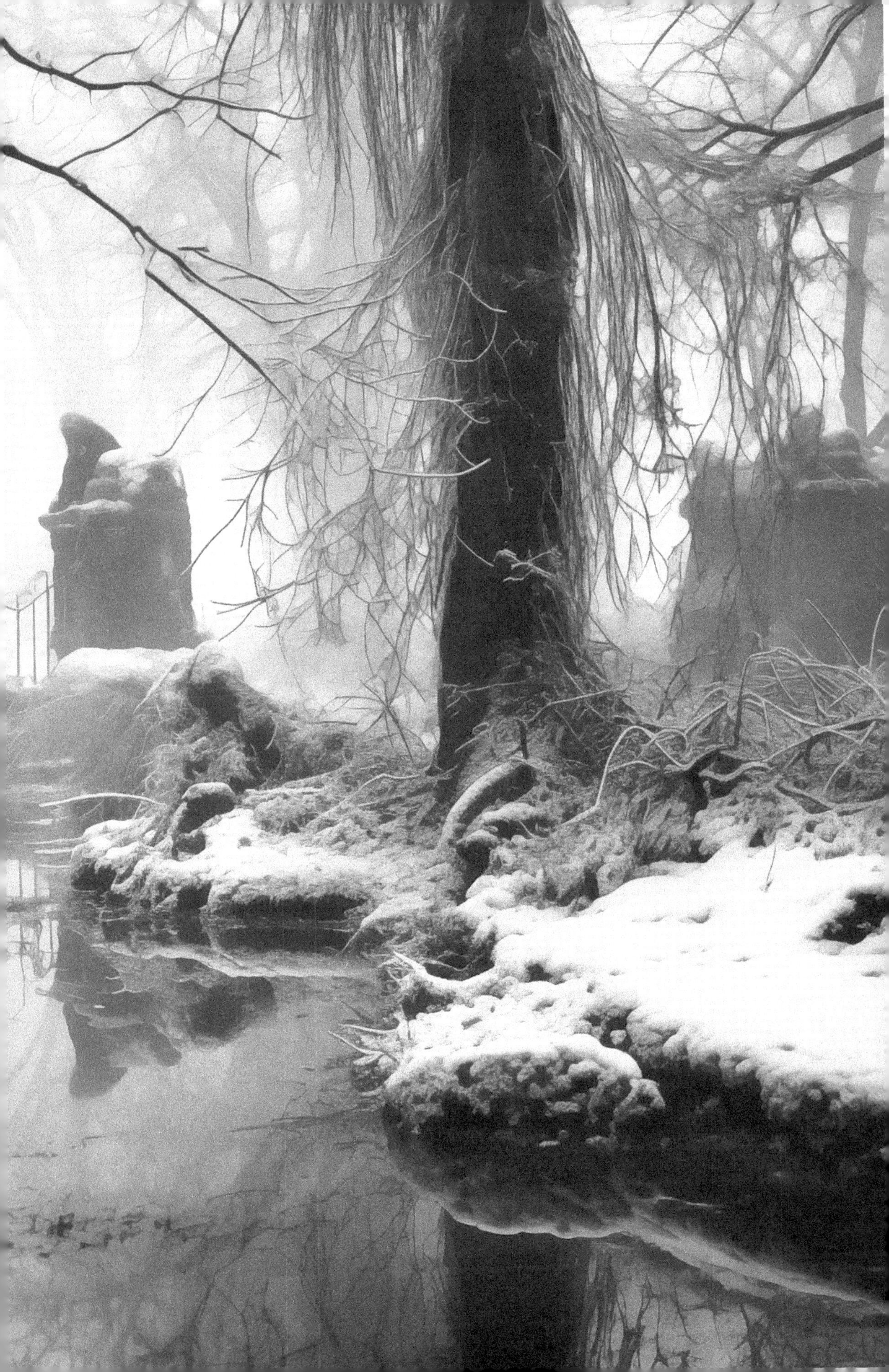

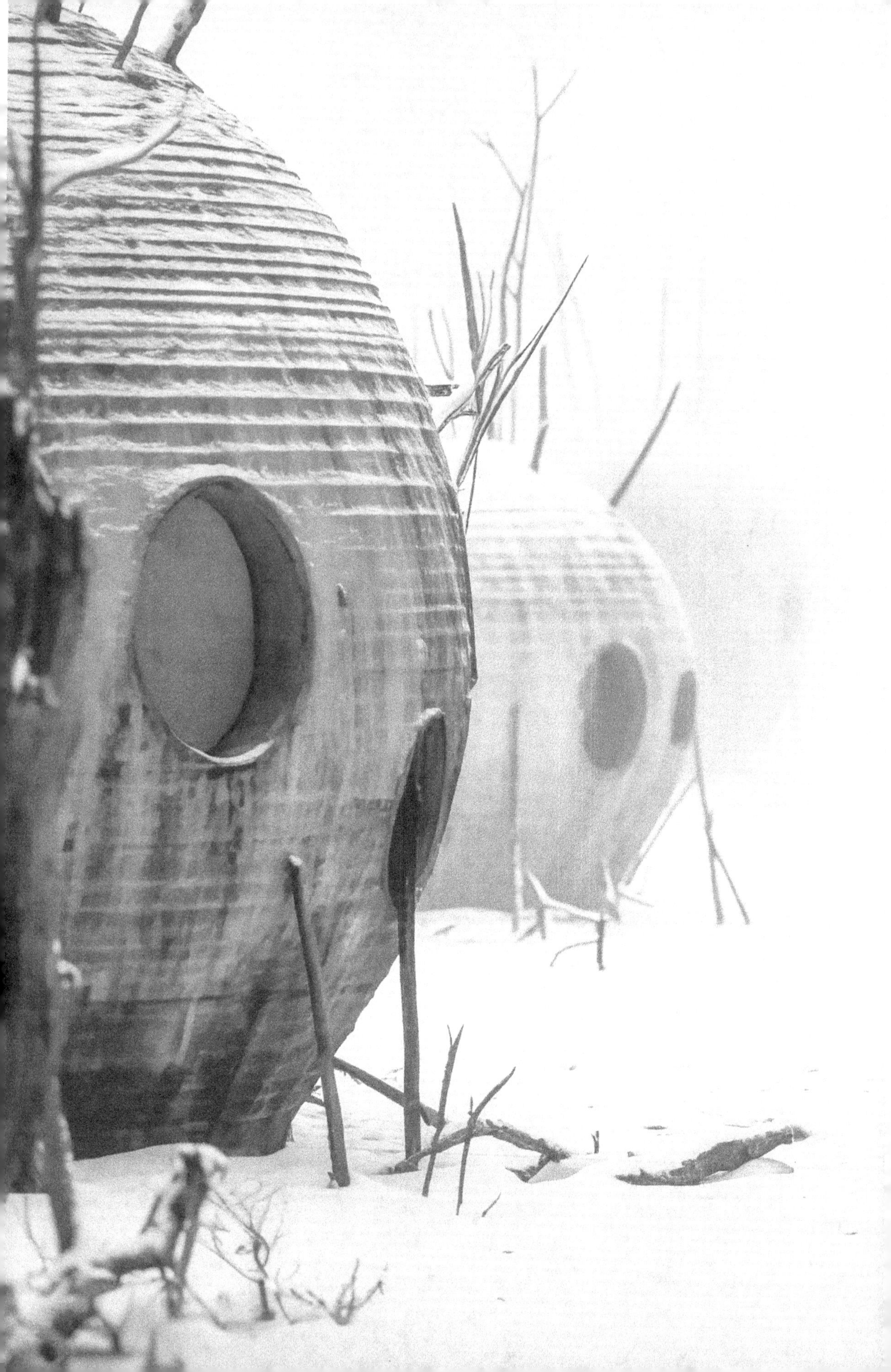

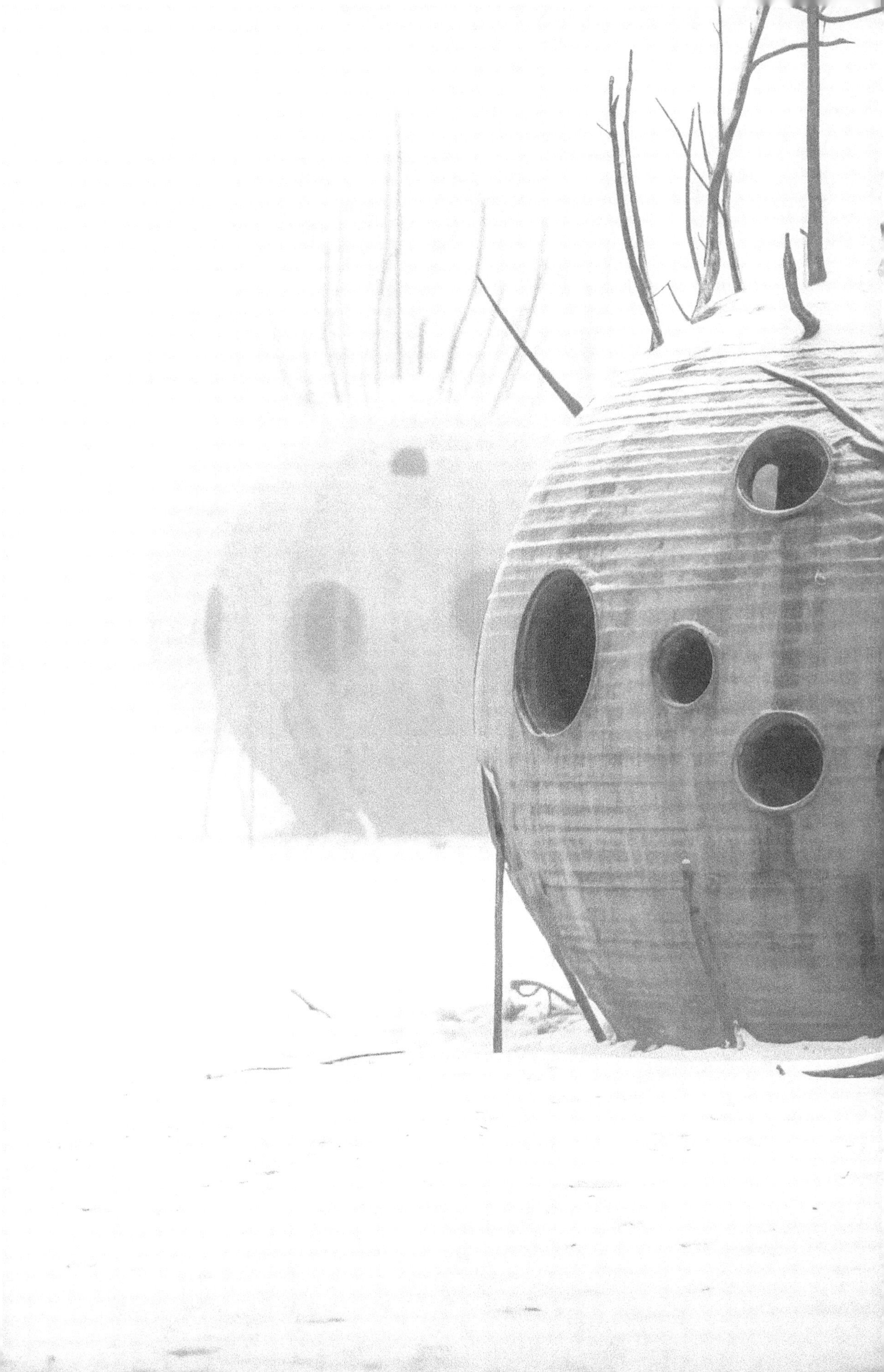

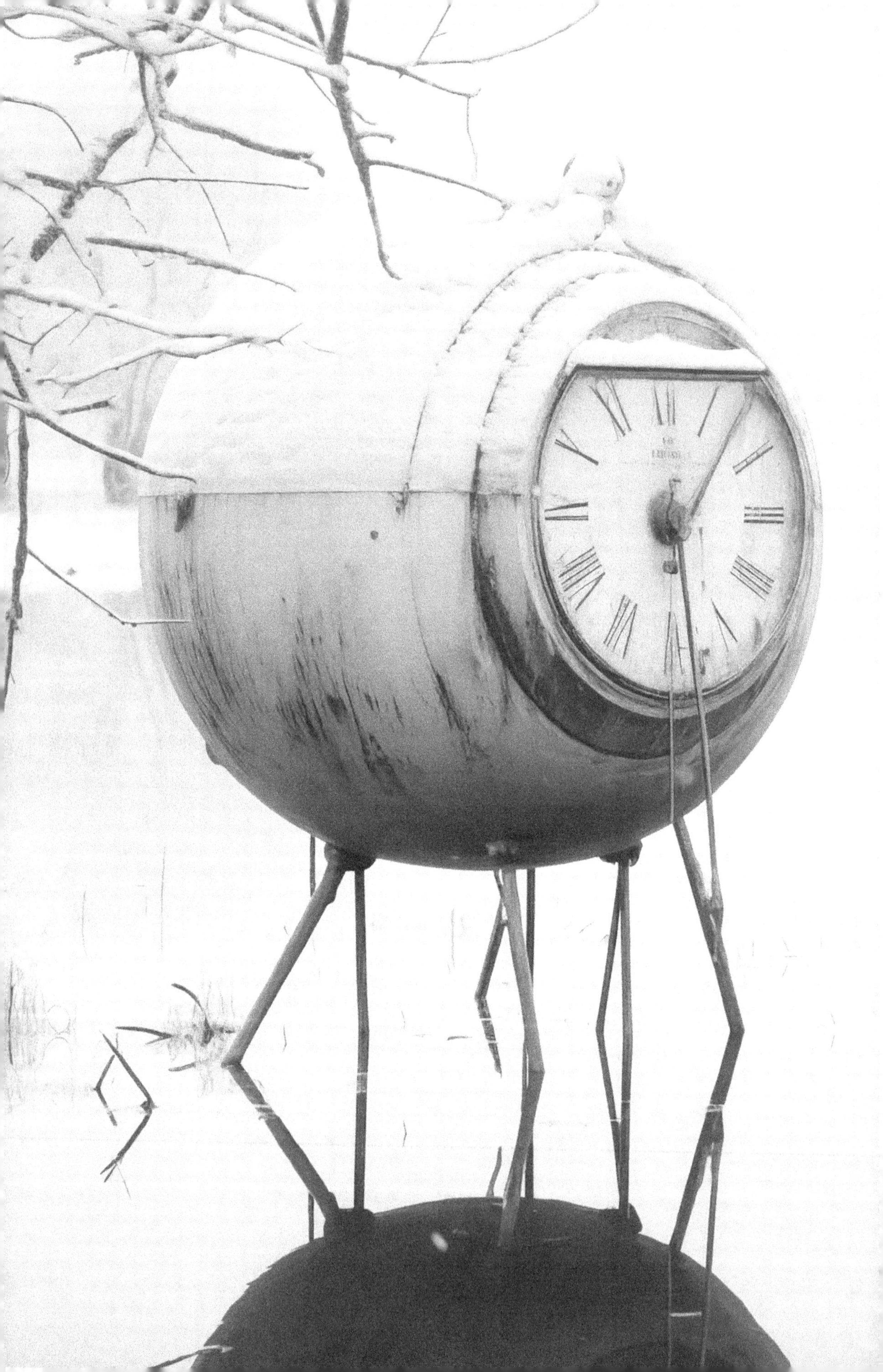

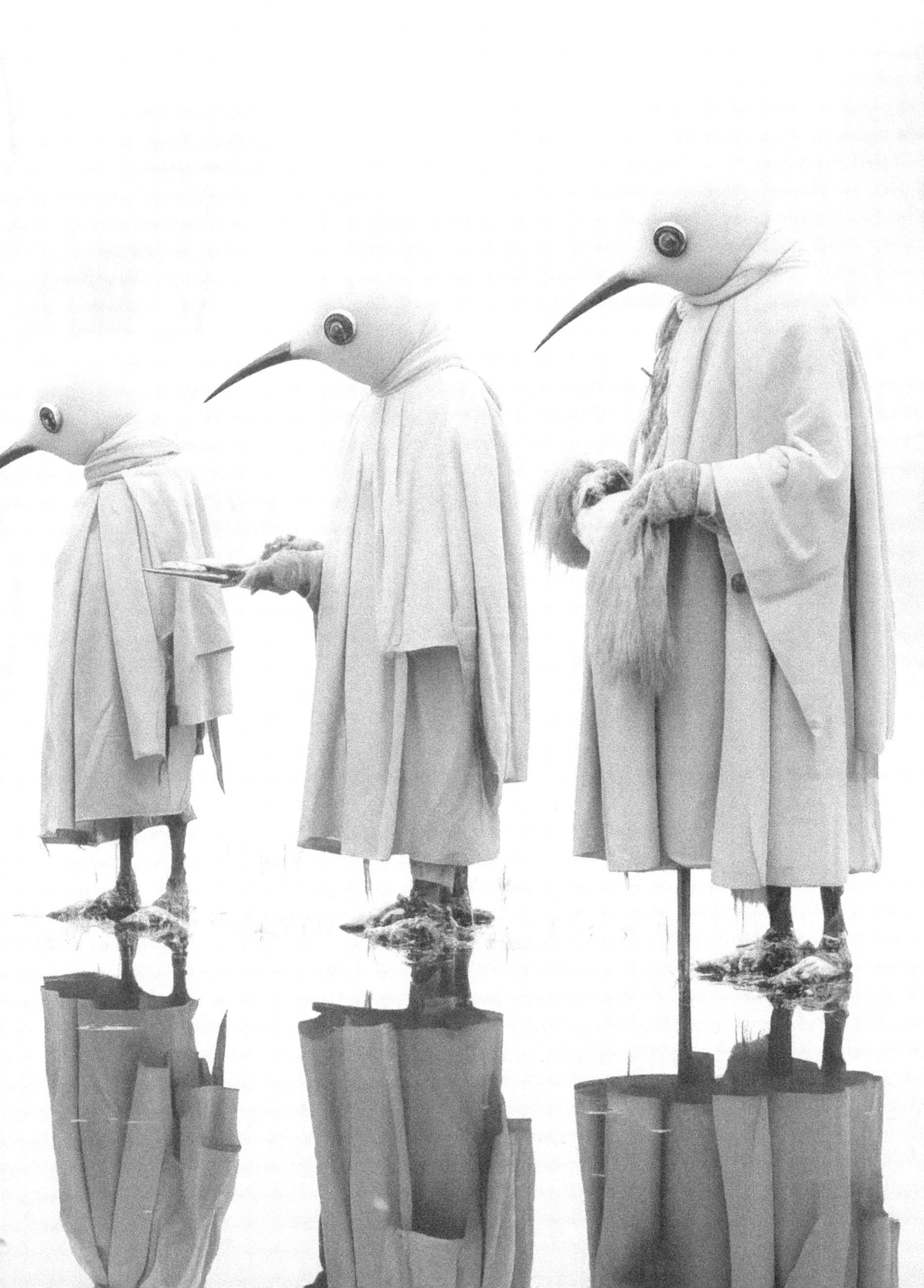

Nothing beats the miracle of a properly running machine.

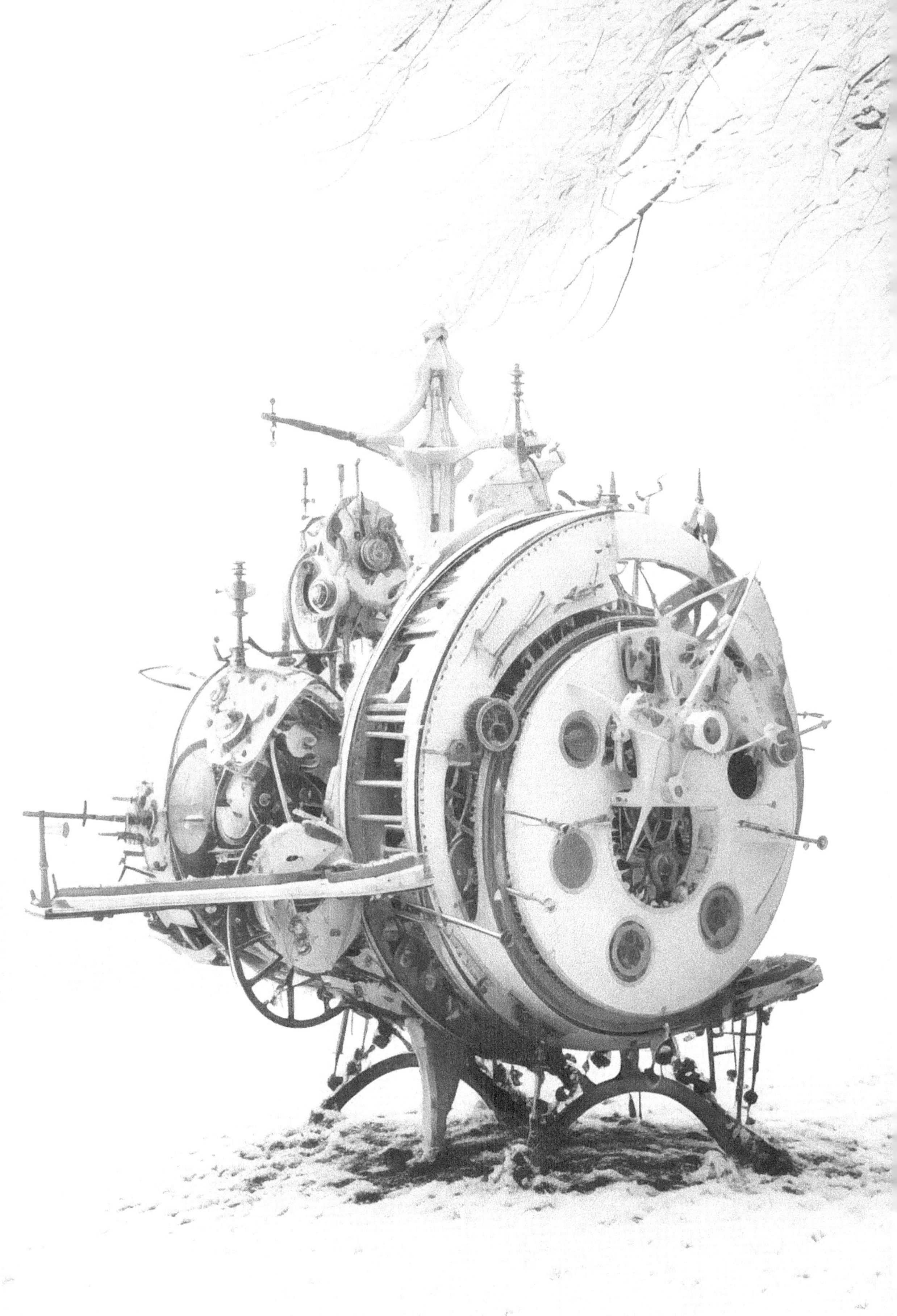

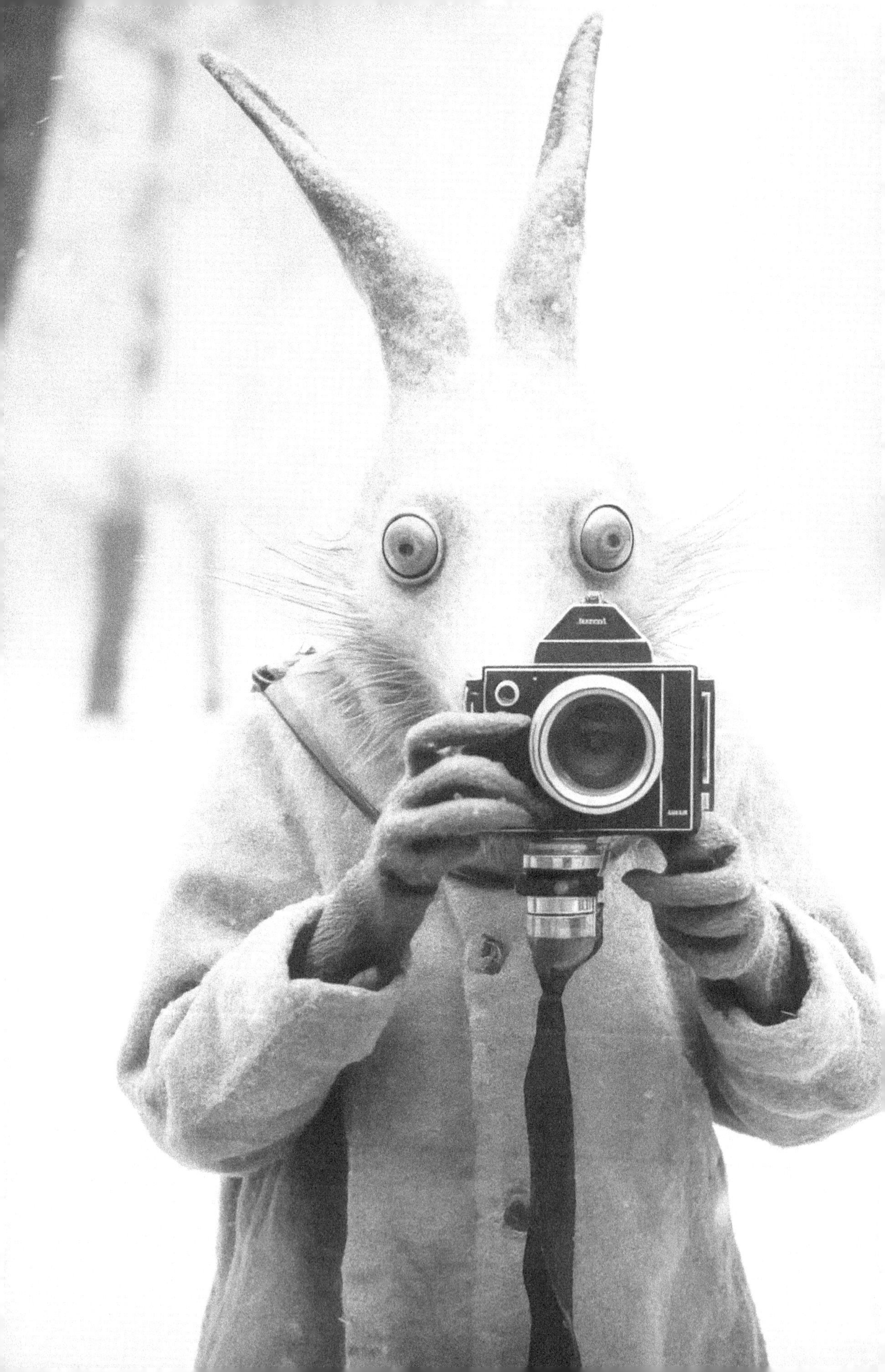

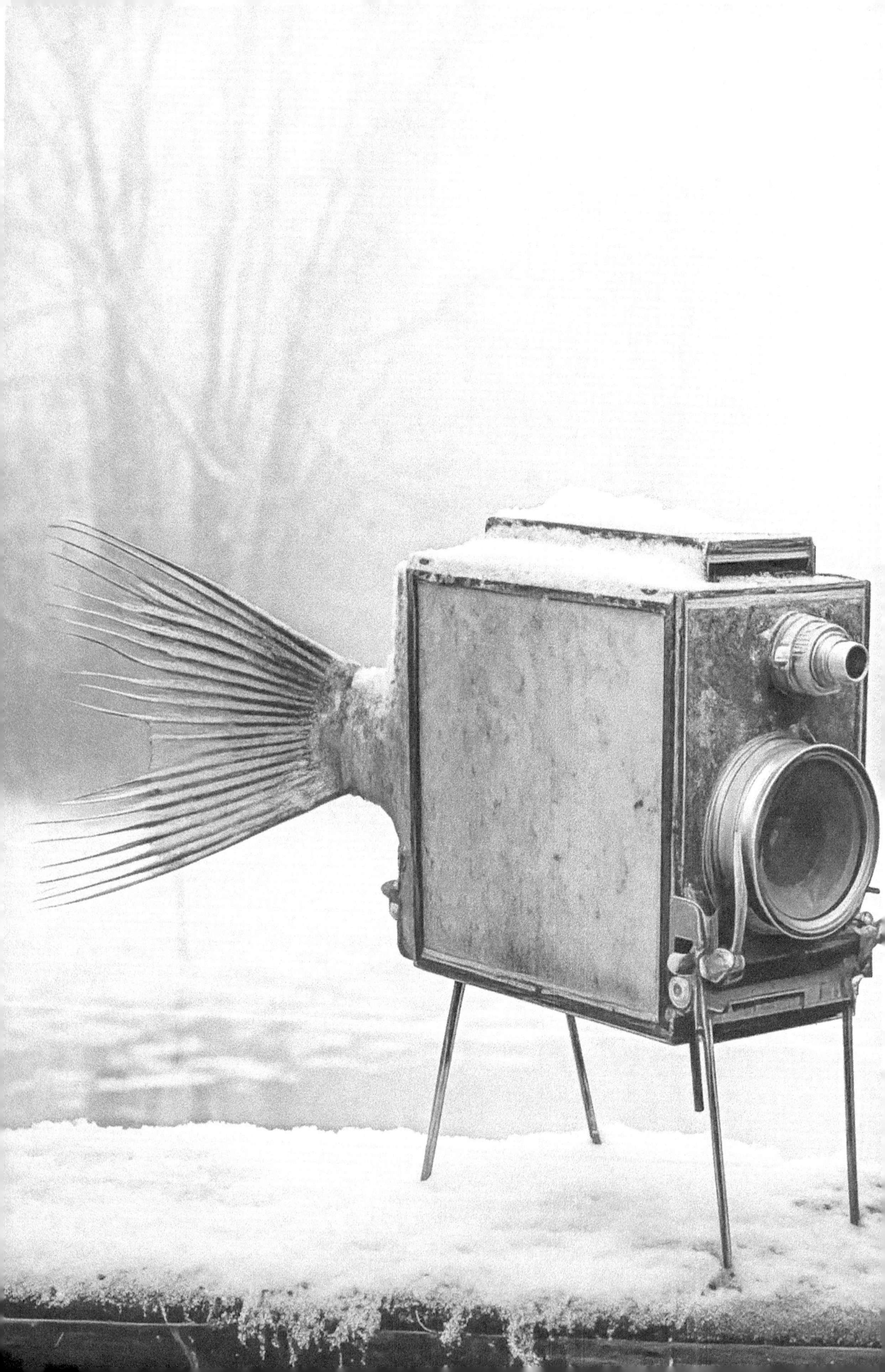

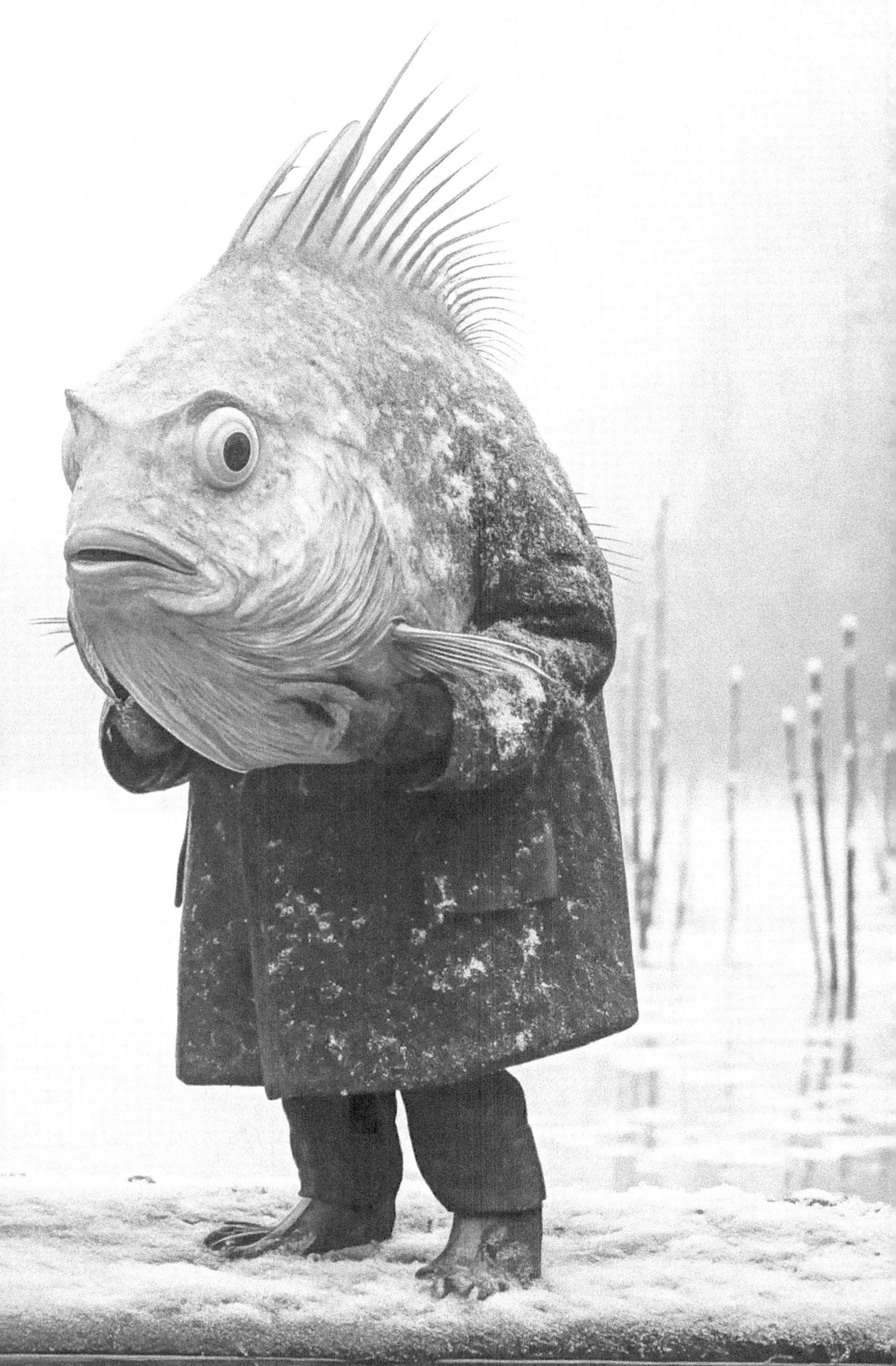

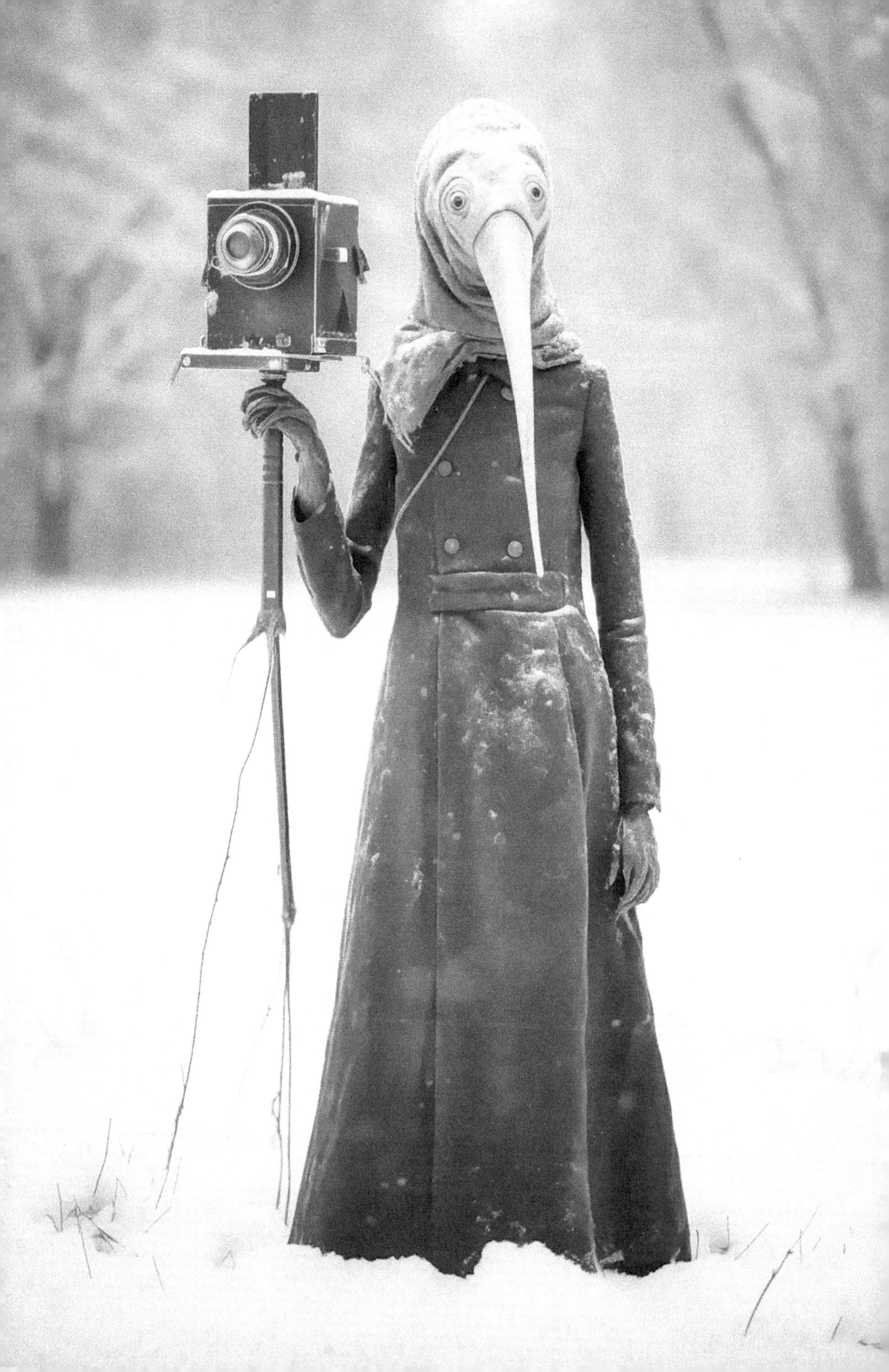

WE
ARE WAGING
A FUTILE WAR
AGAINST
THE FUGACITY
OF THE
MOMENT.

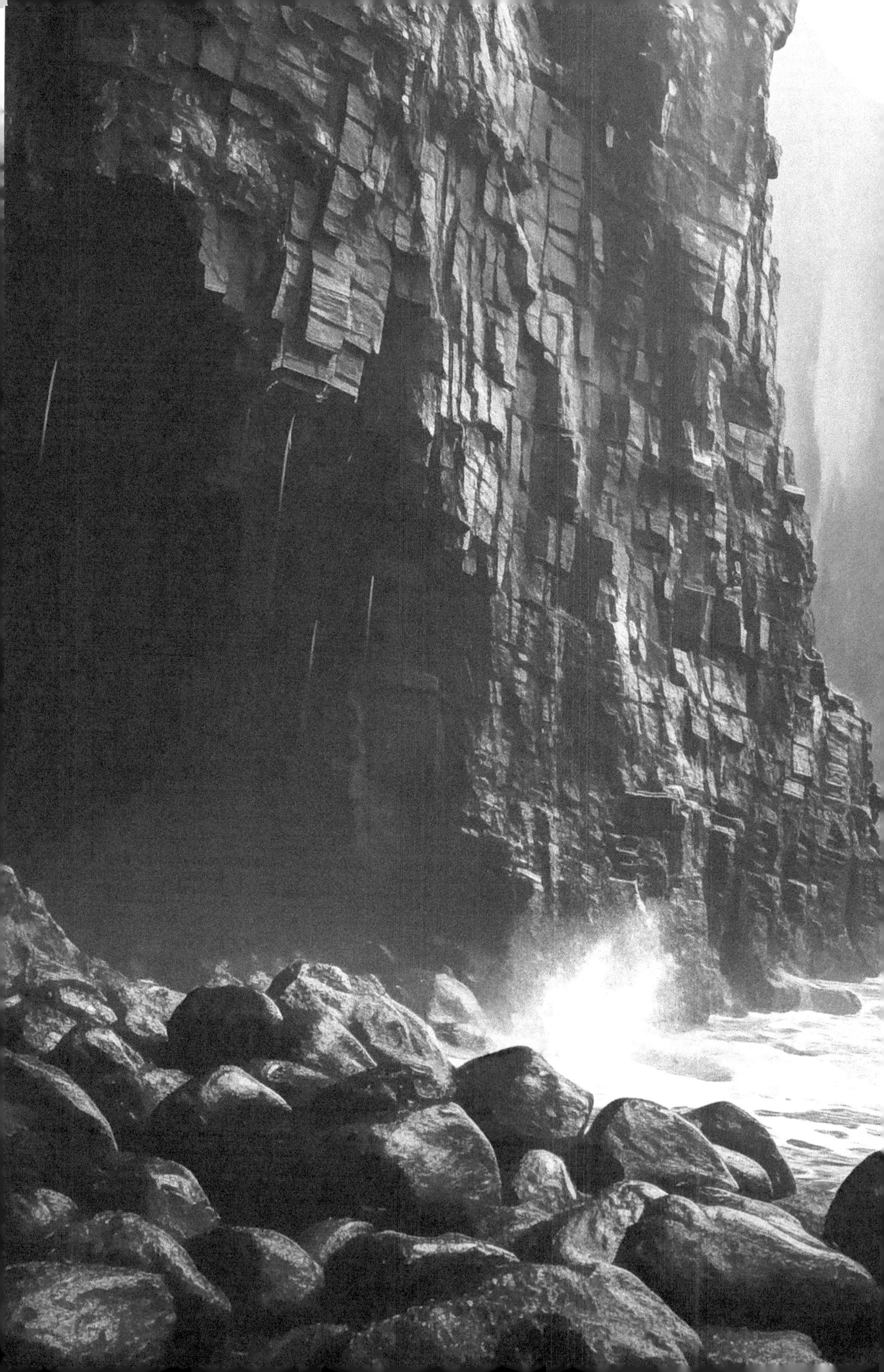

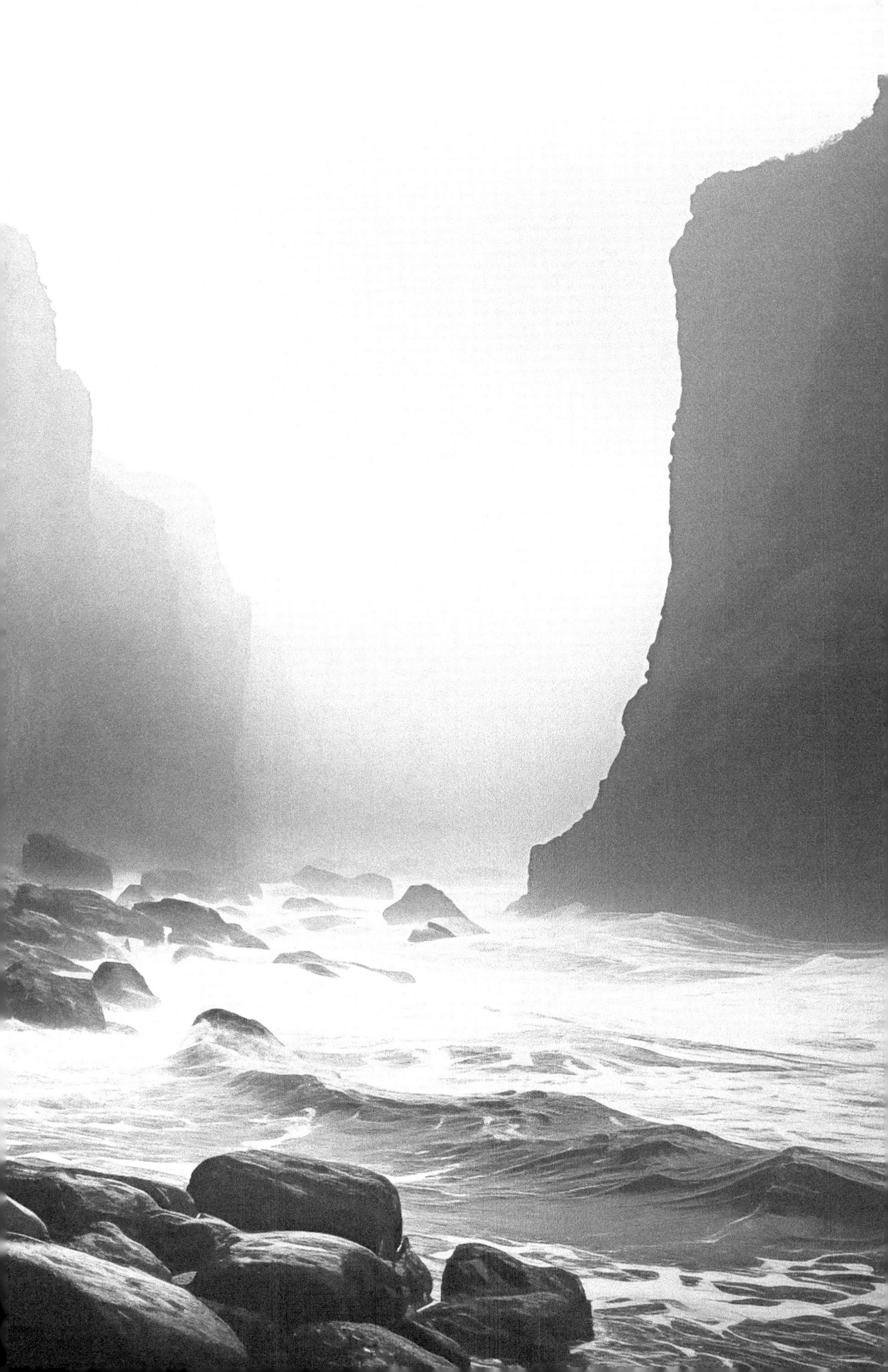

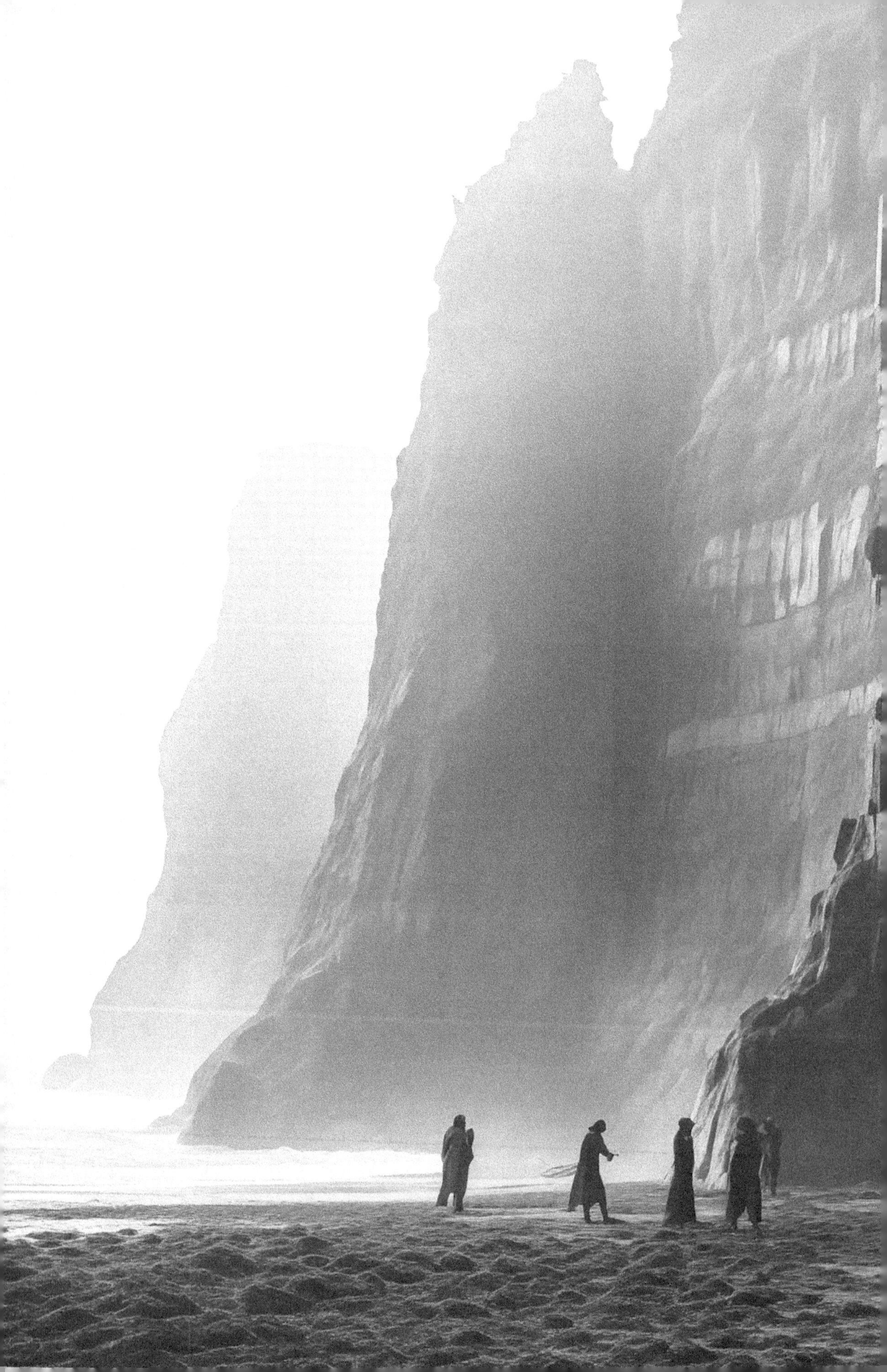

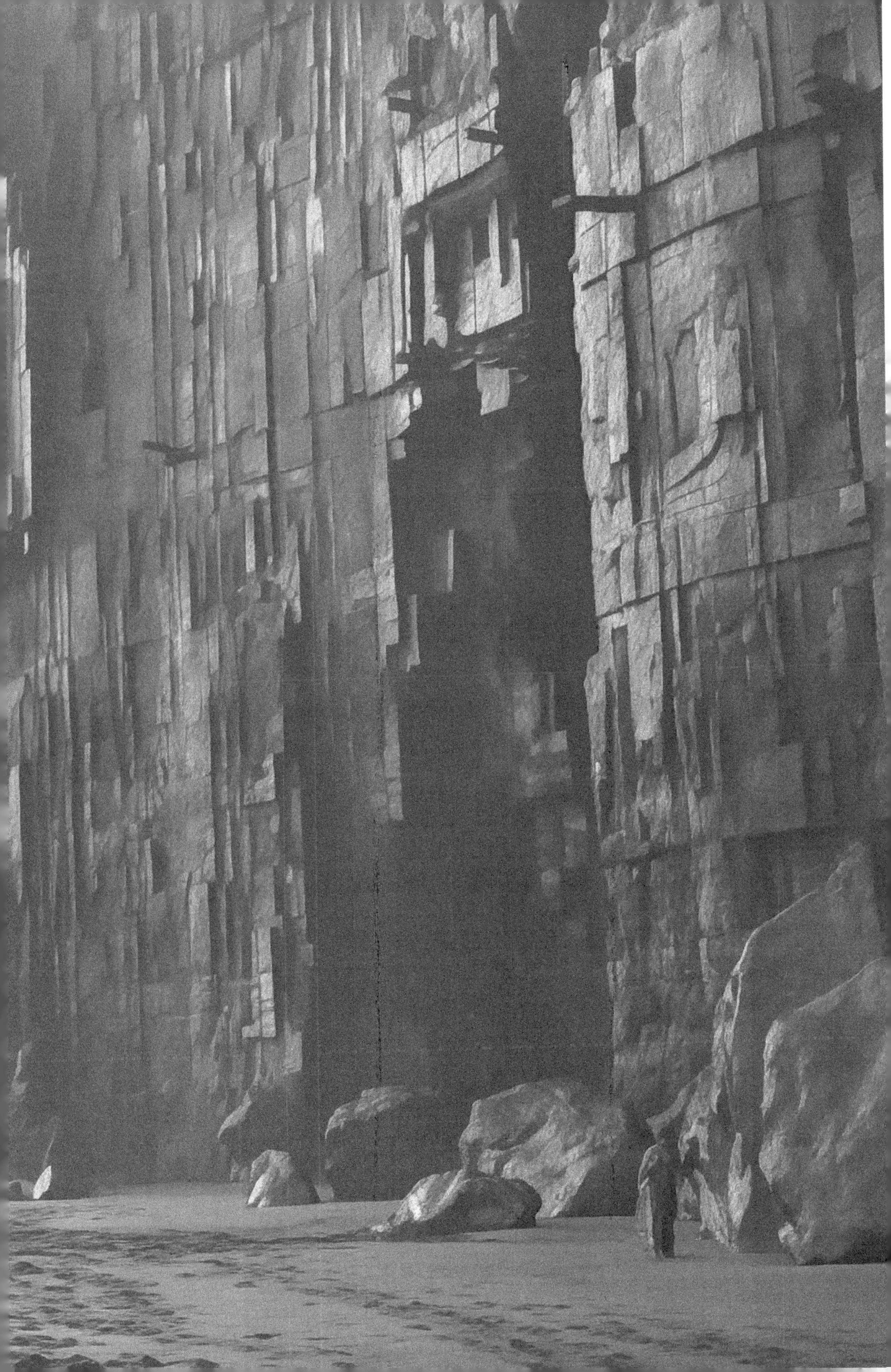

Oh sweet death!
Thy kiss shall
be the dark
echo of joy.

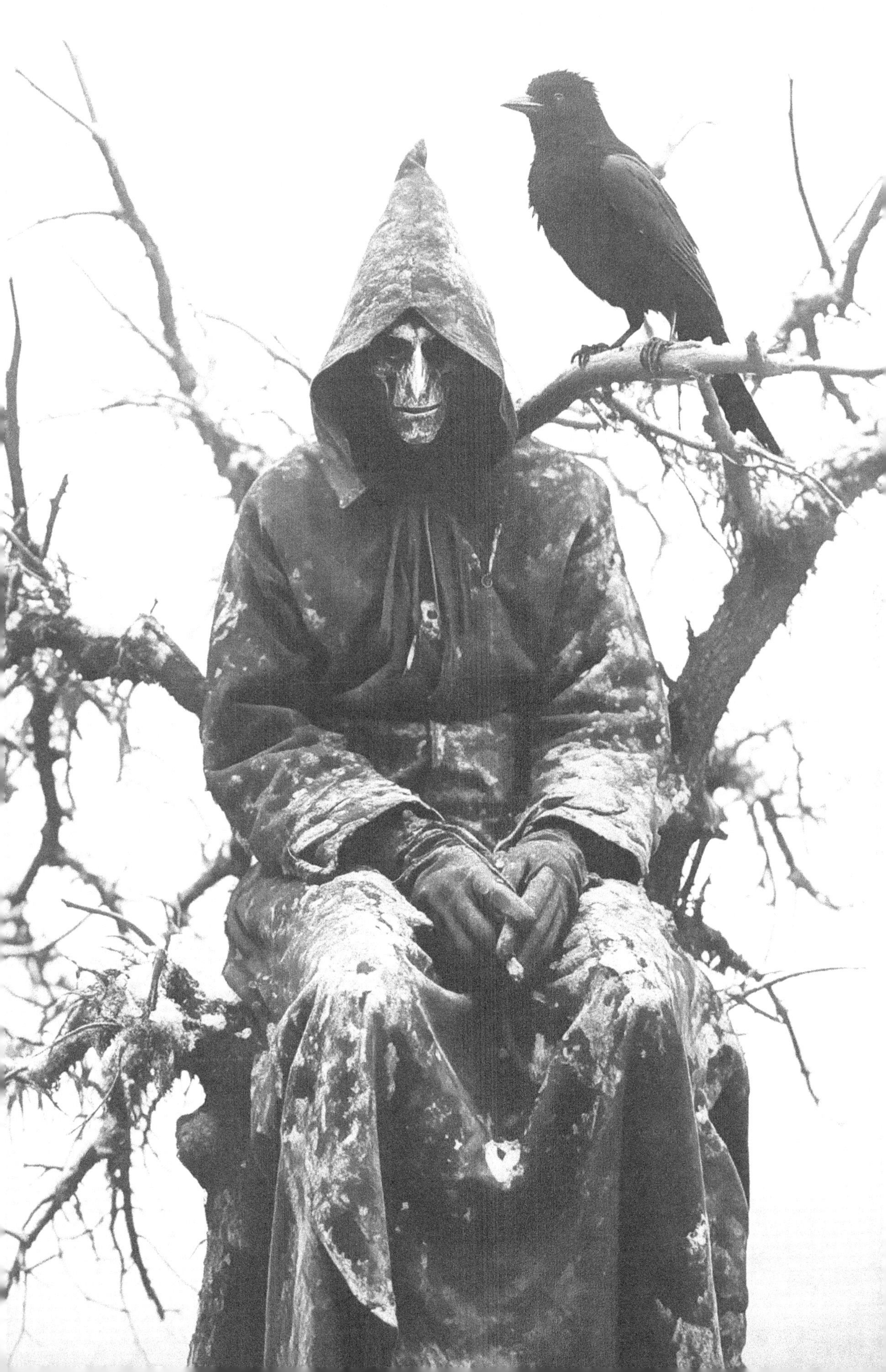

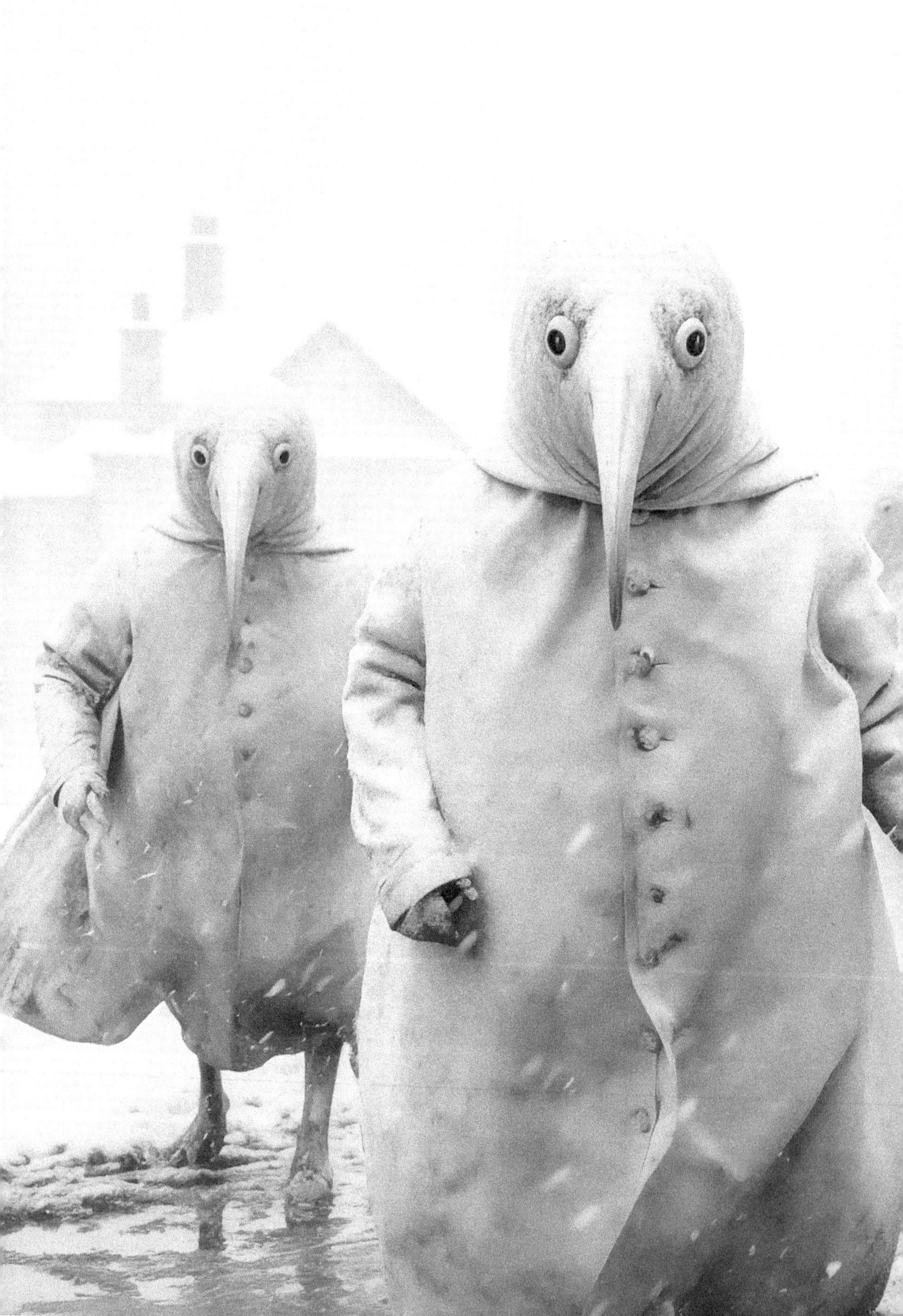

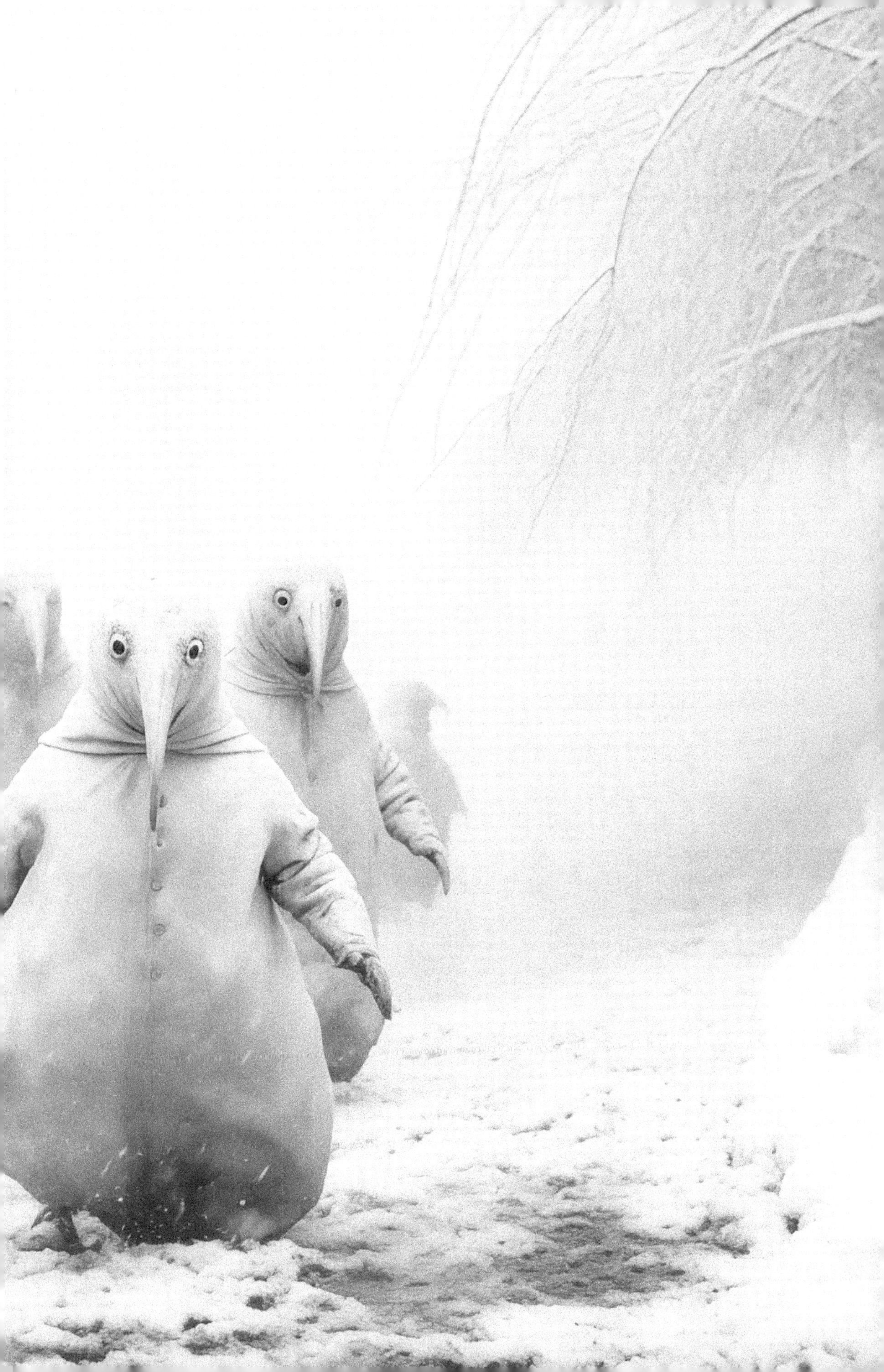

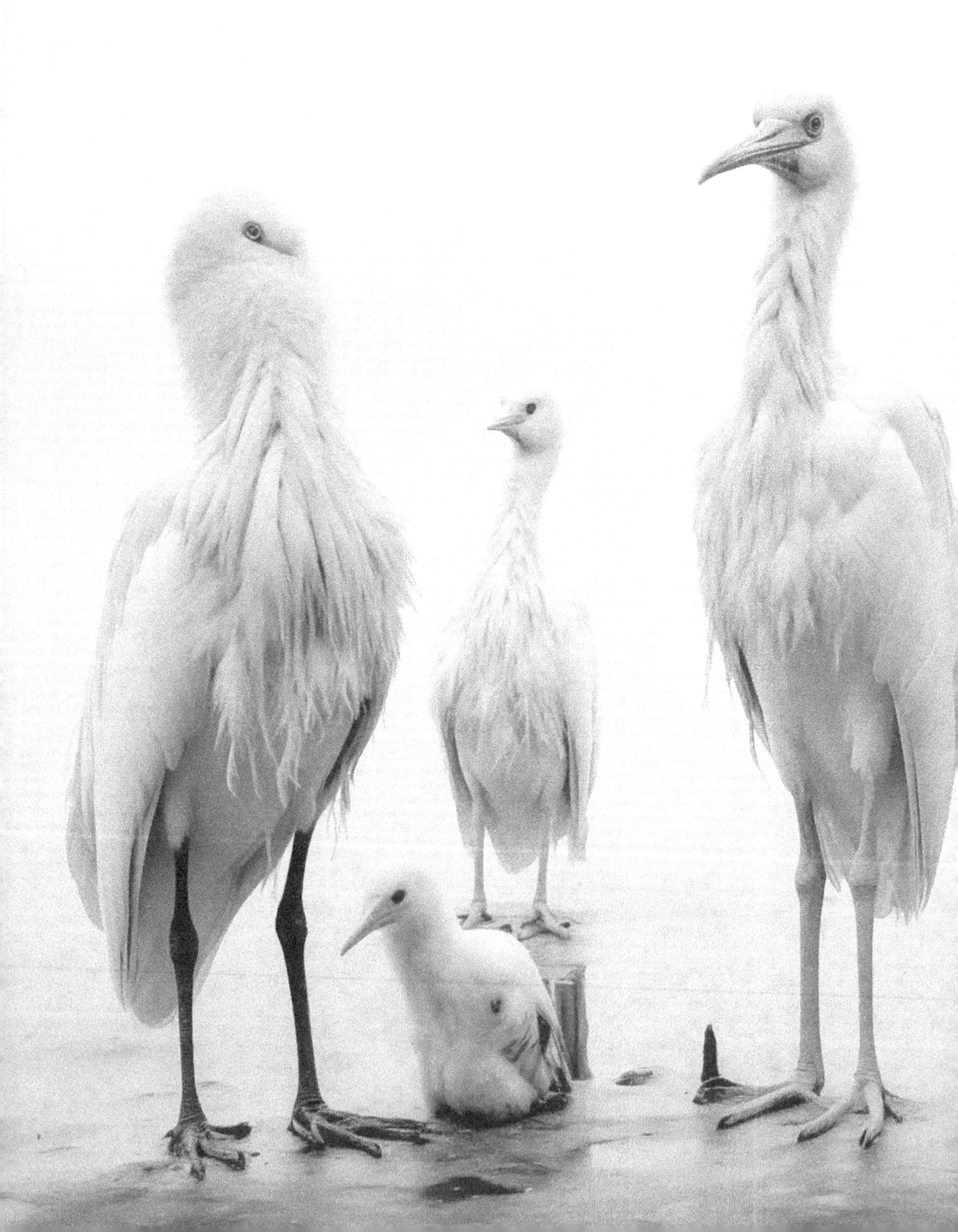

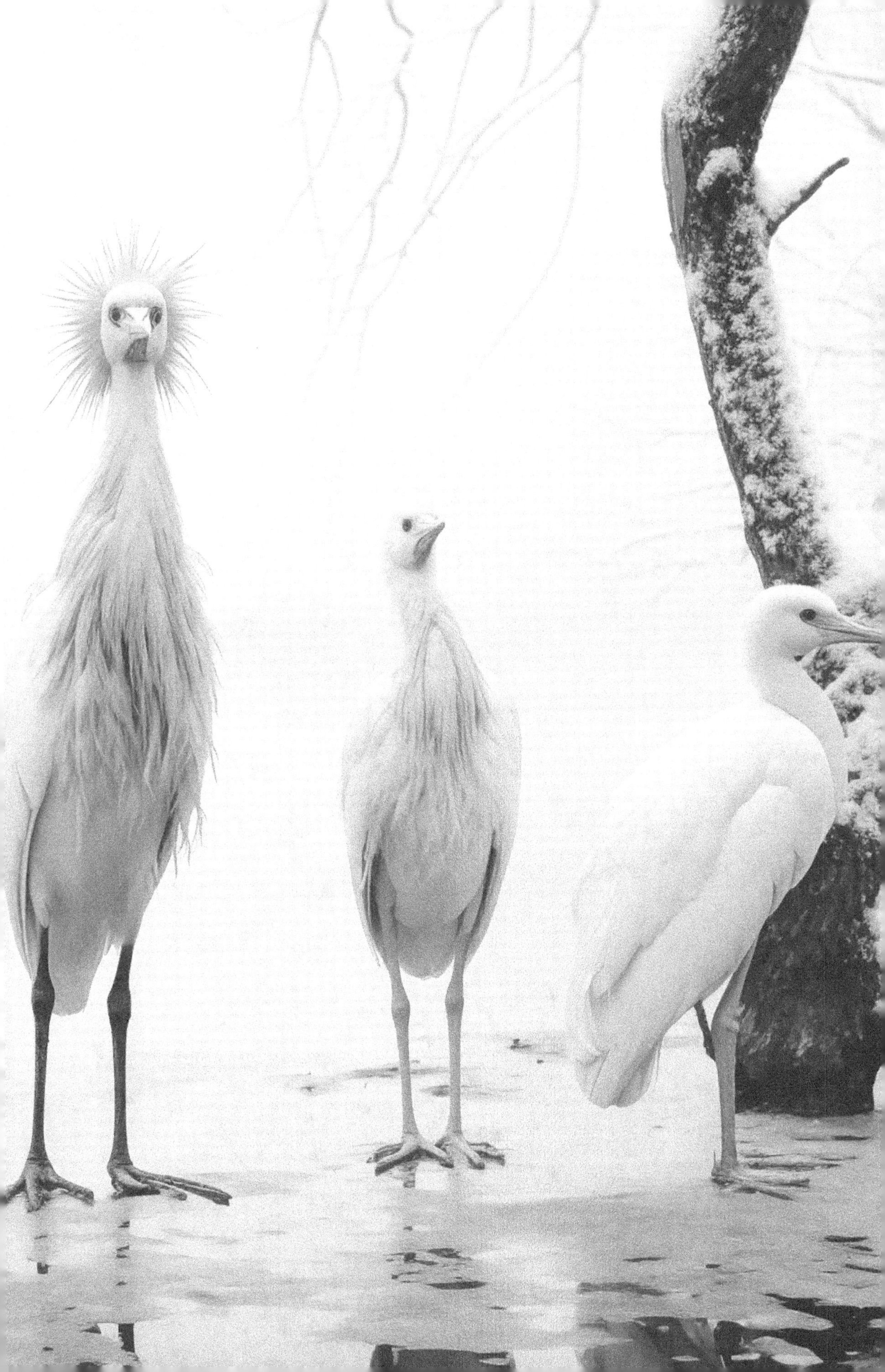

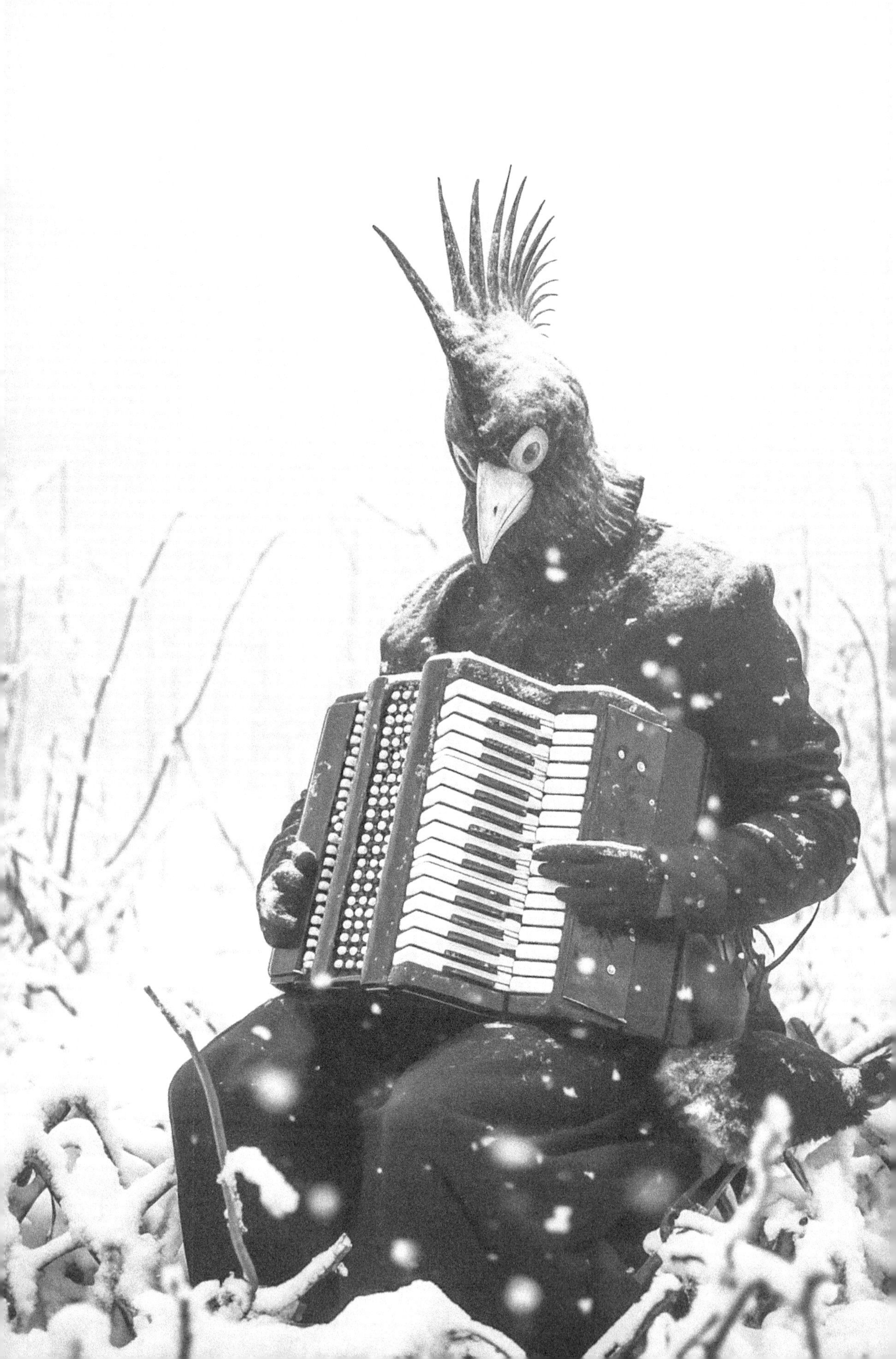

Capturing silence.

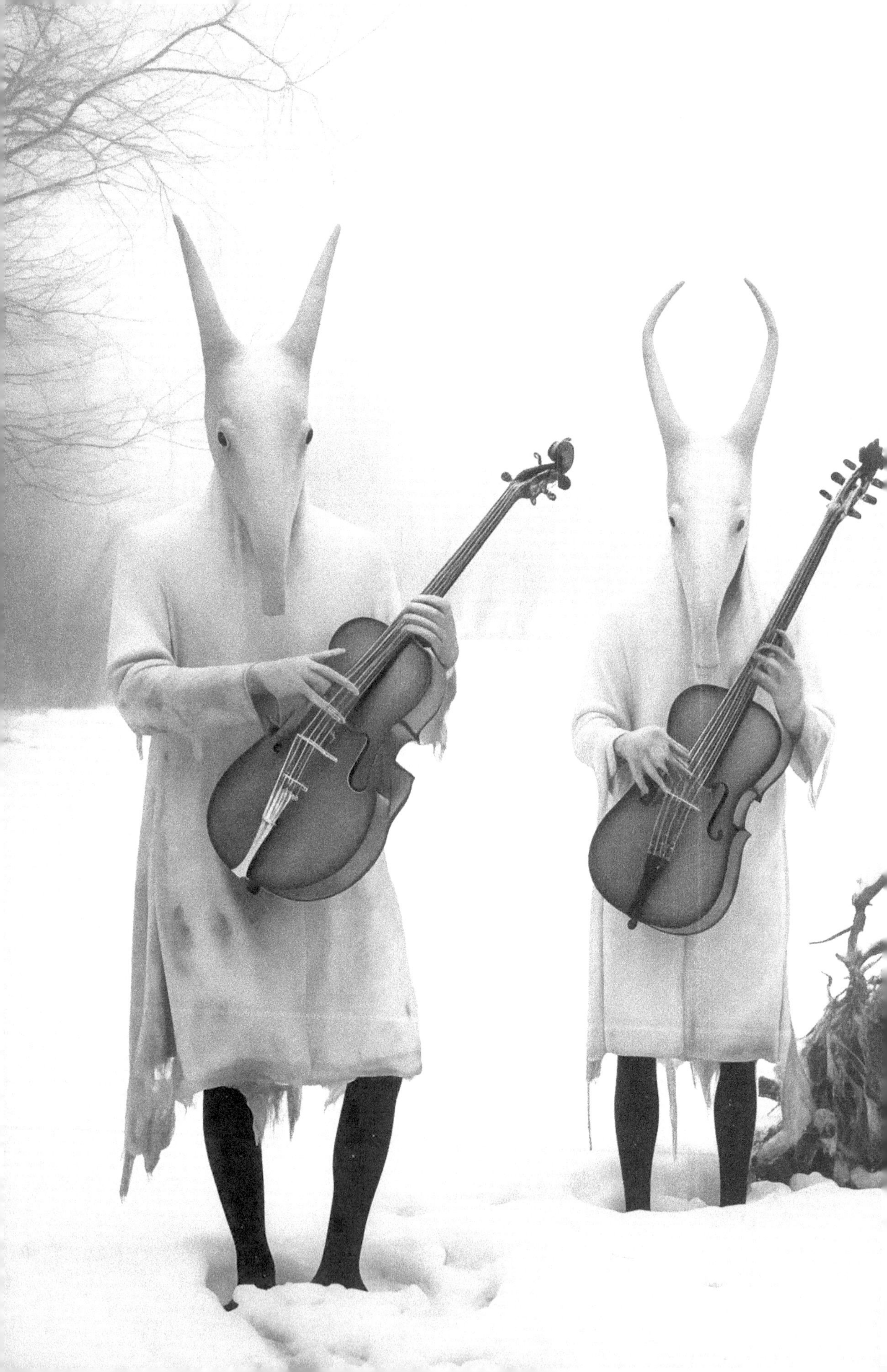

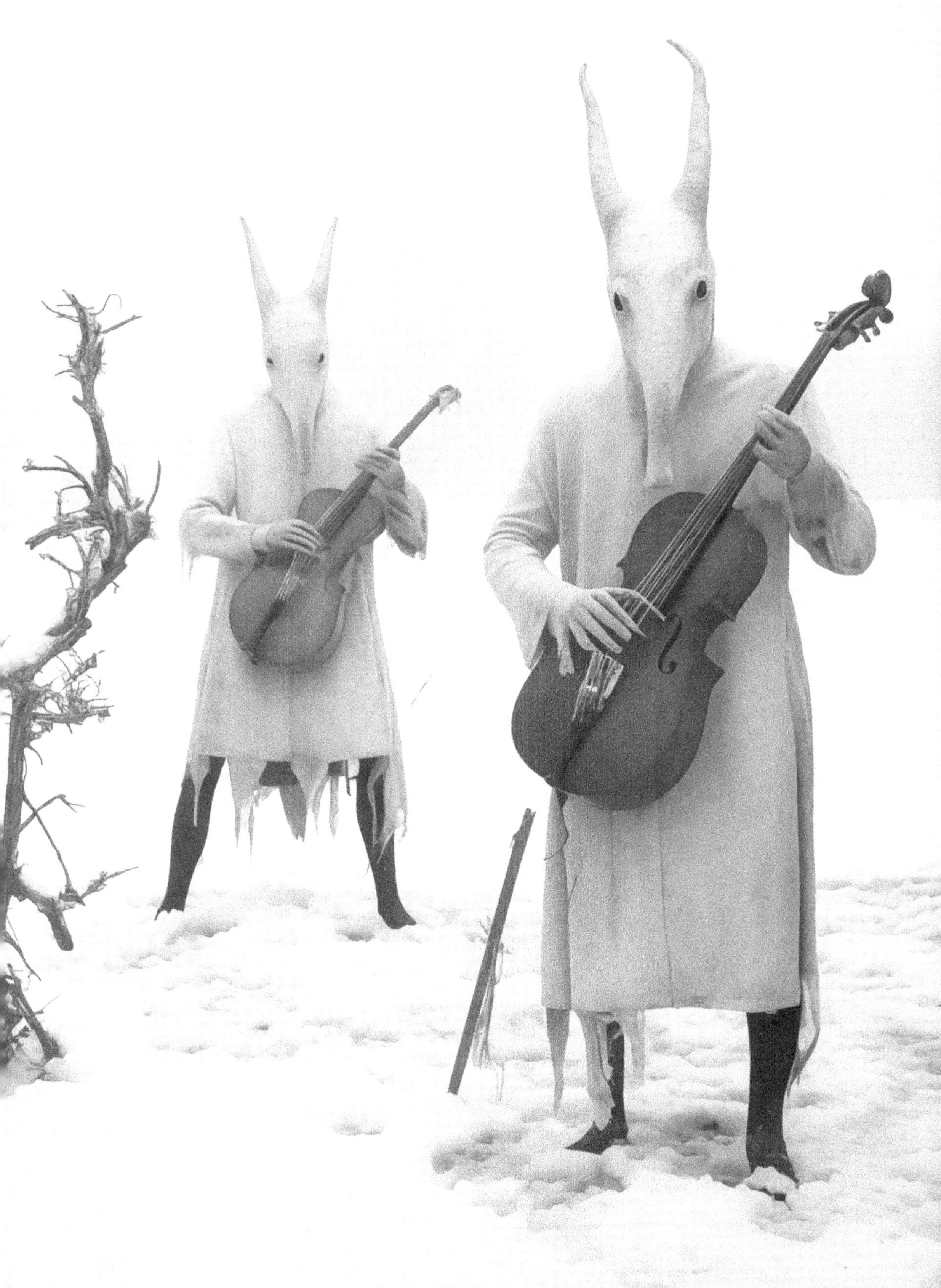

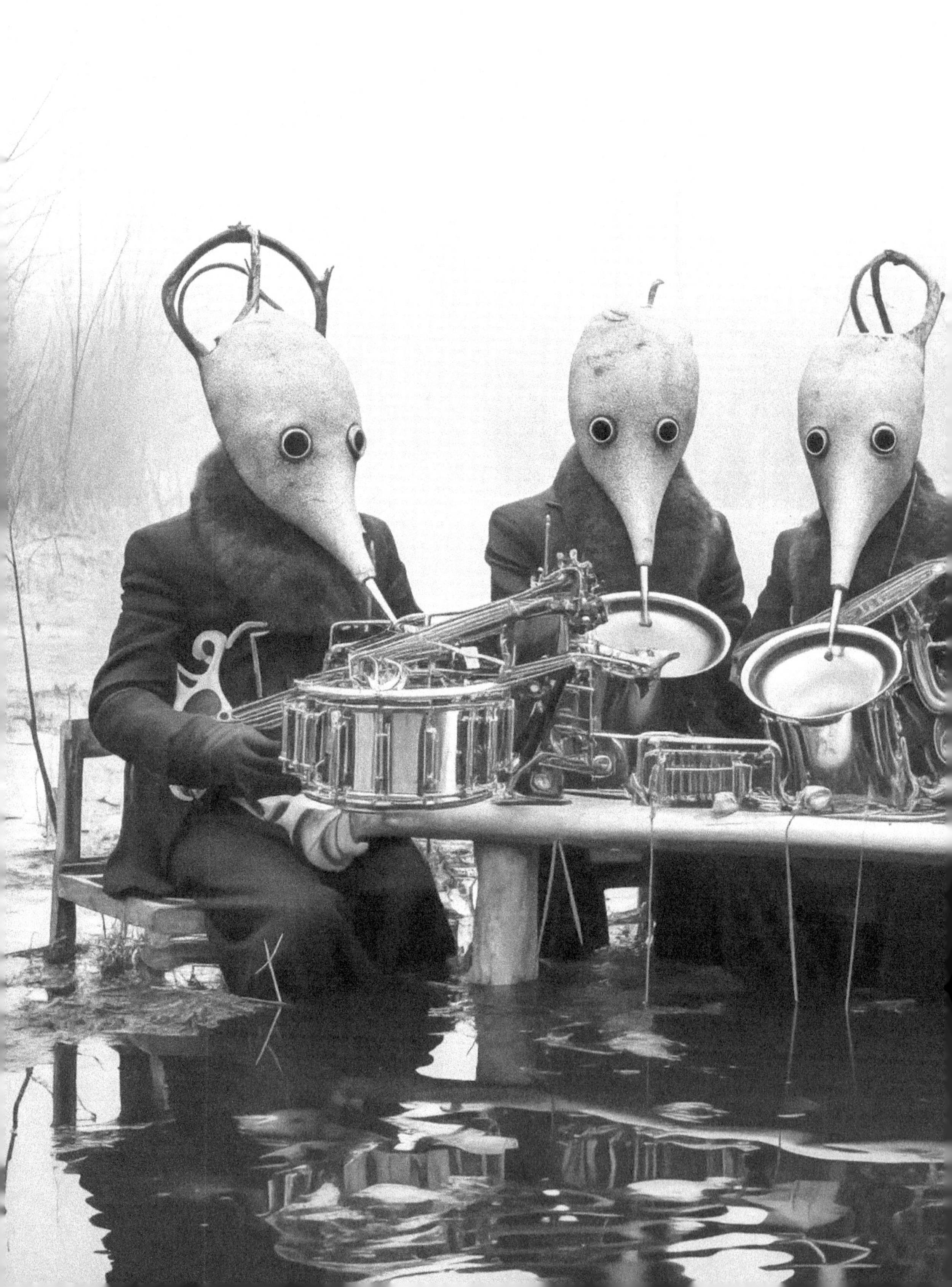

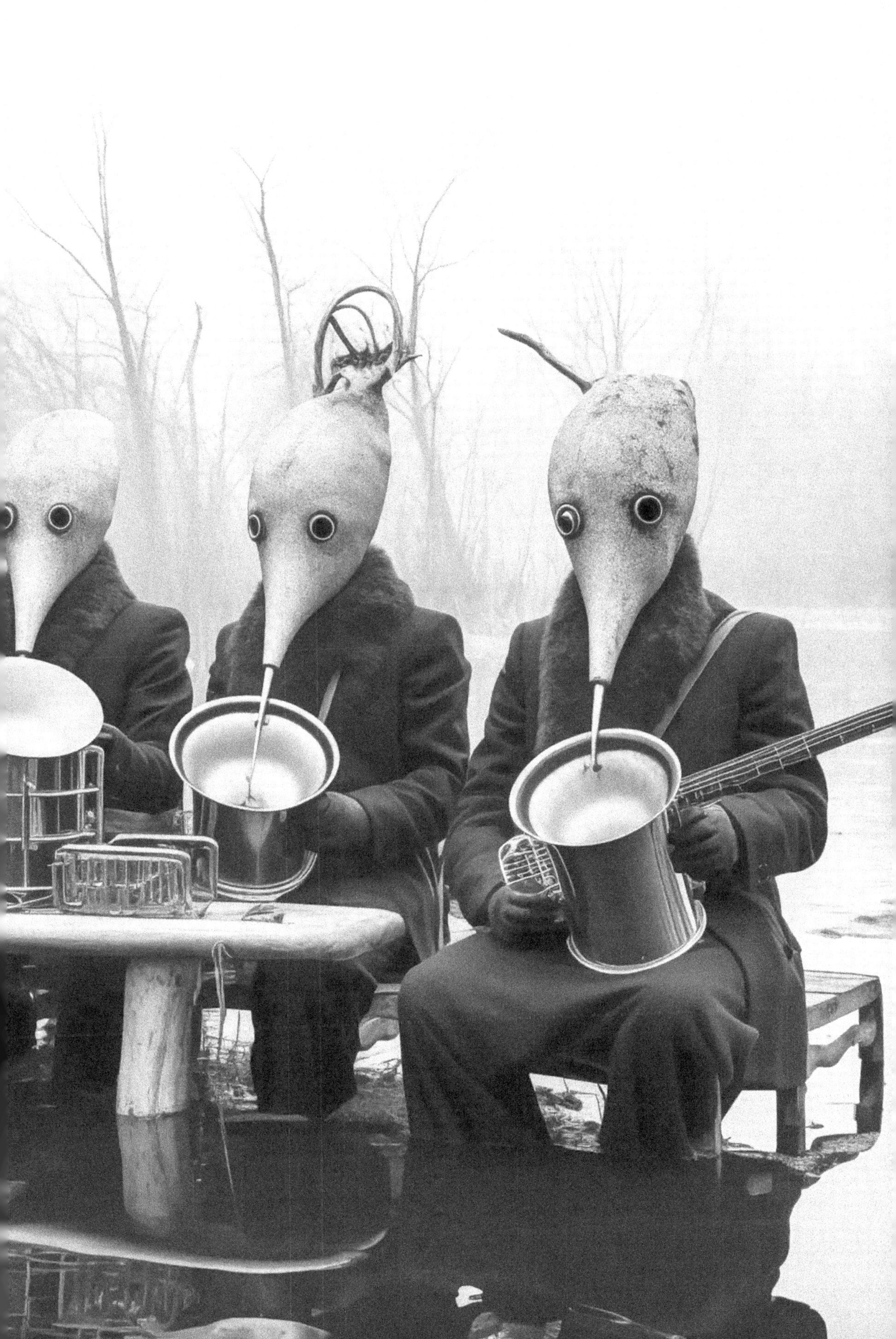

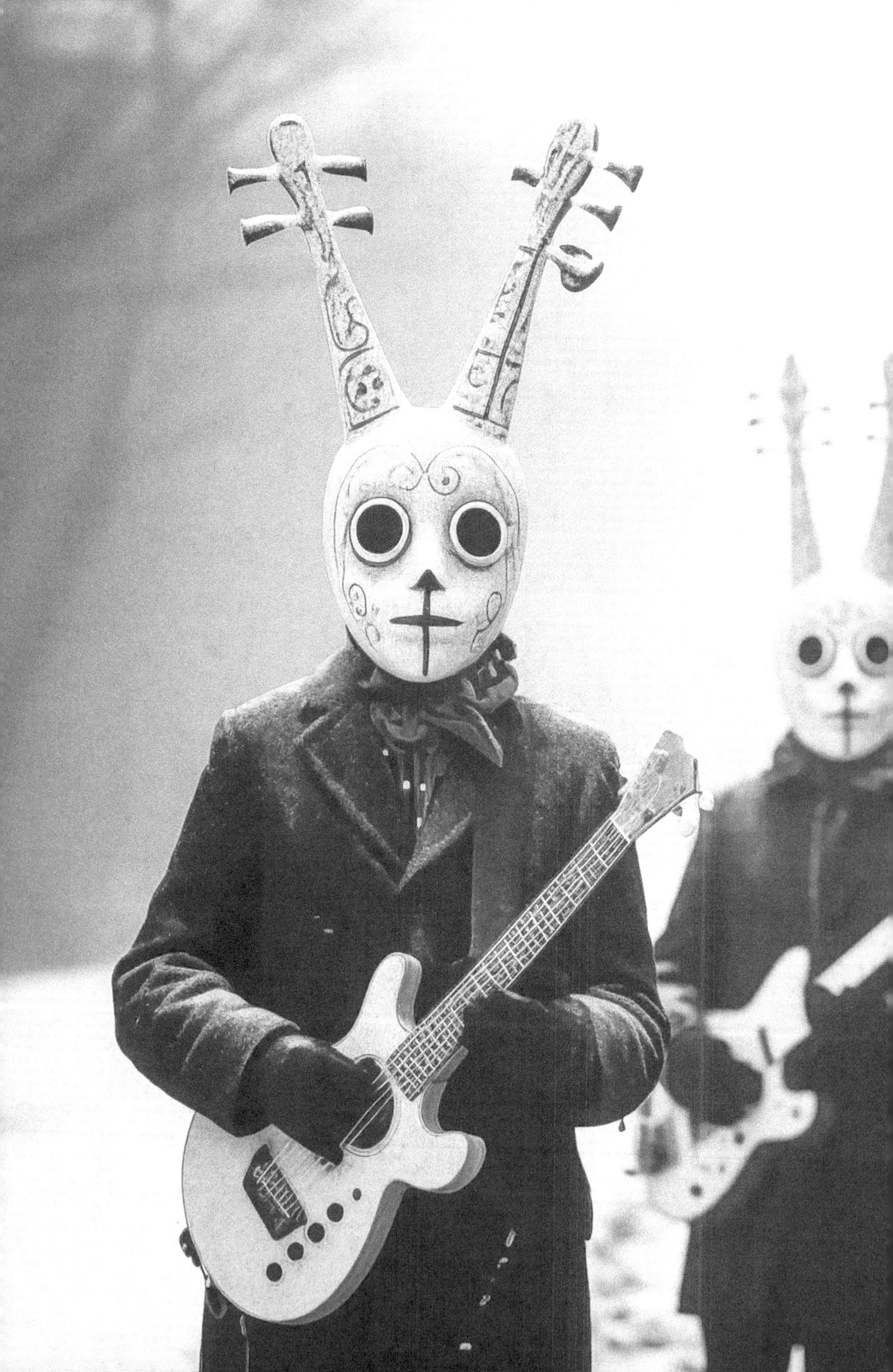

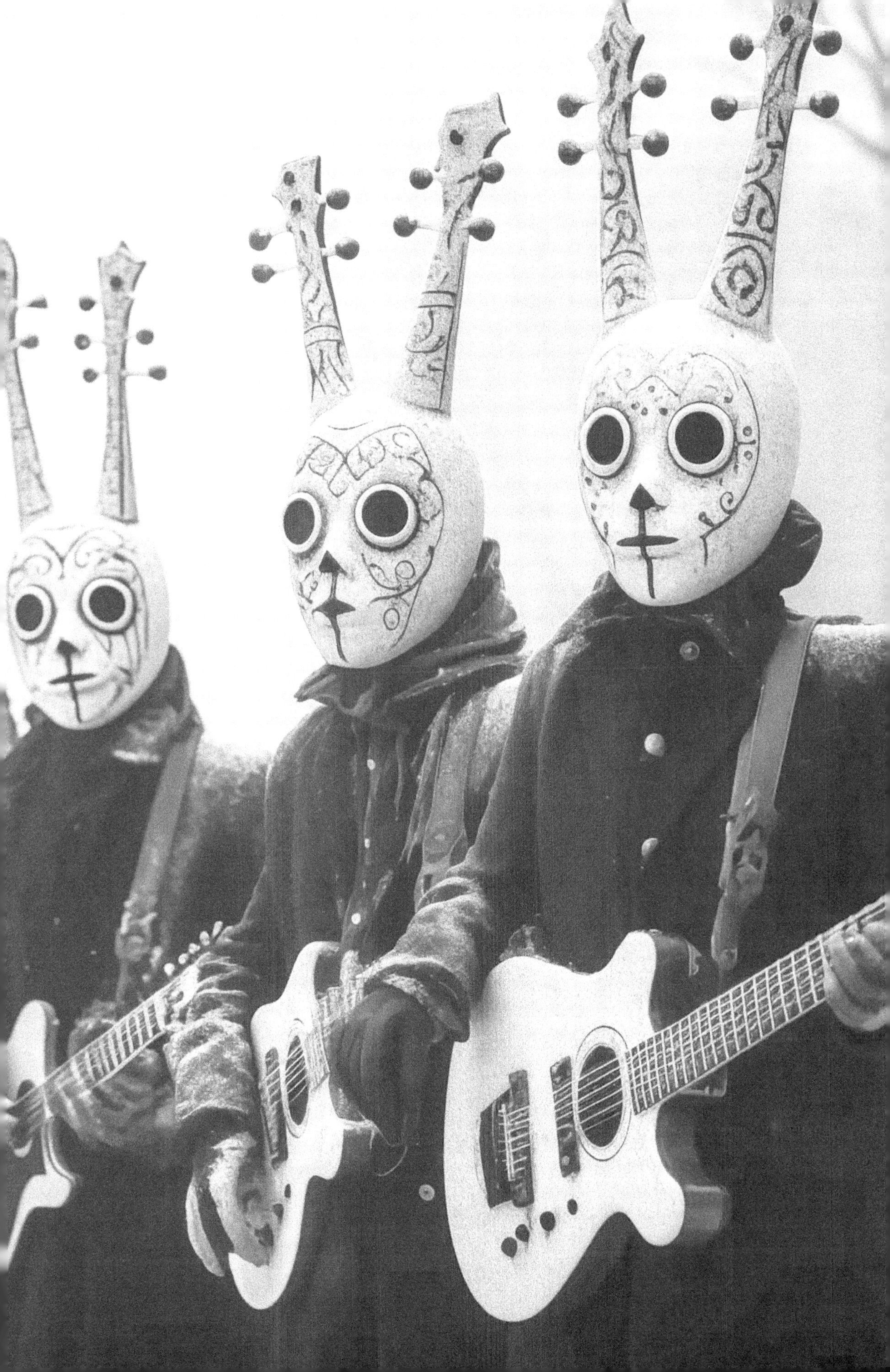

ONLY BY
PLAYING
CAN WE
ABANDON
OURSELVES

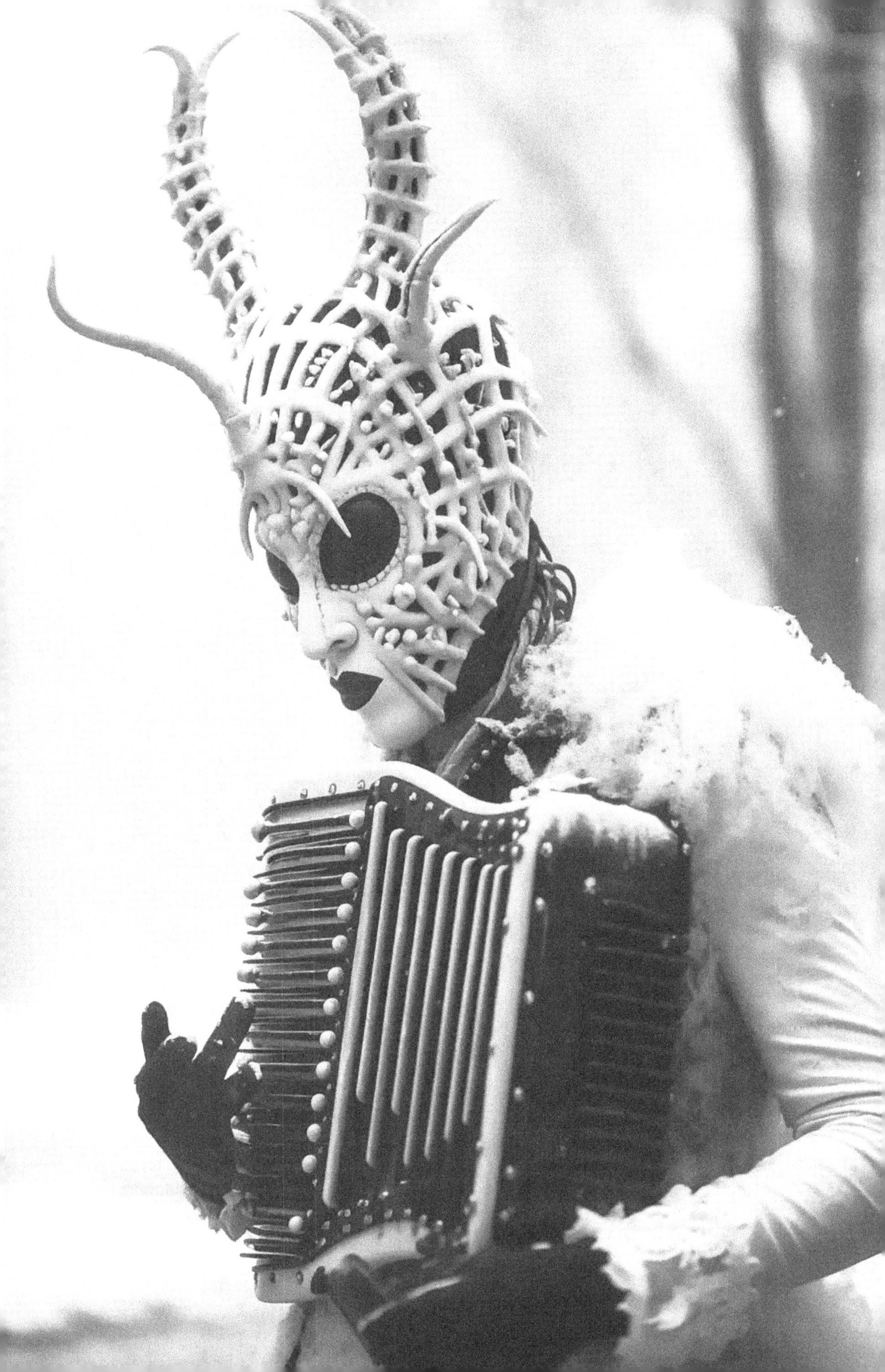

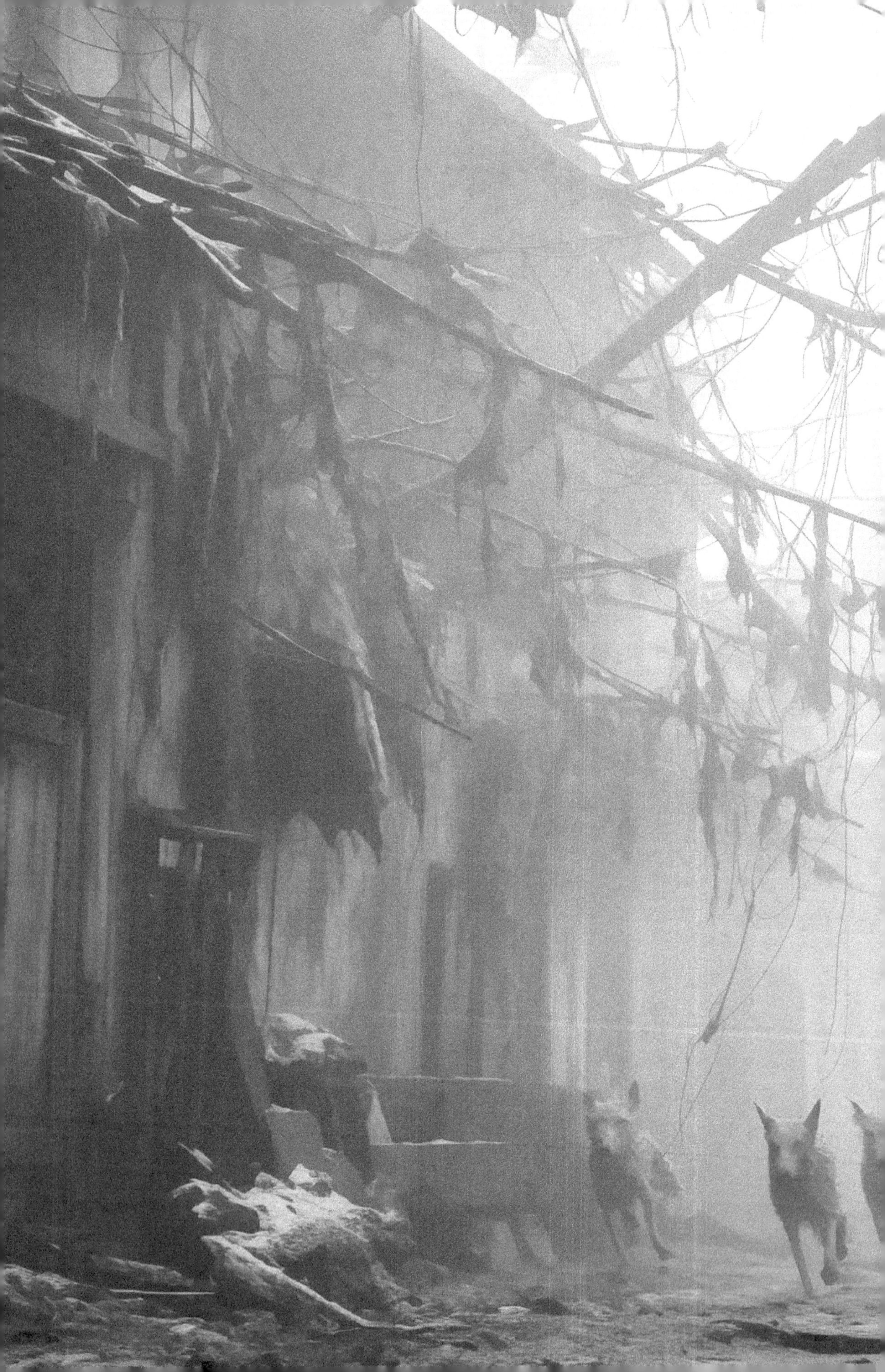

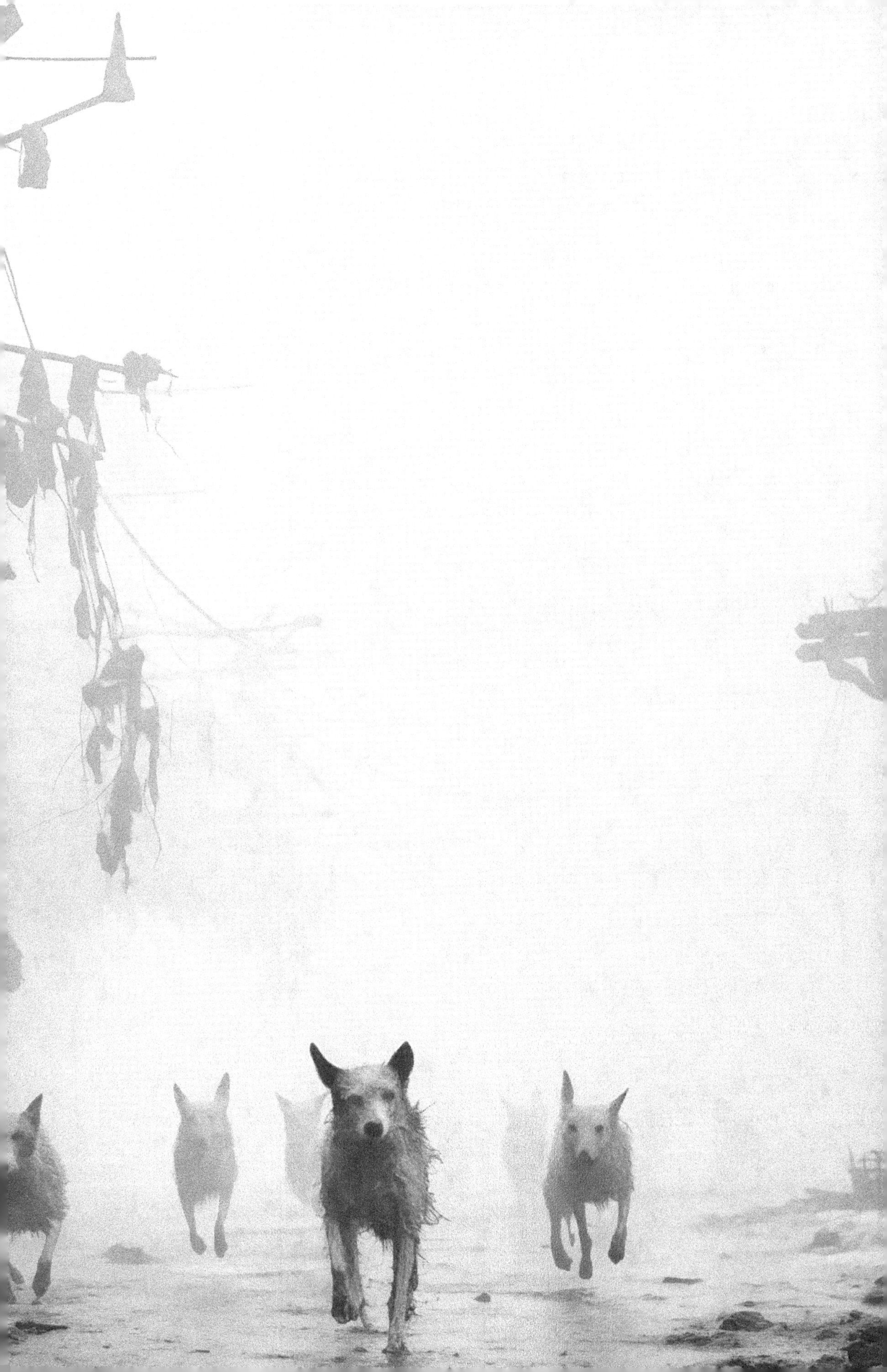

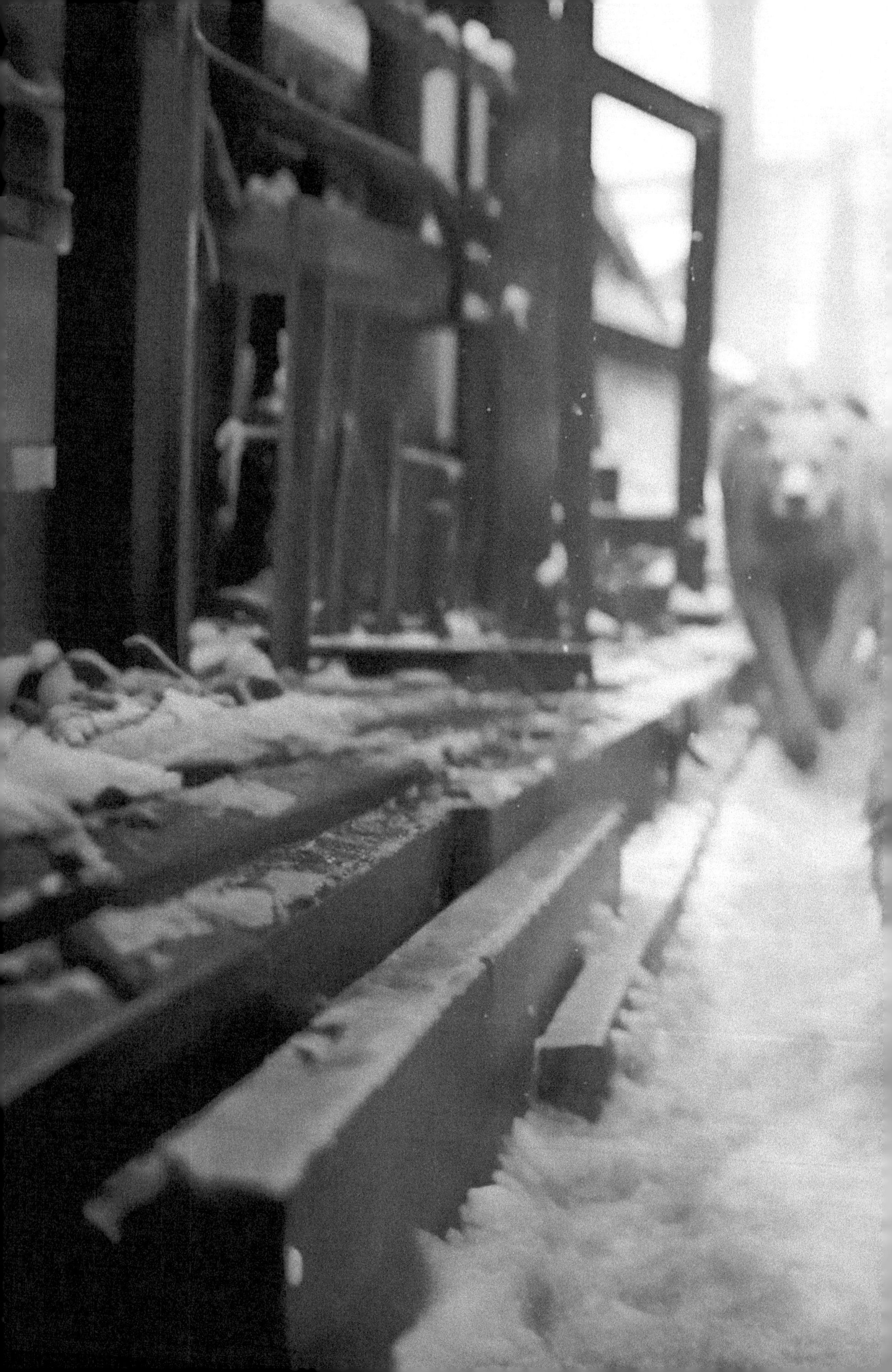

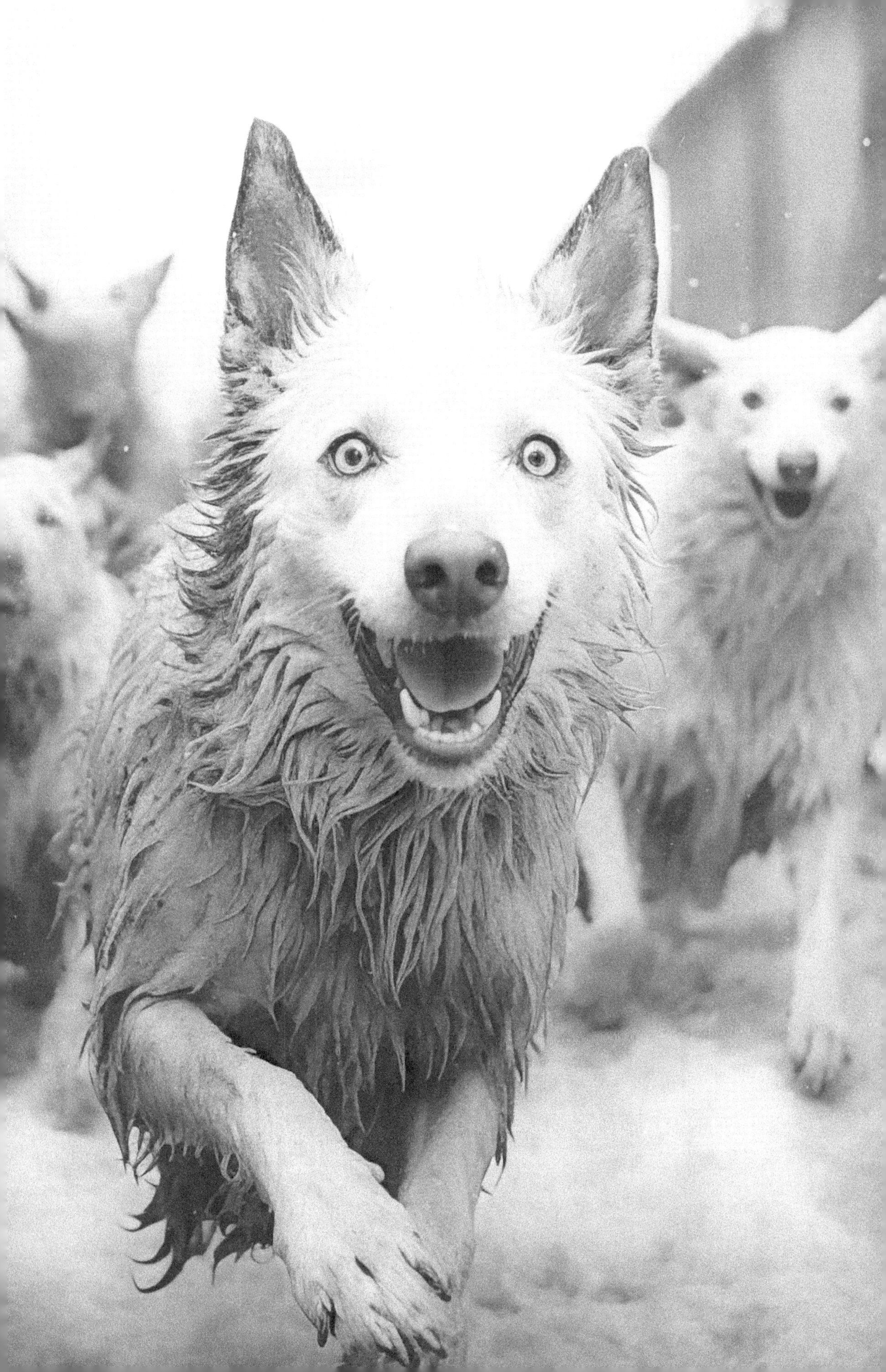

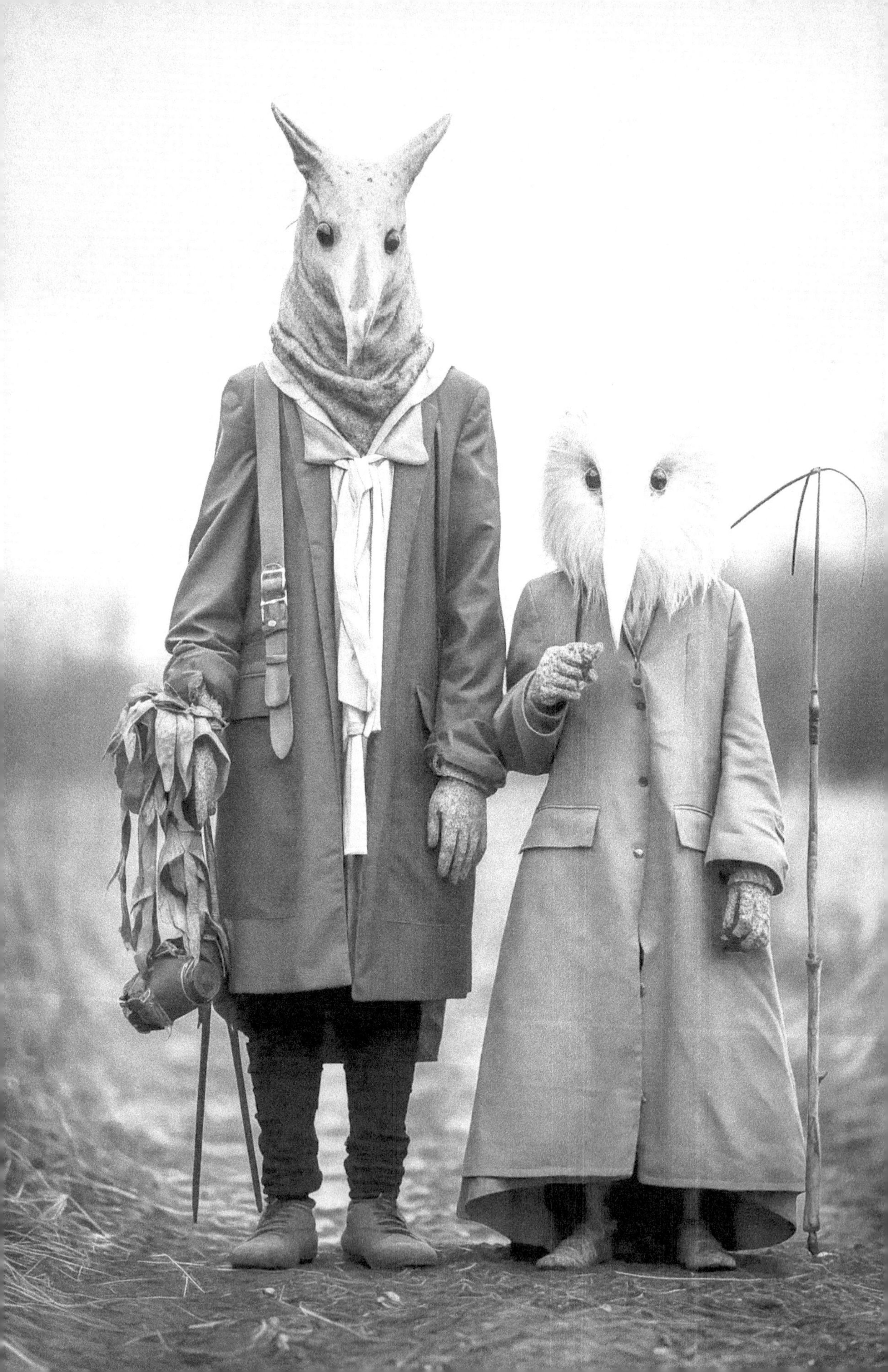

THIS UNCERTAINTY OF THE JOURNEY

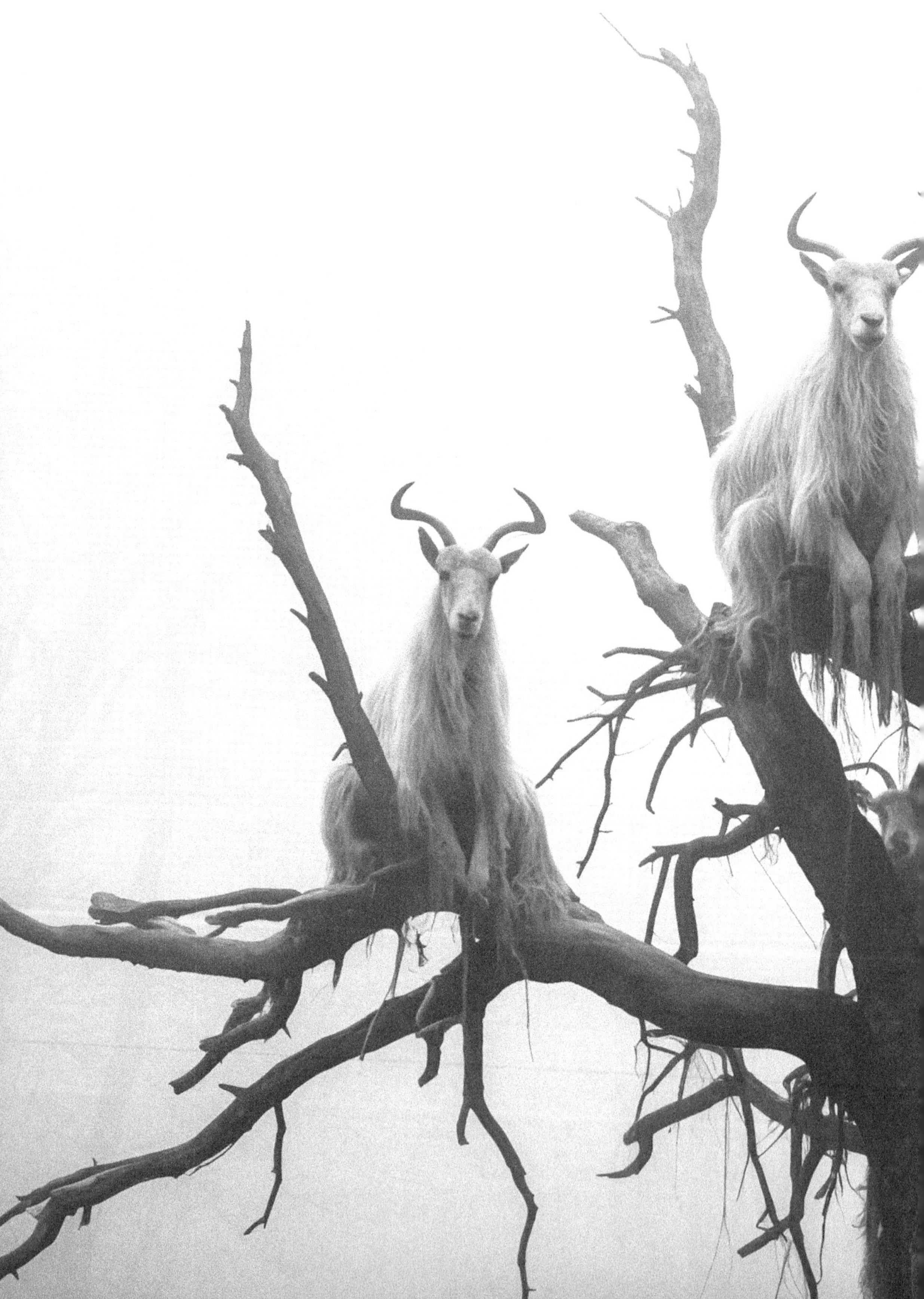

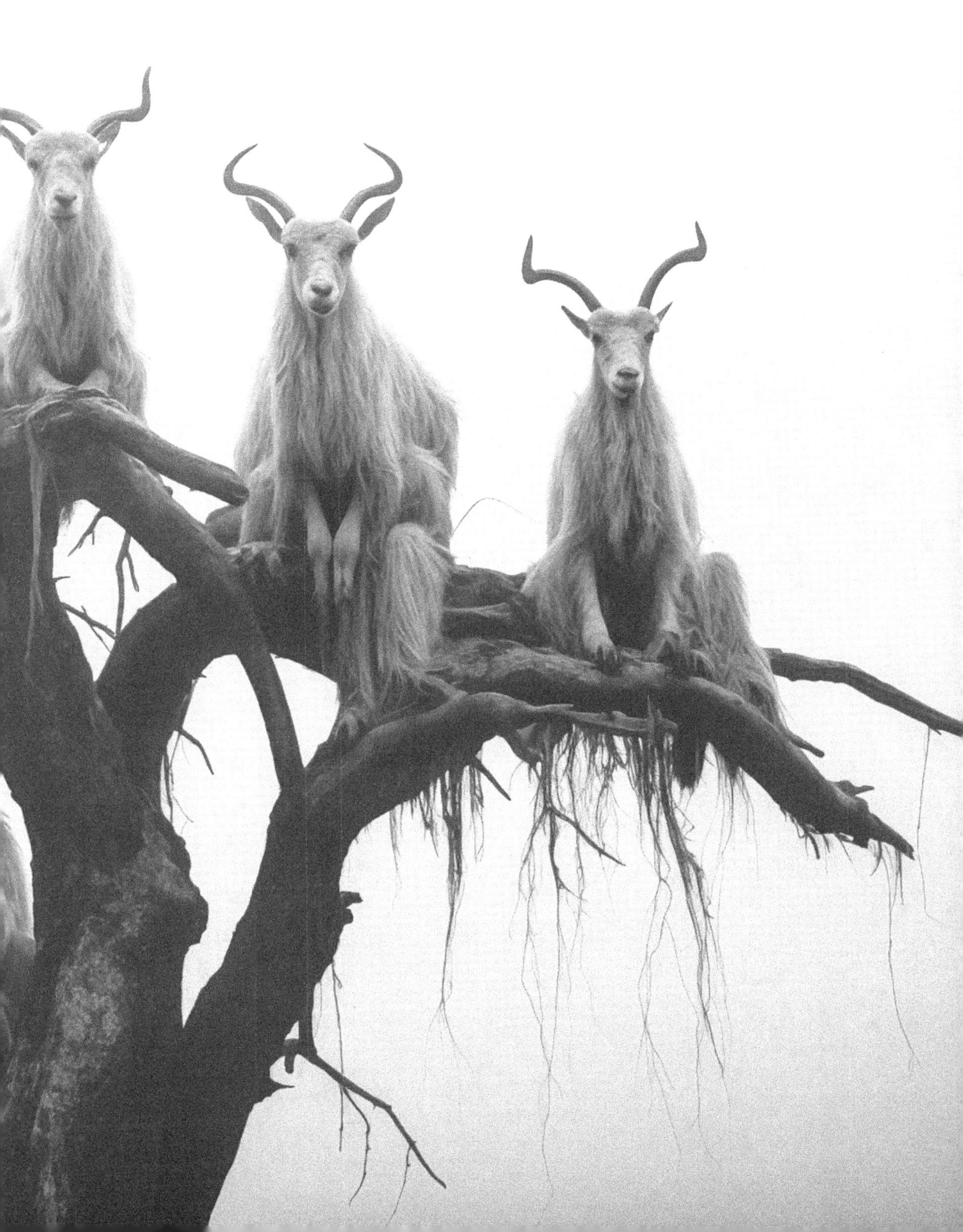

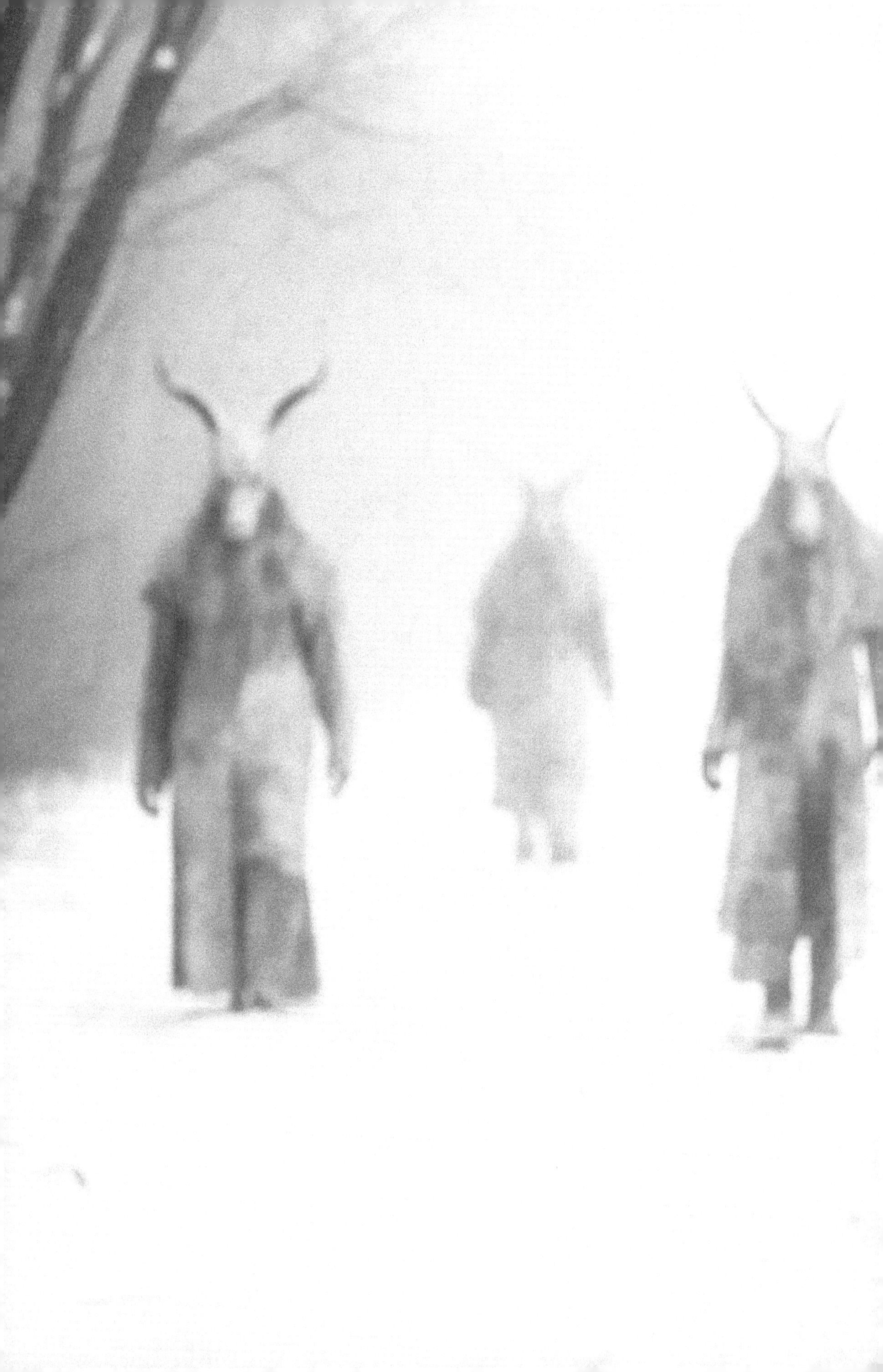

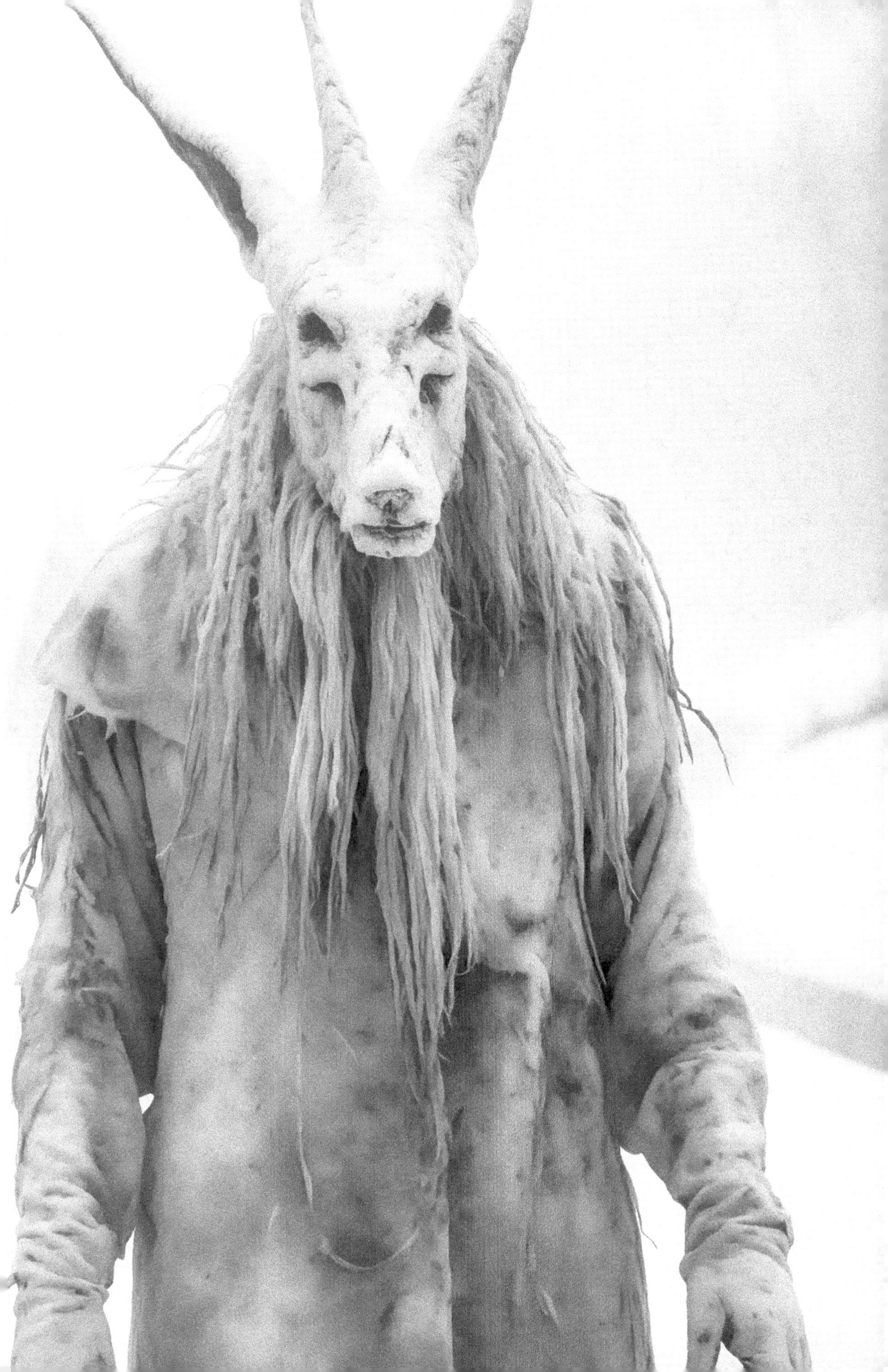

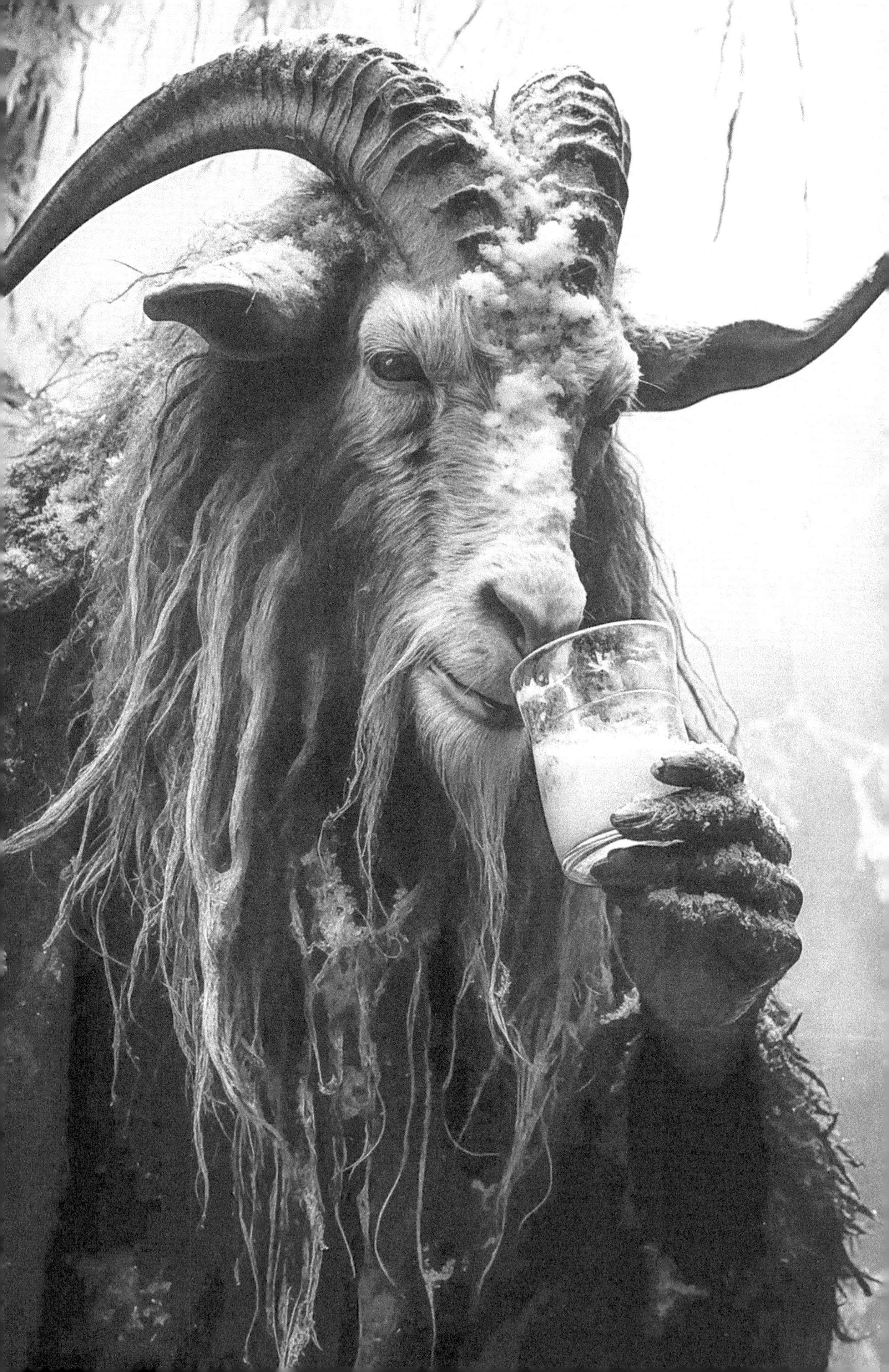

UNQUENCHABLE THIRST

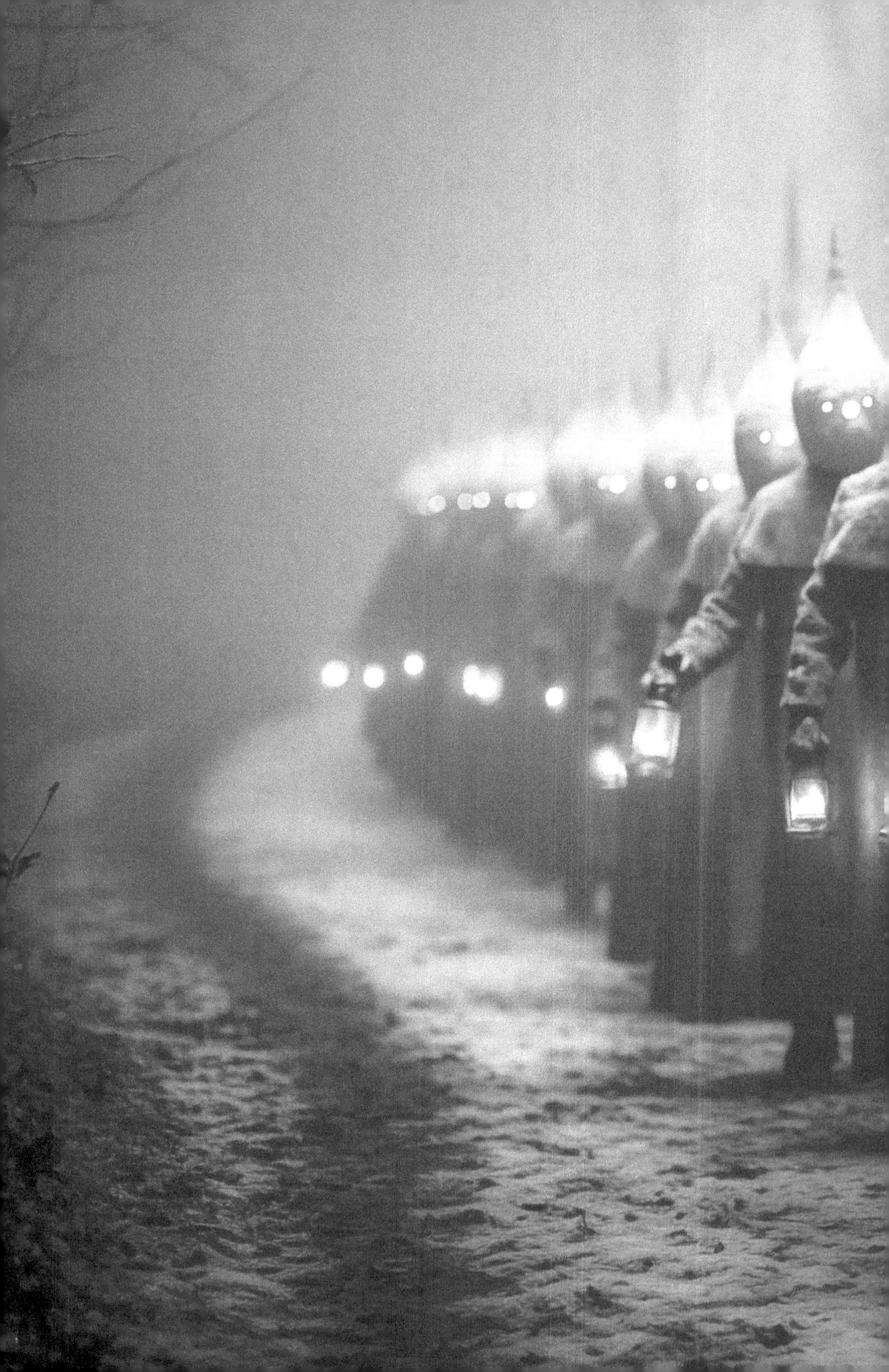

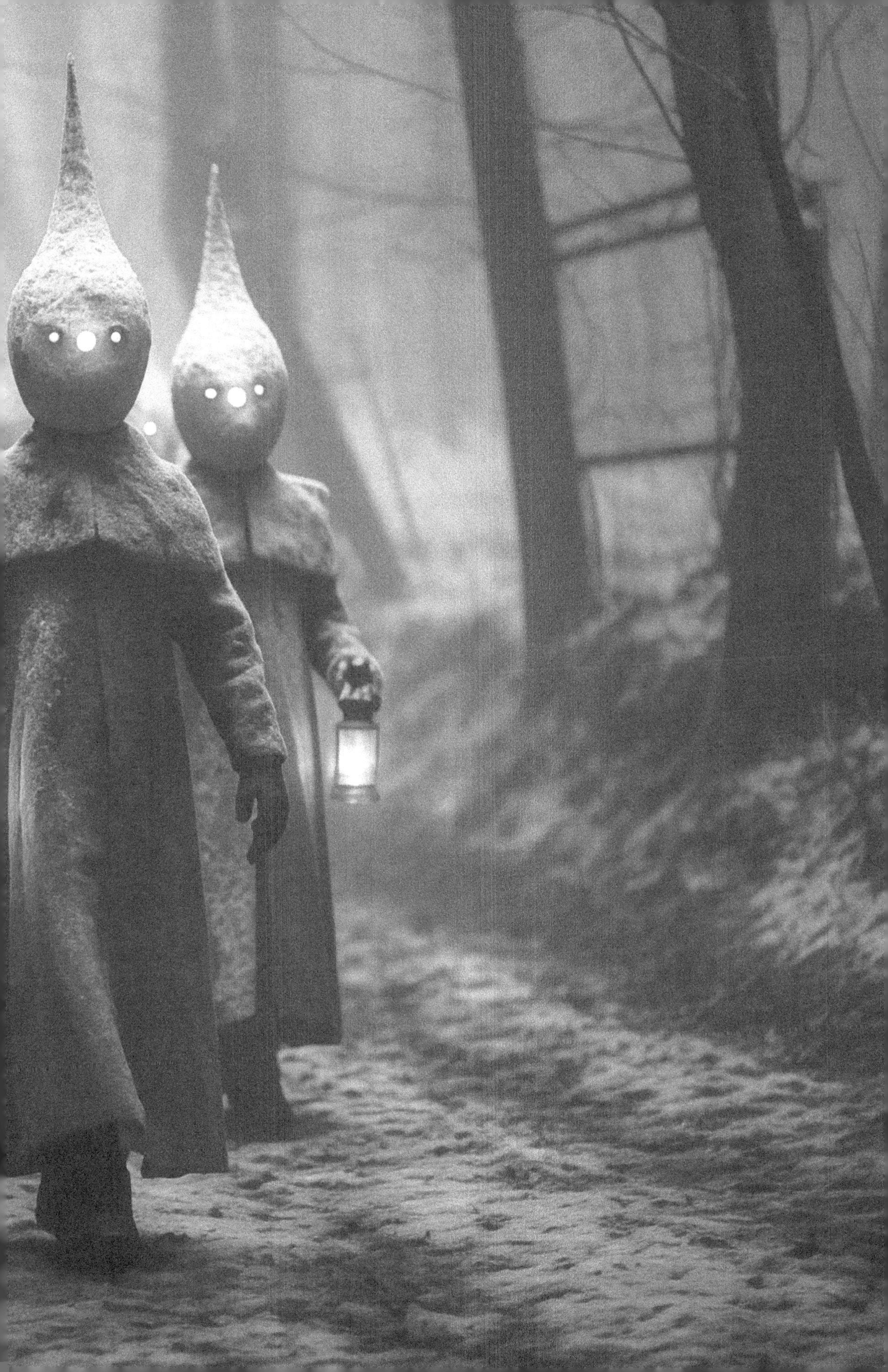

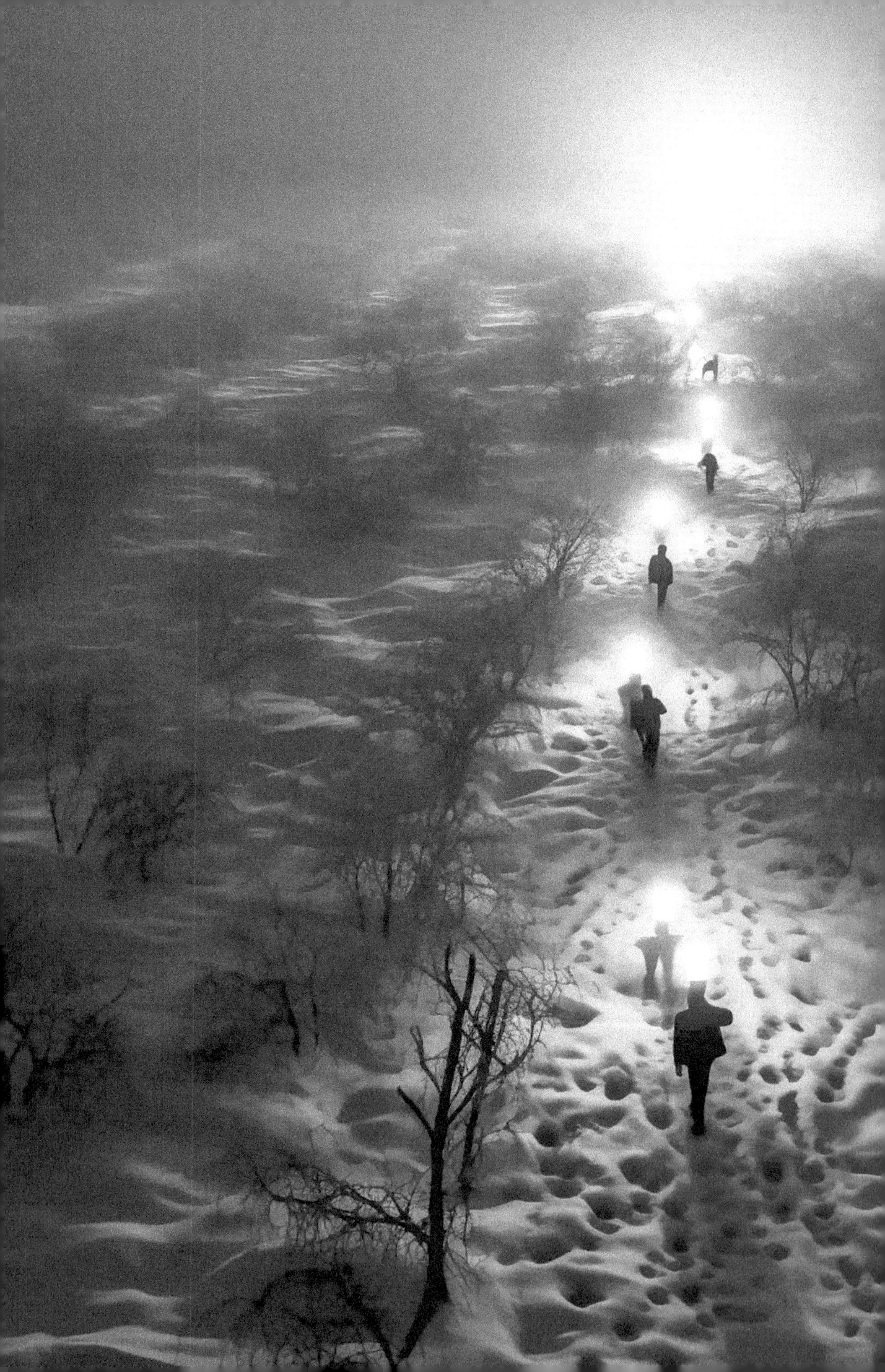

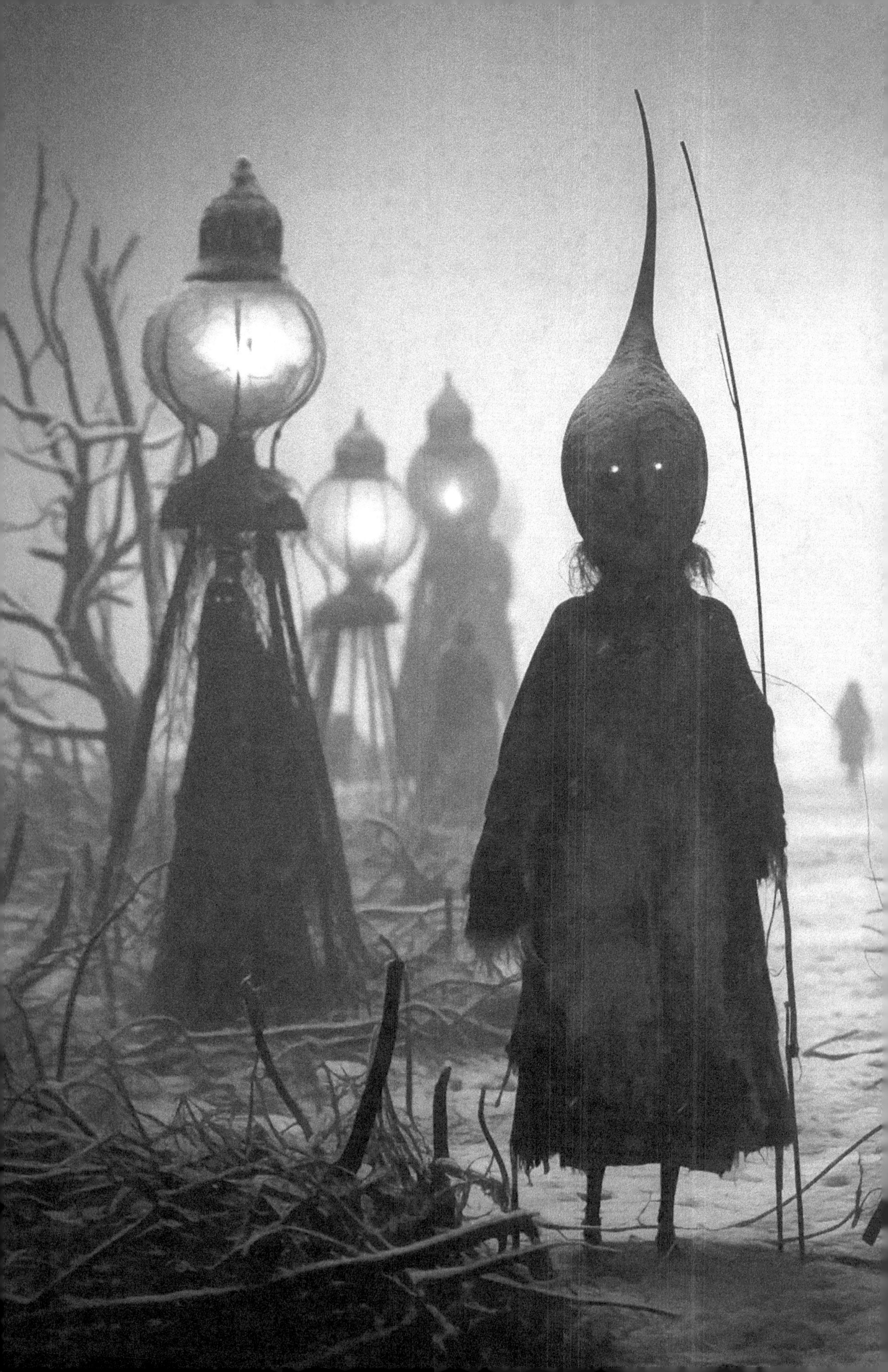

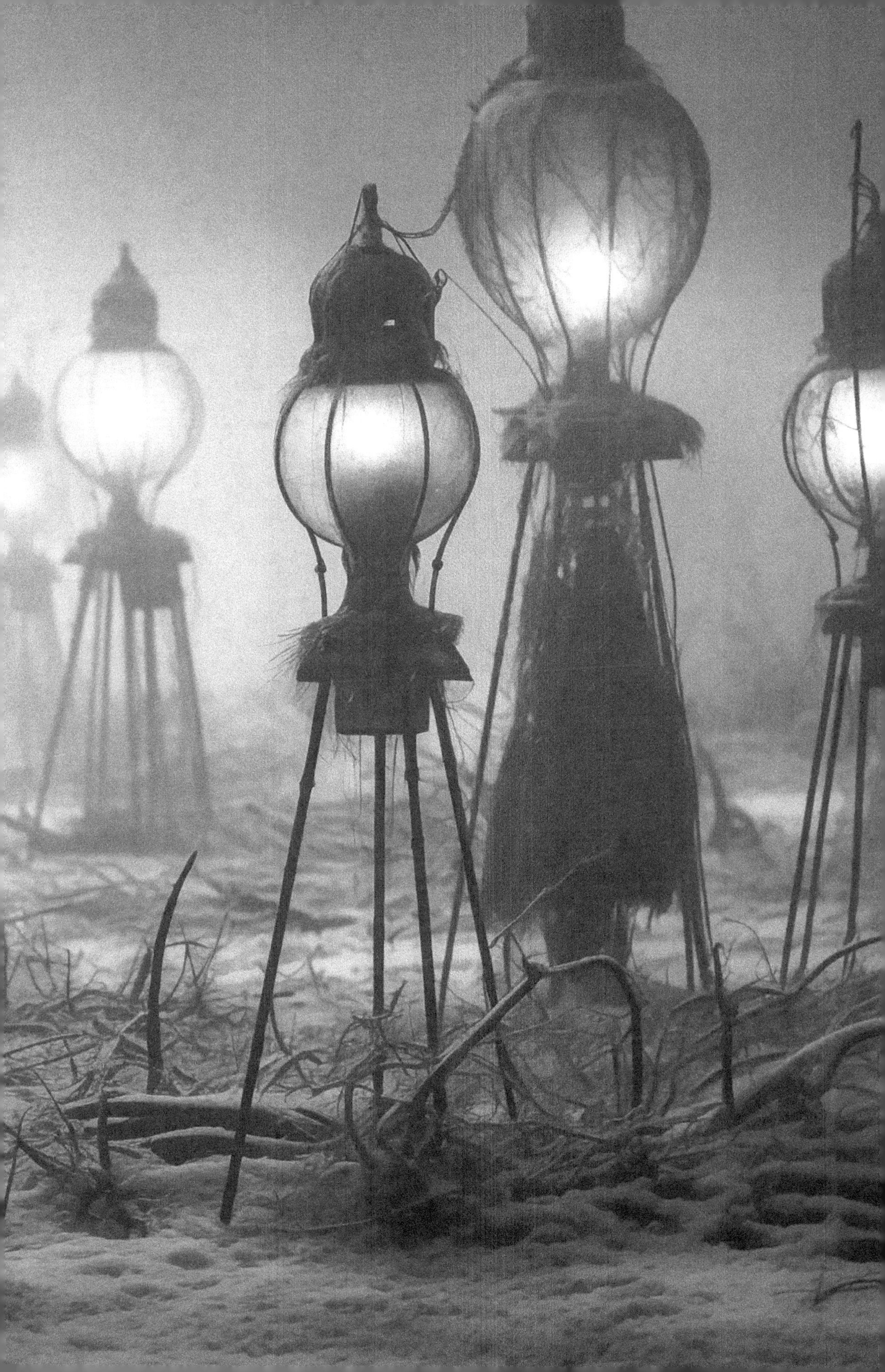

Walk in
silence.

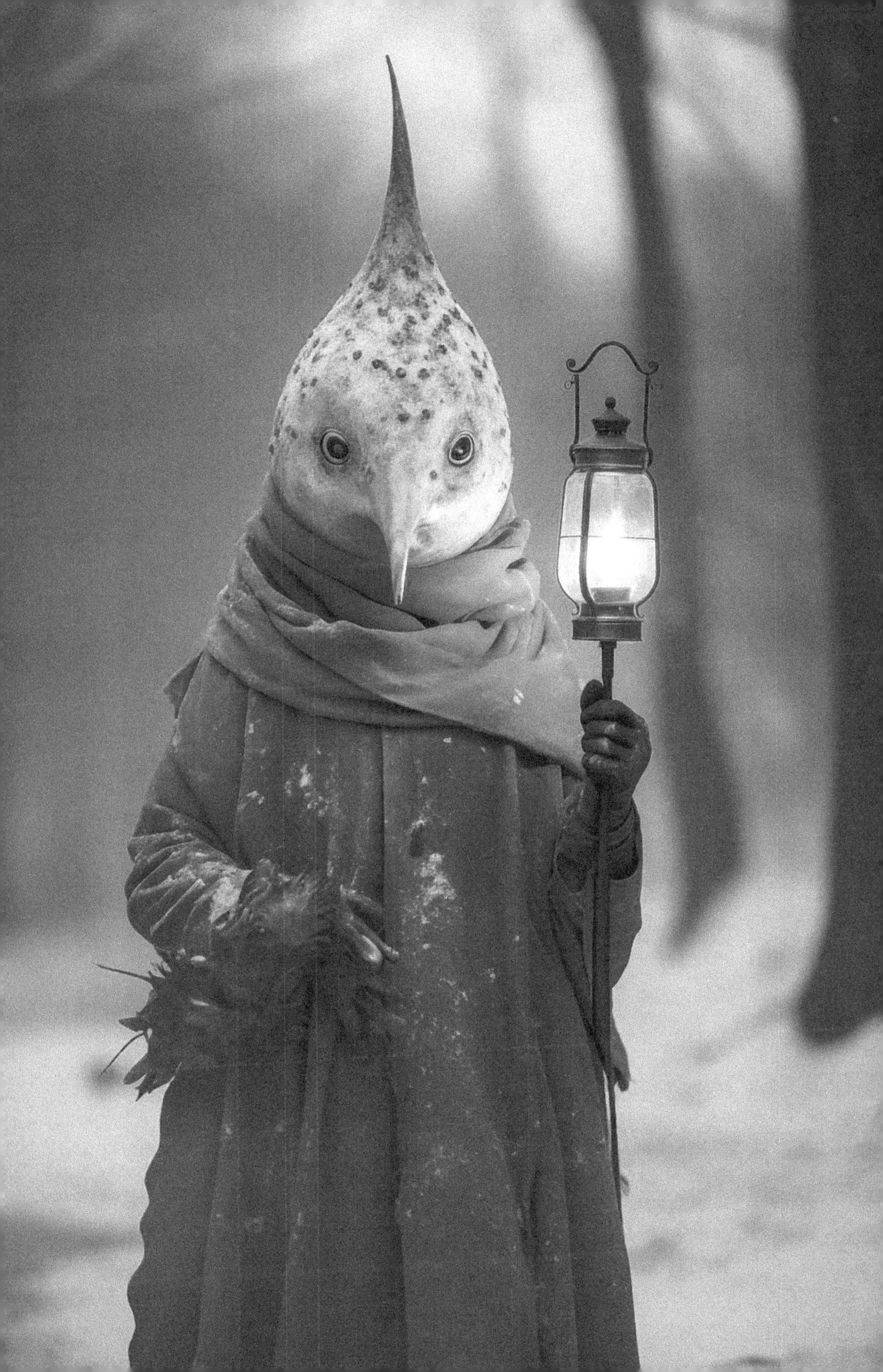

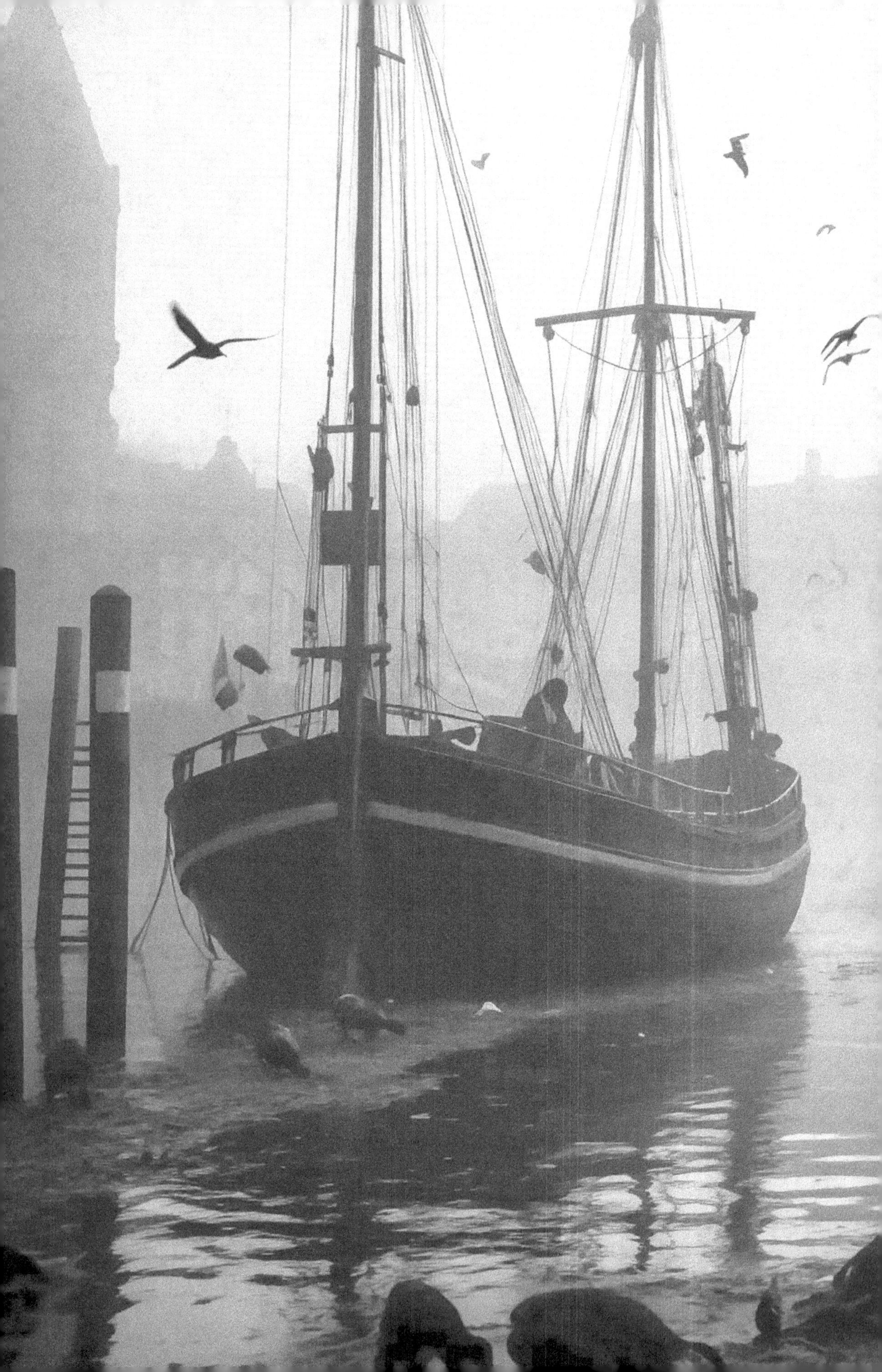

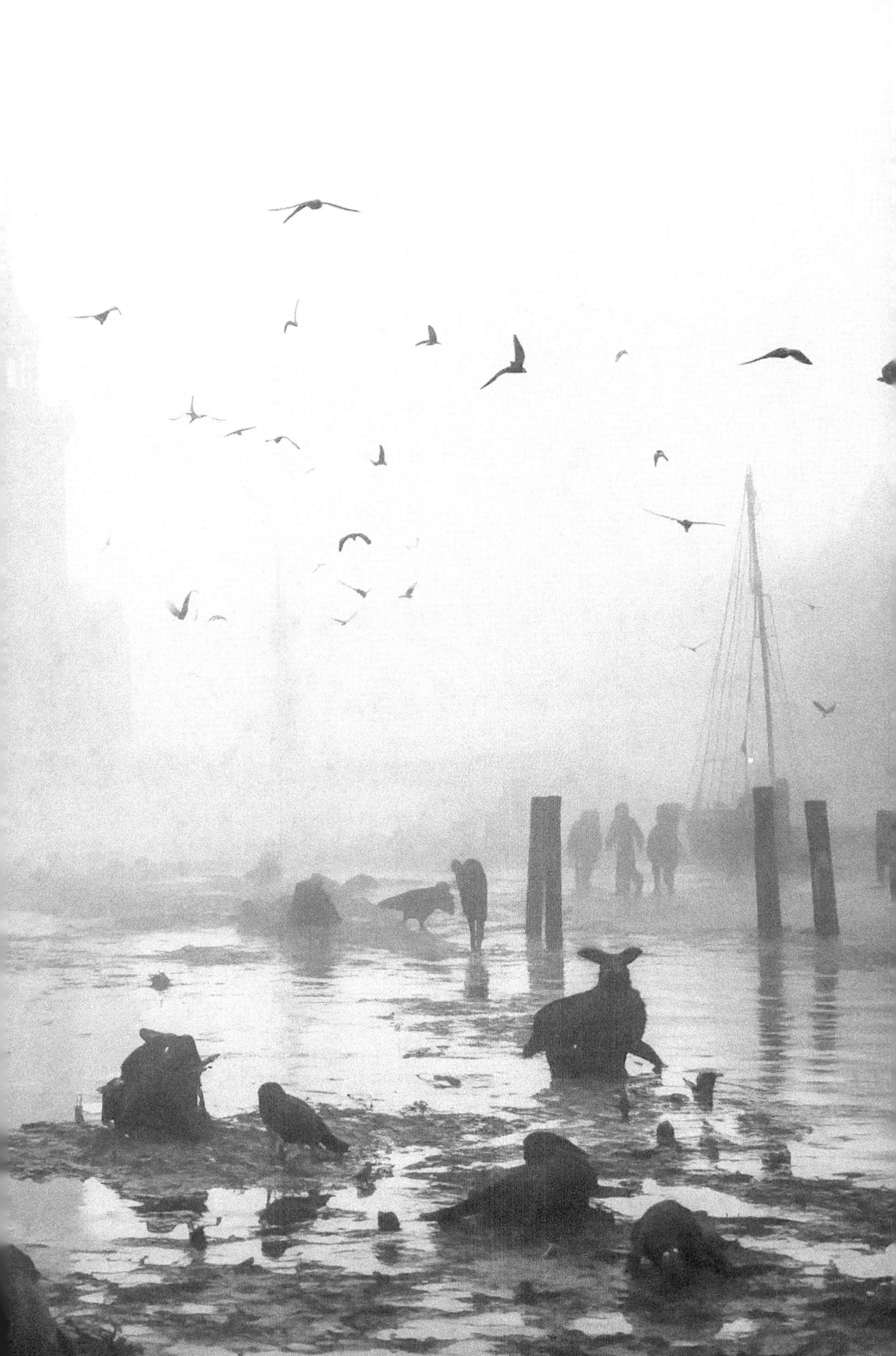

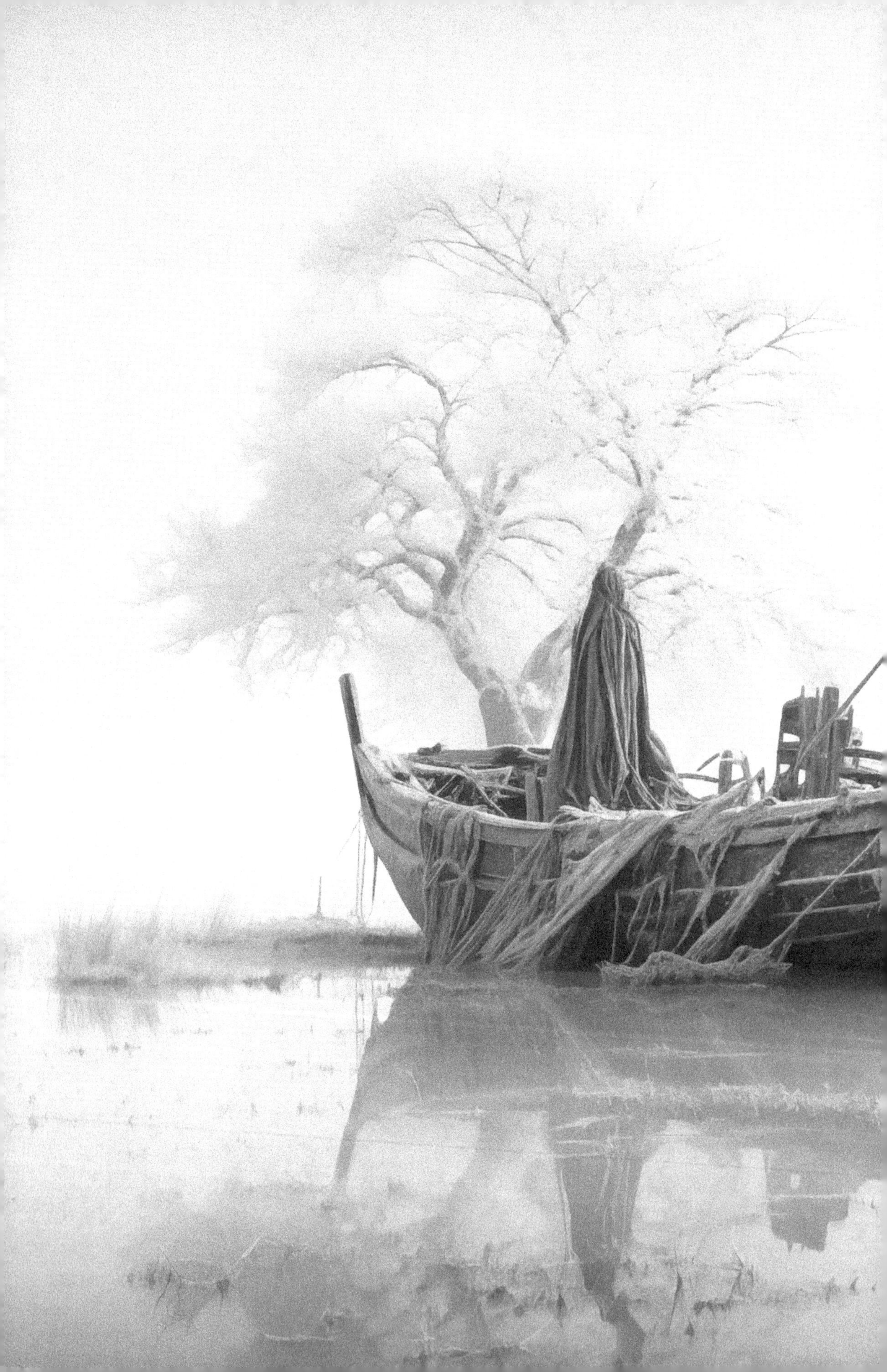

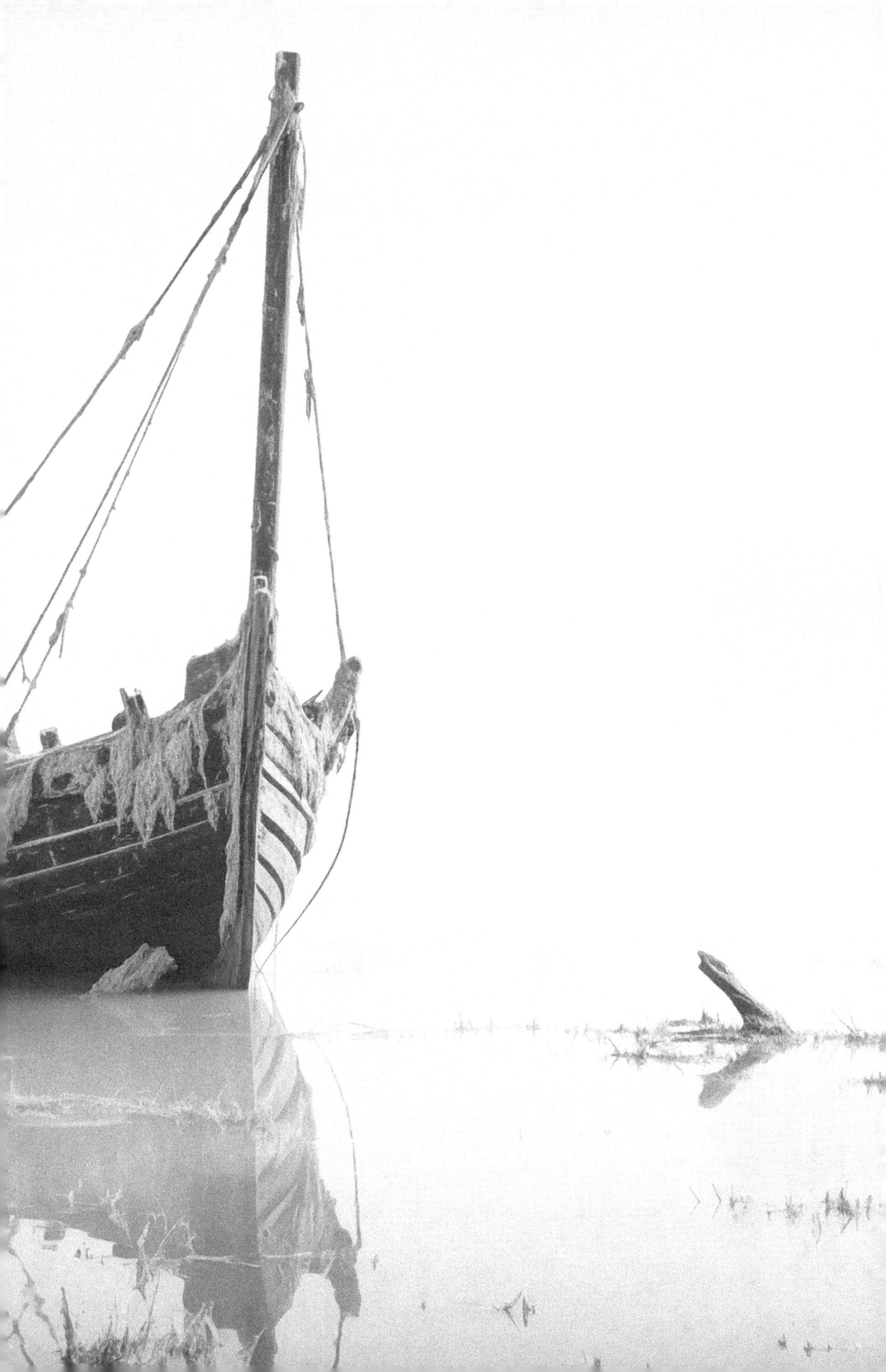

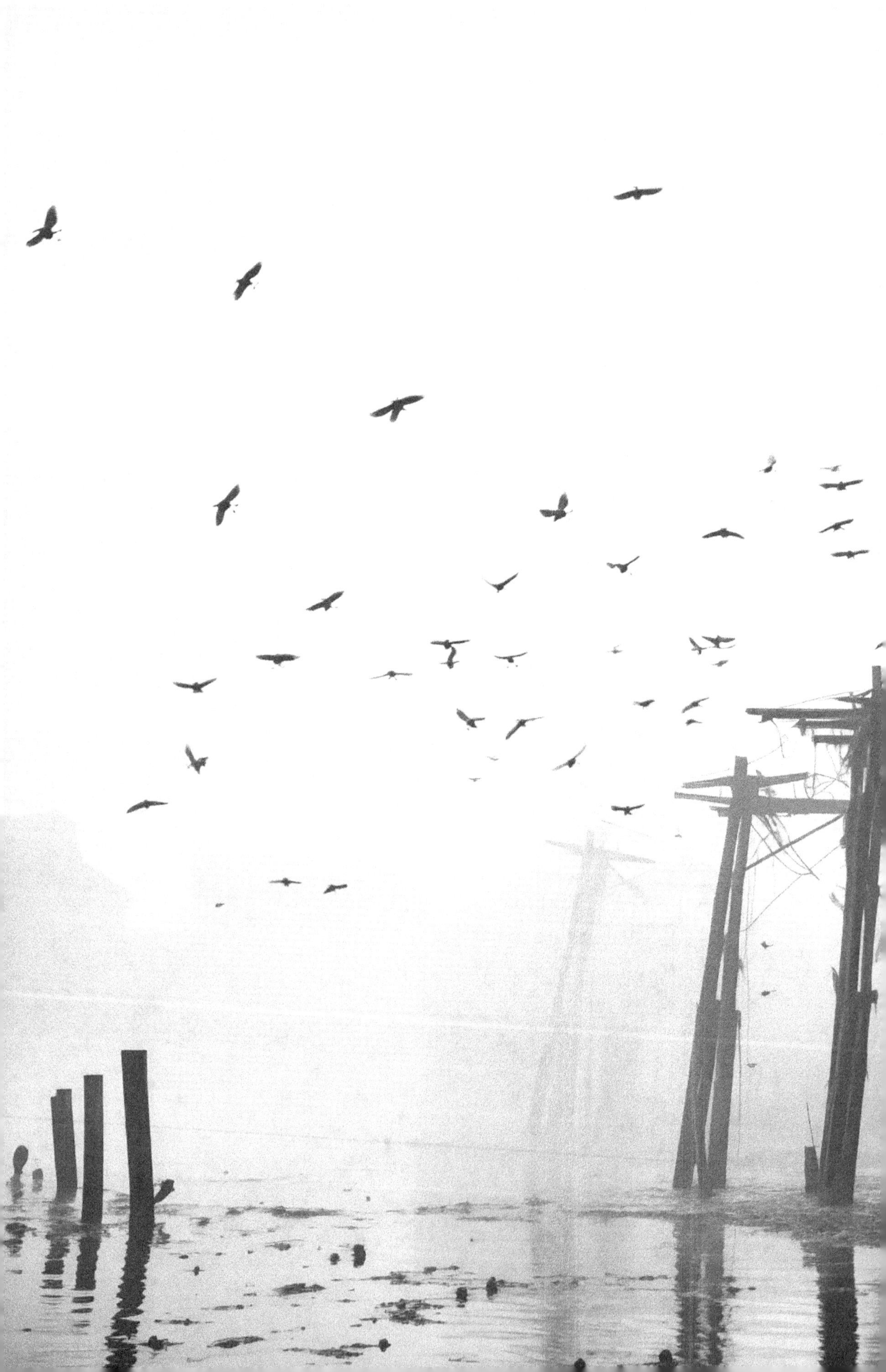

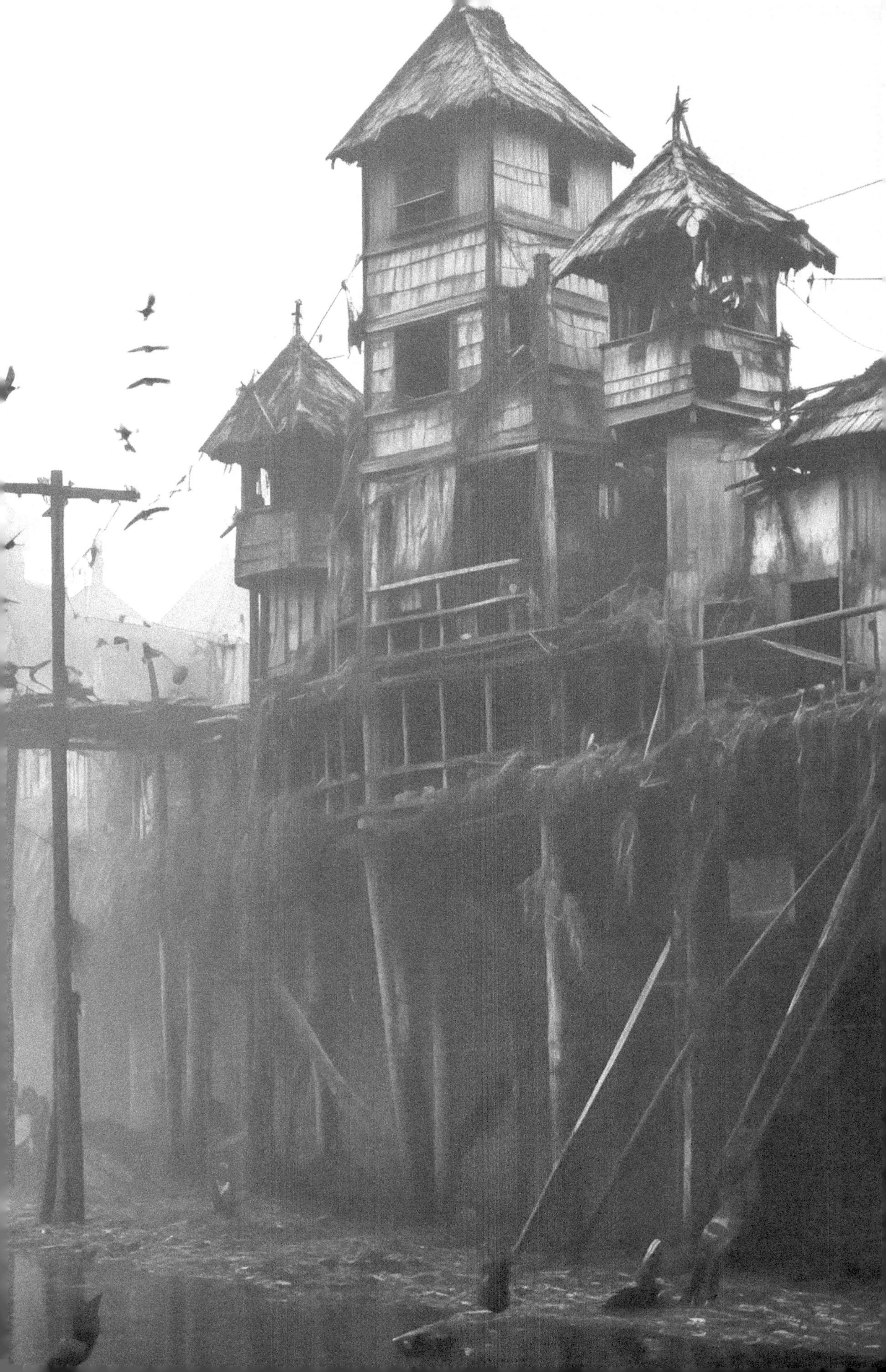

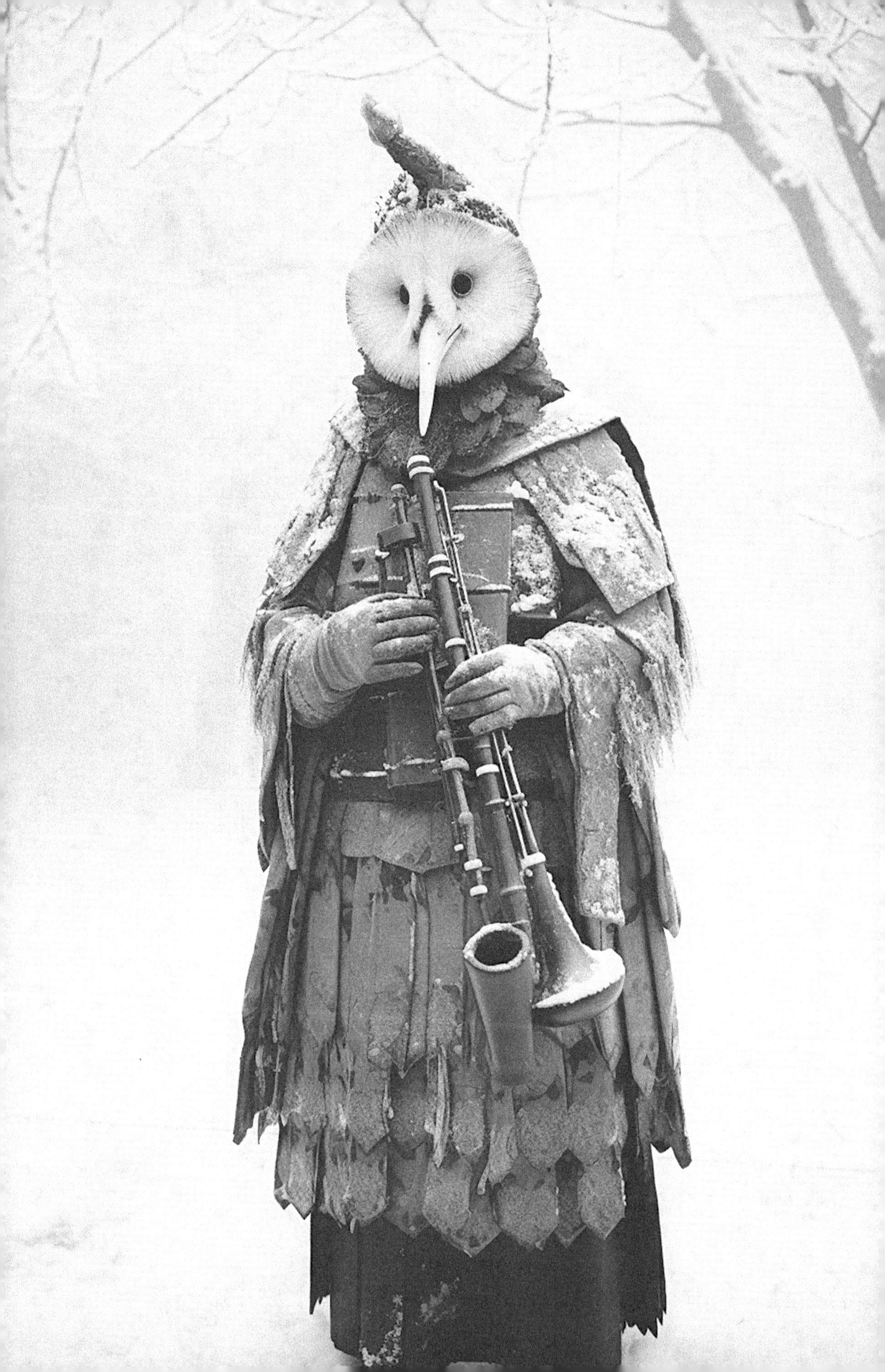

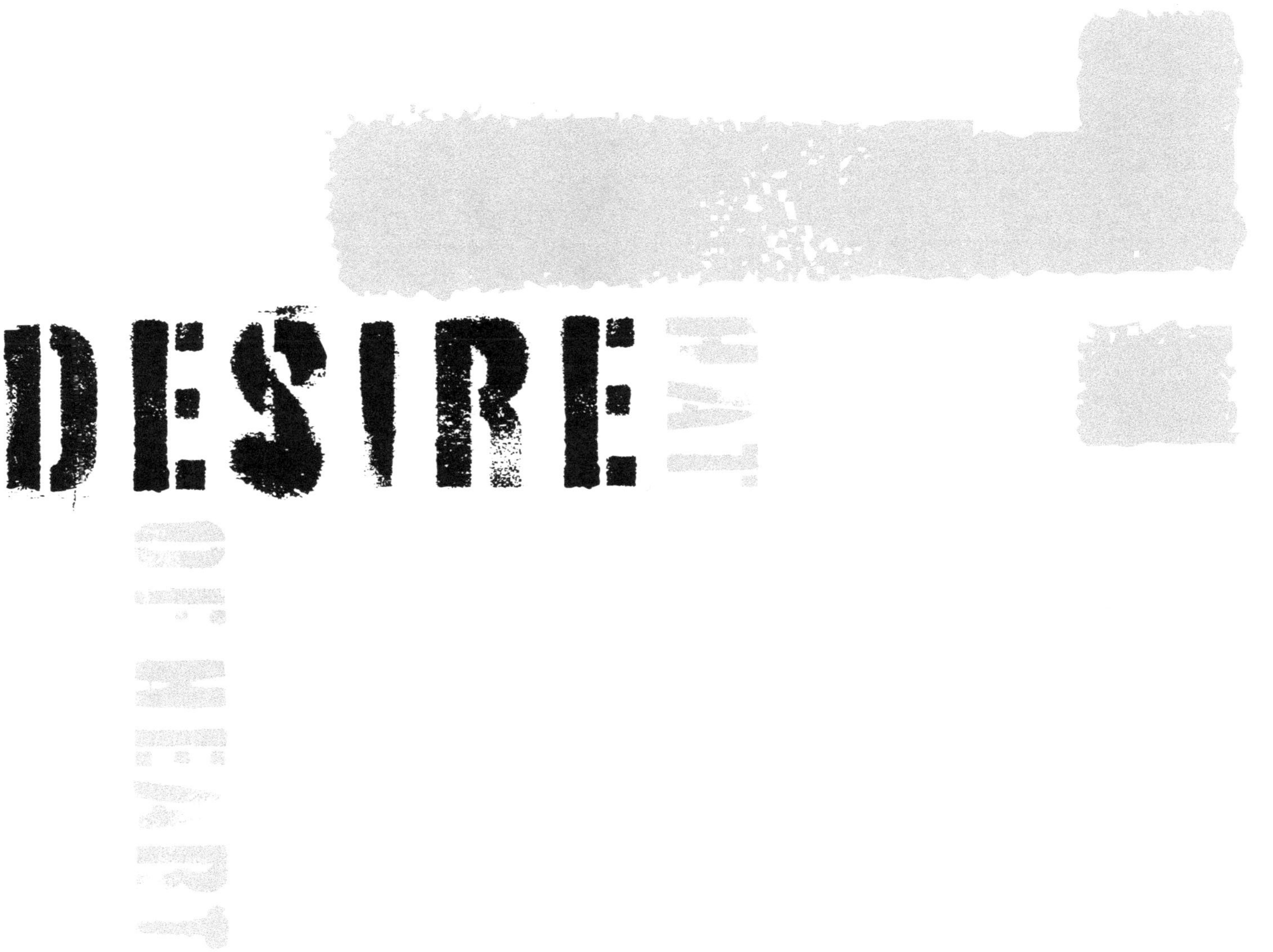
17
DESIRE
PAT
OF HEART

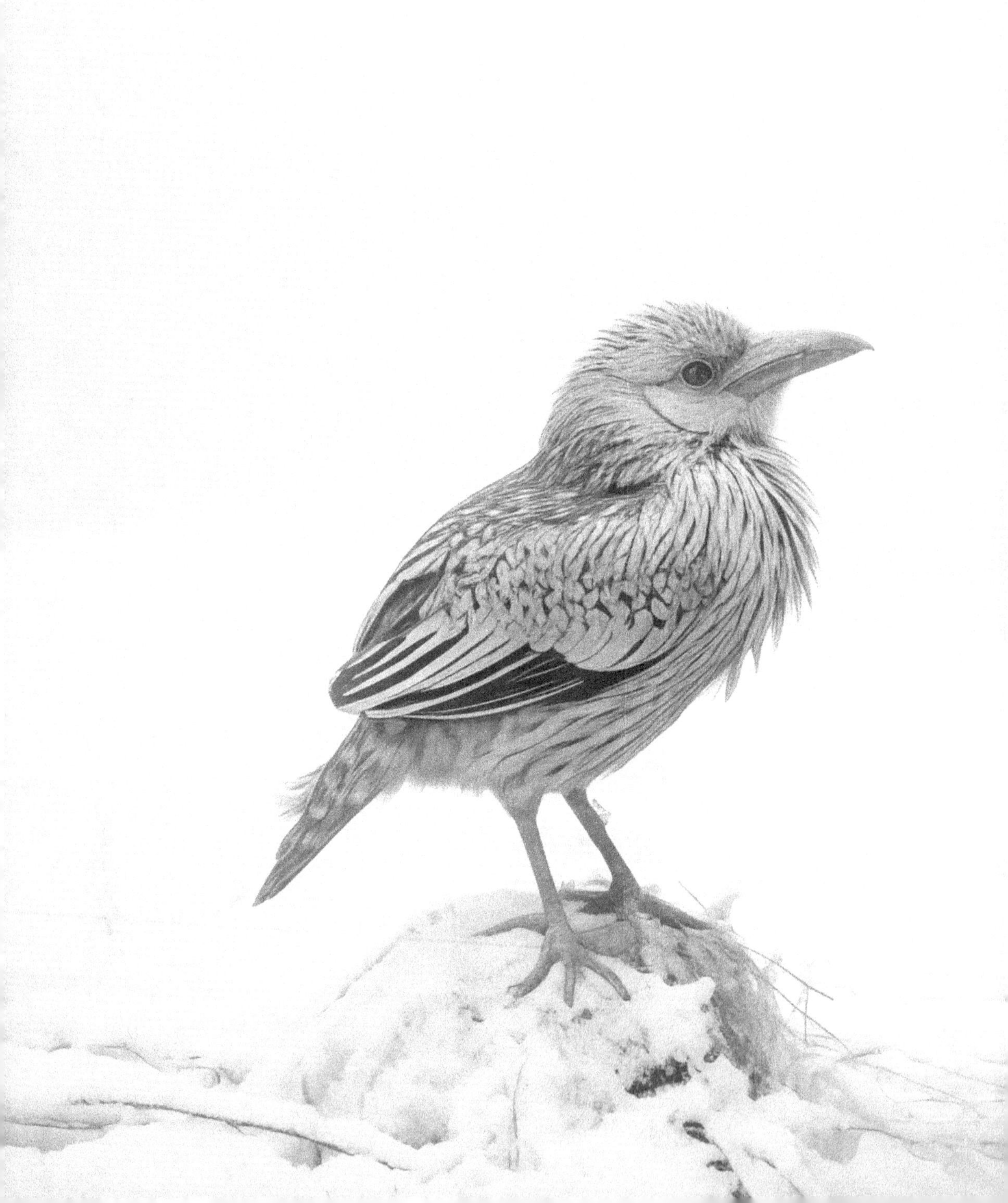

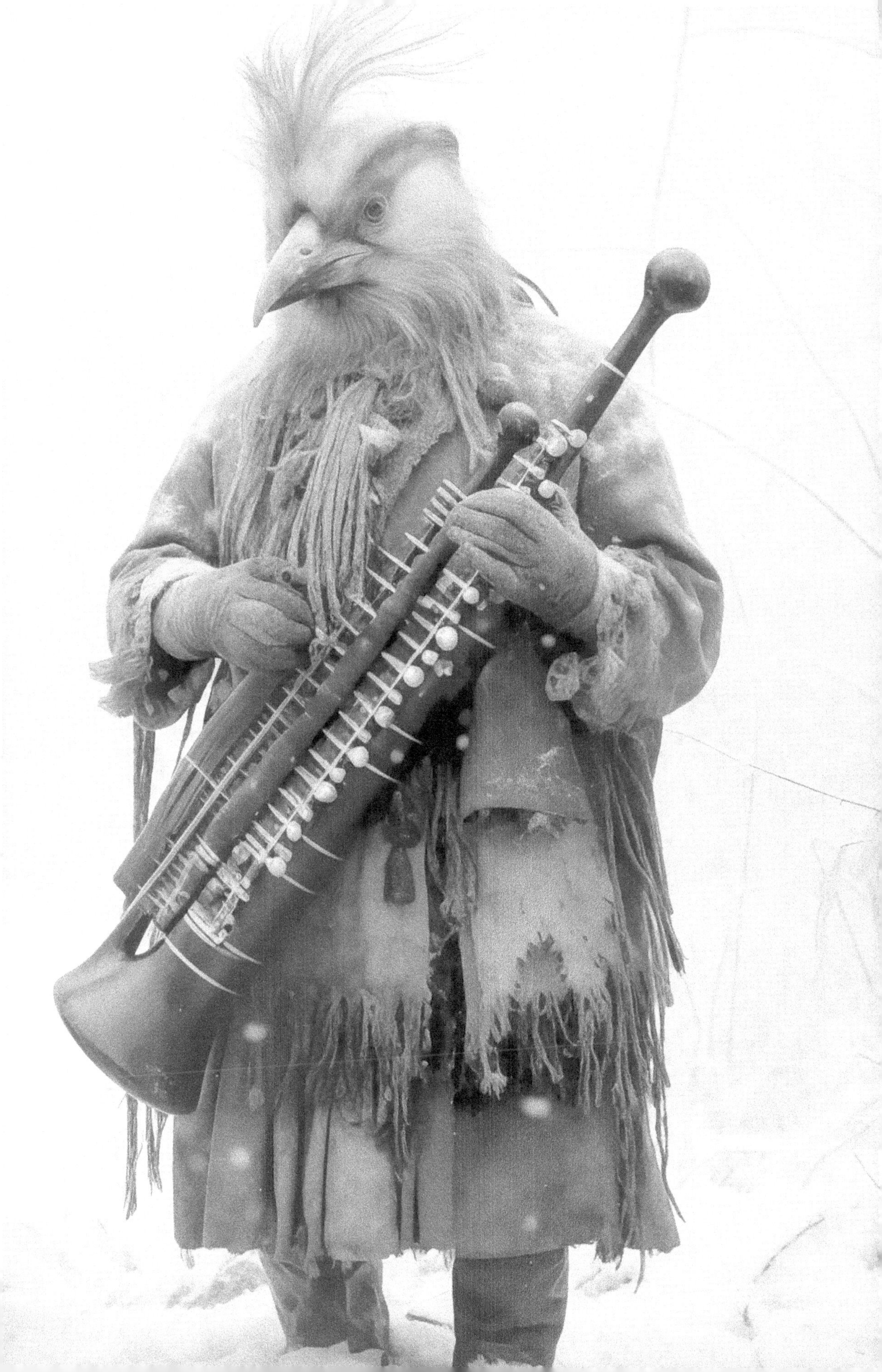

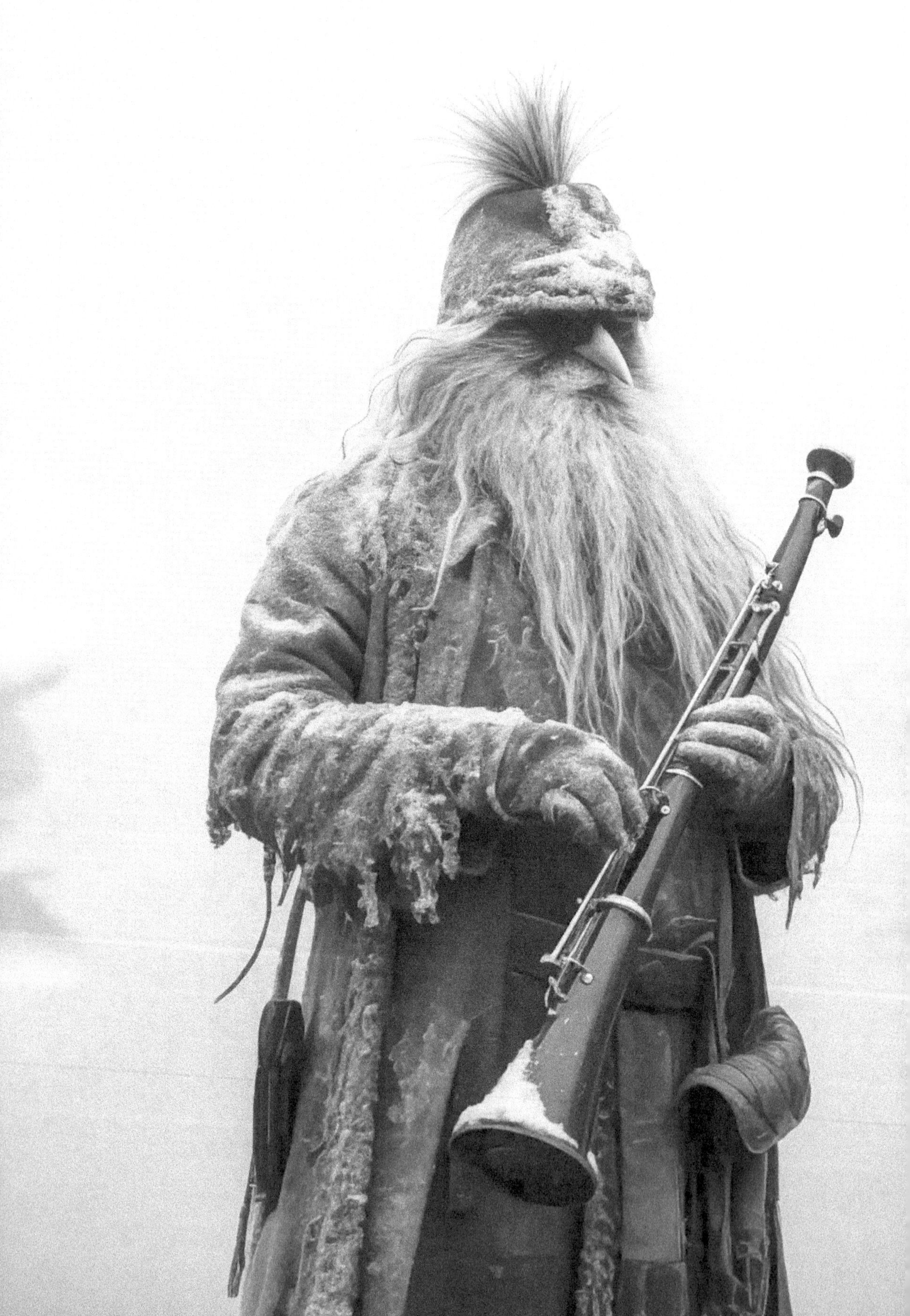

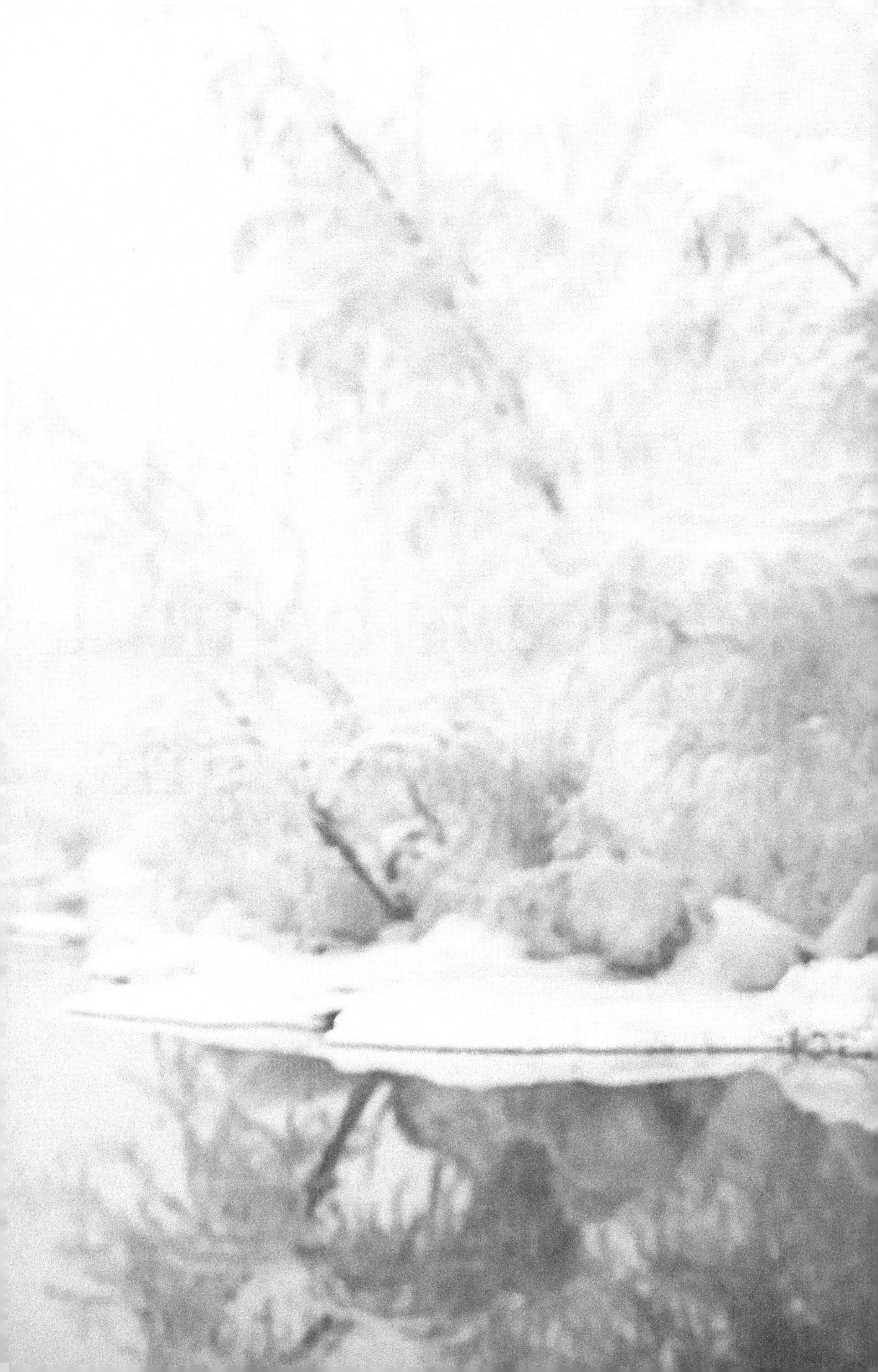

The last thing
we leave behind
are signs.

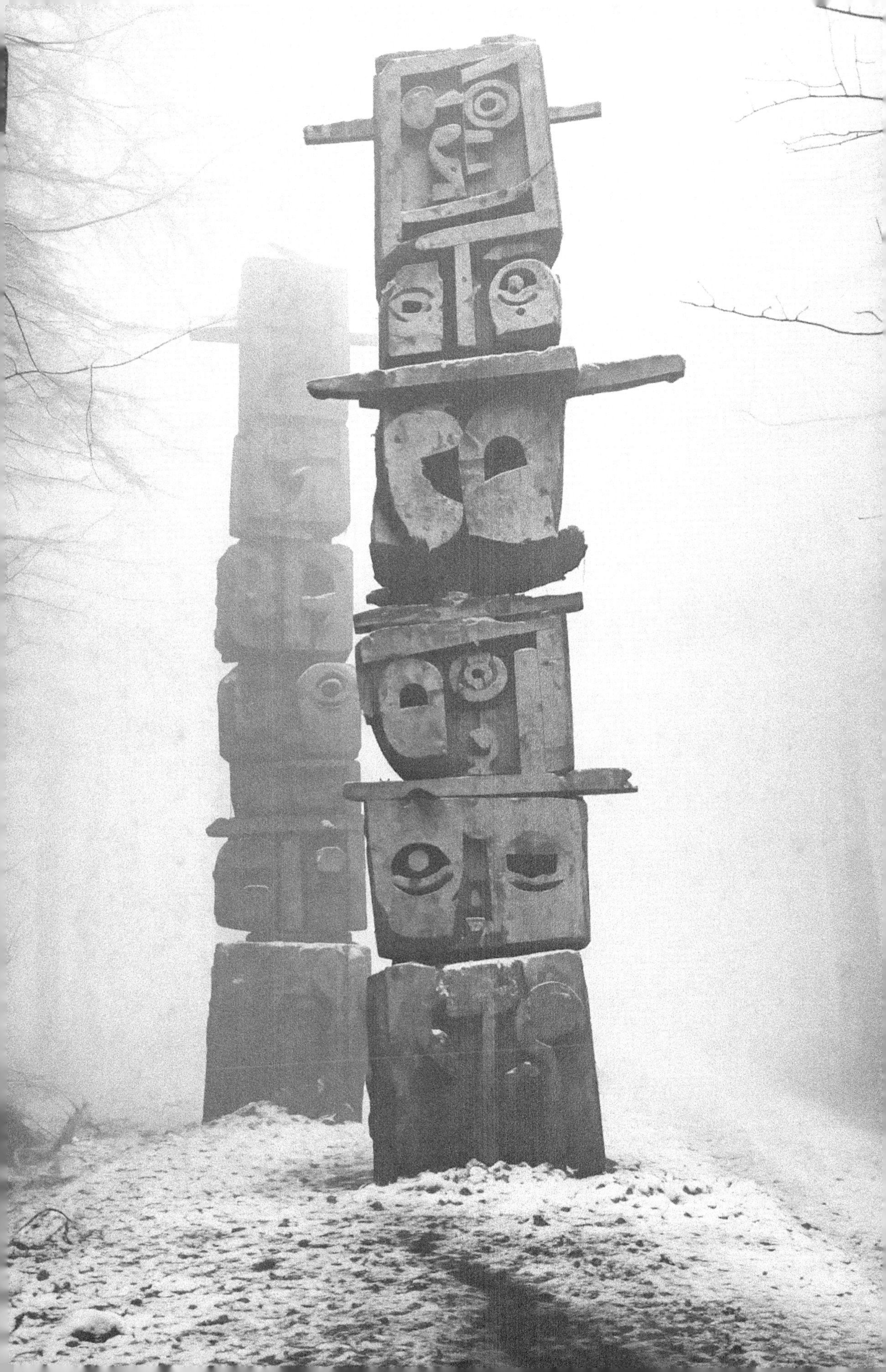

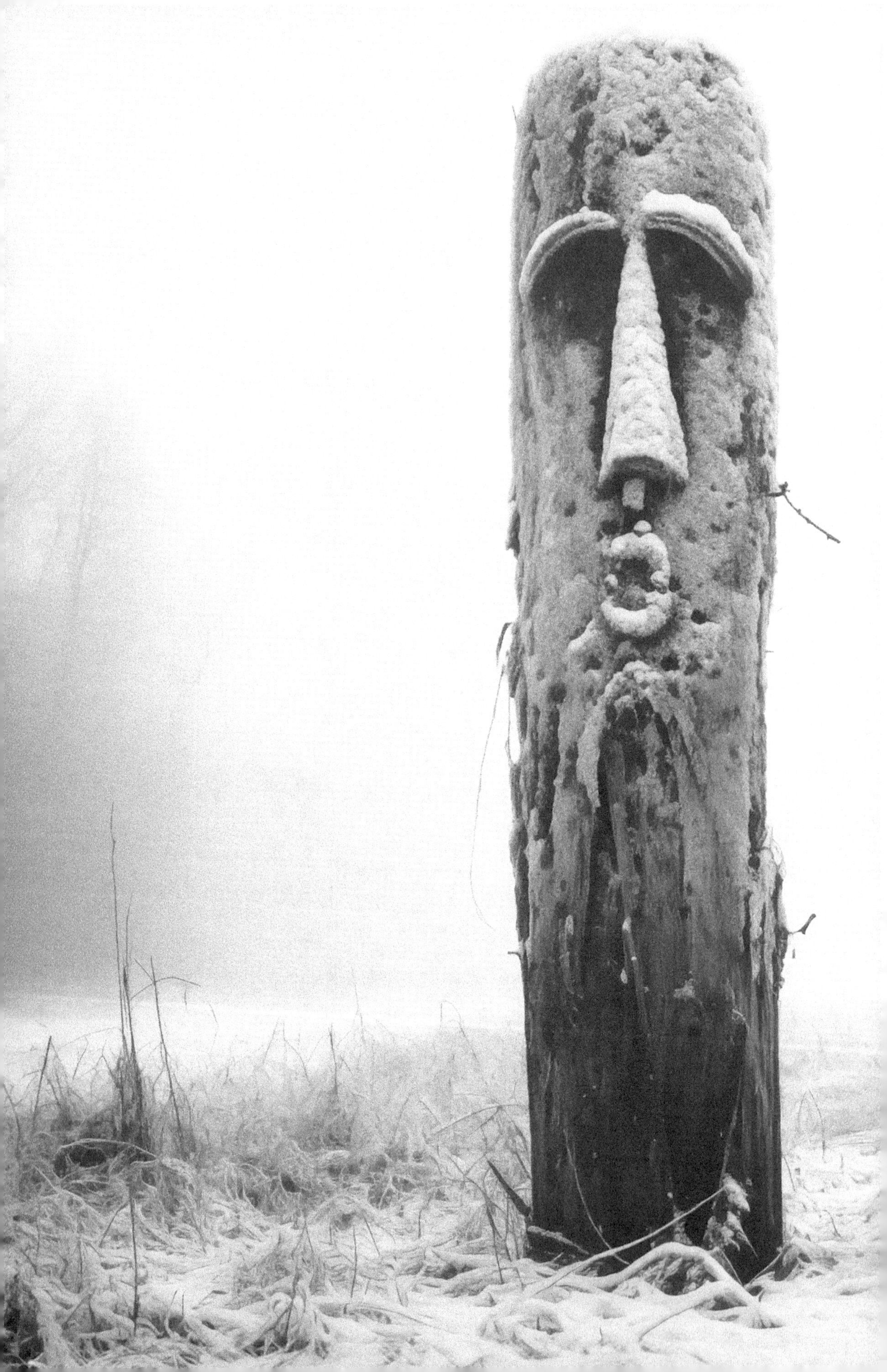

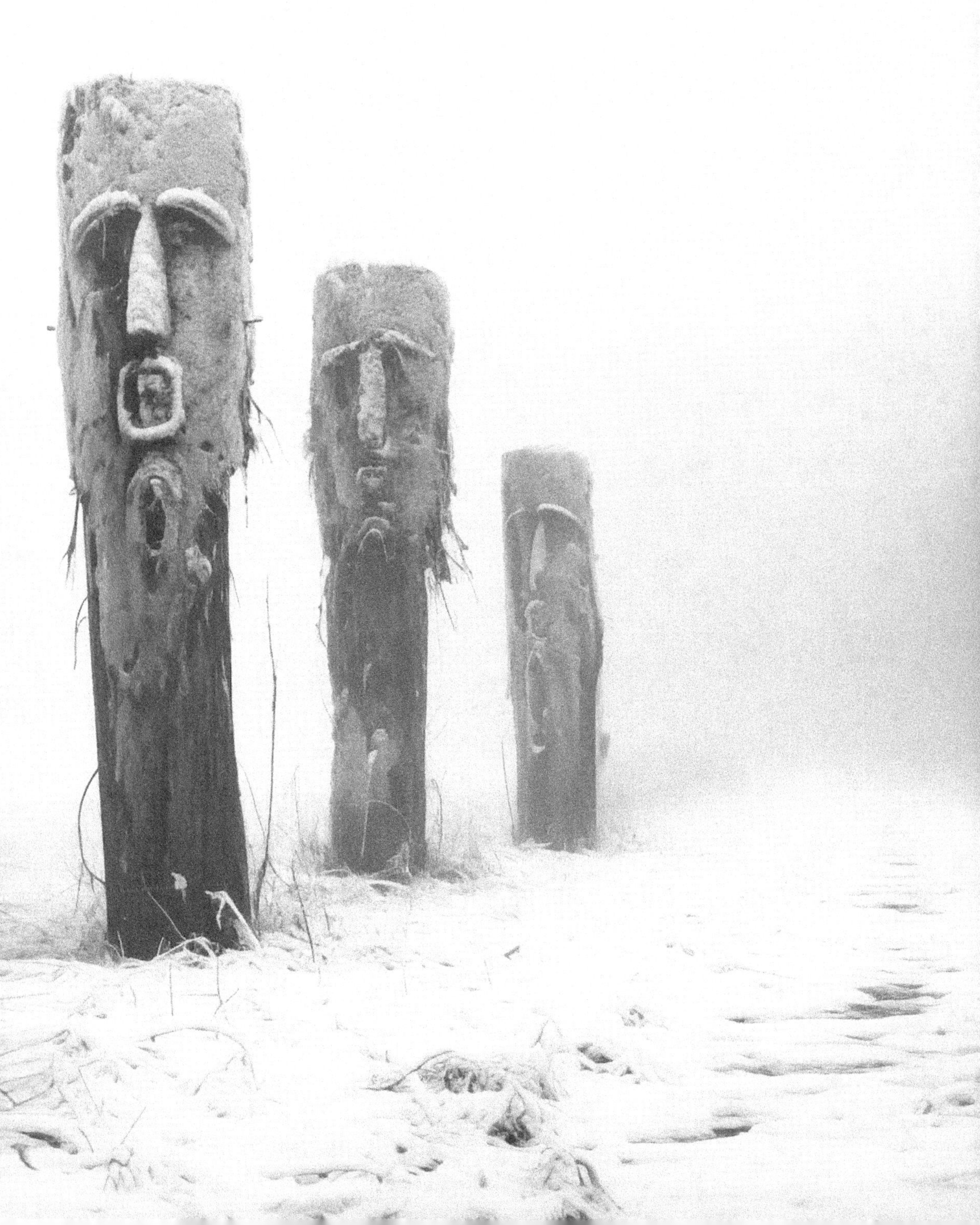

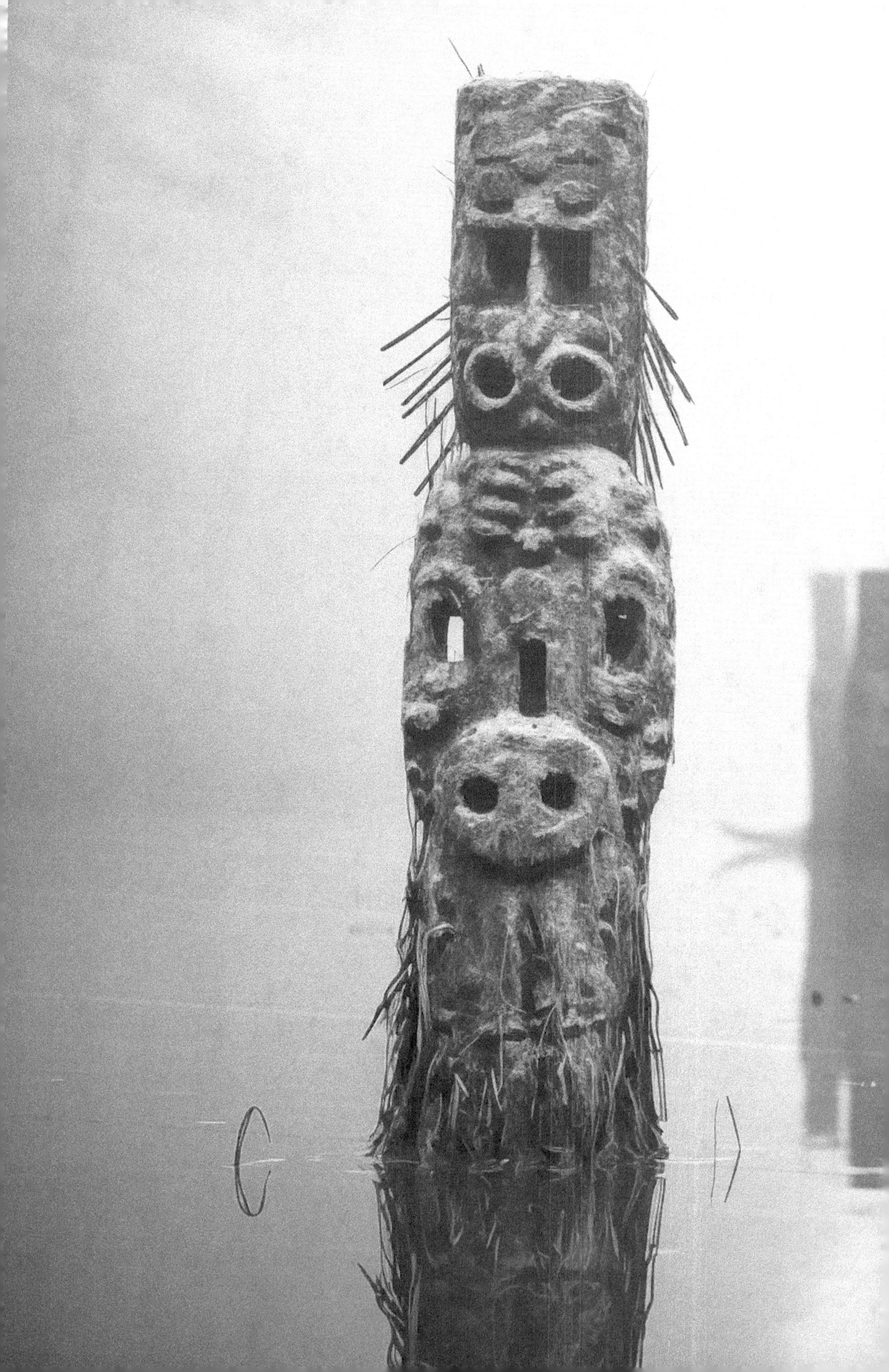

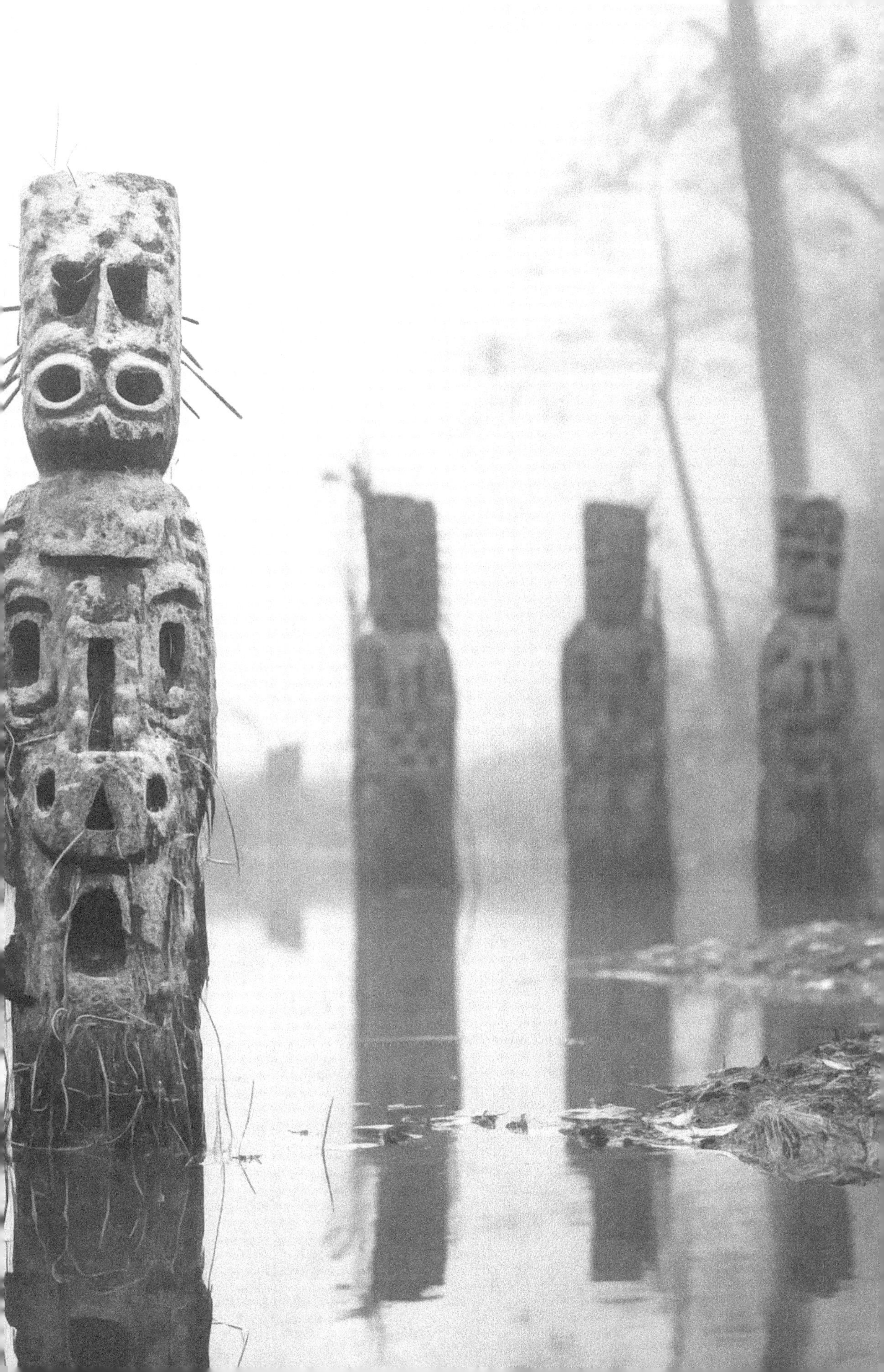

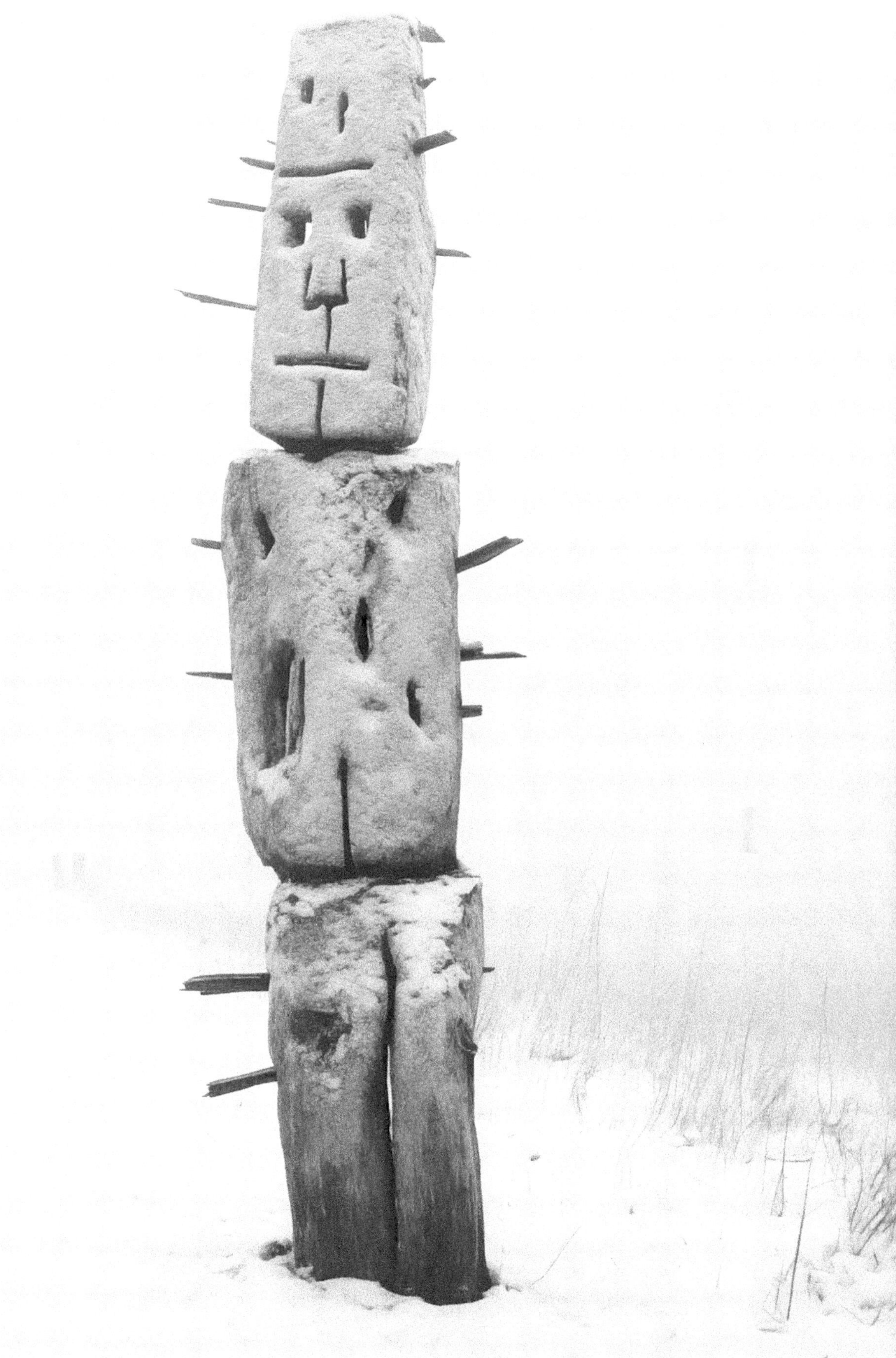

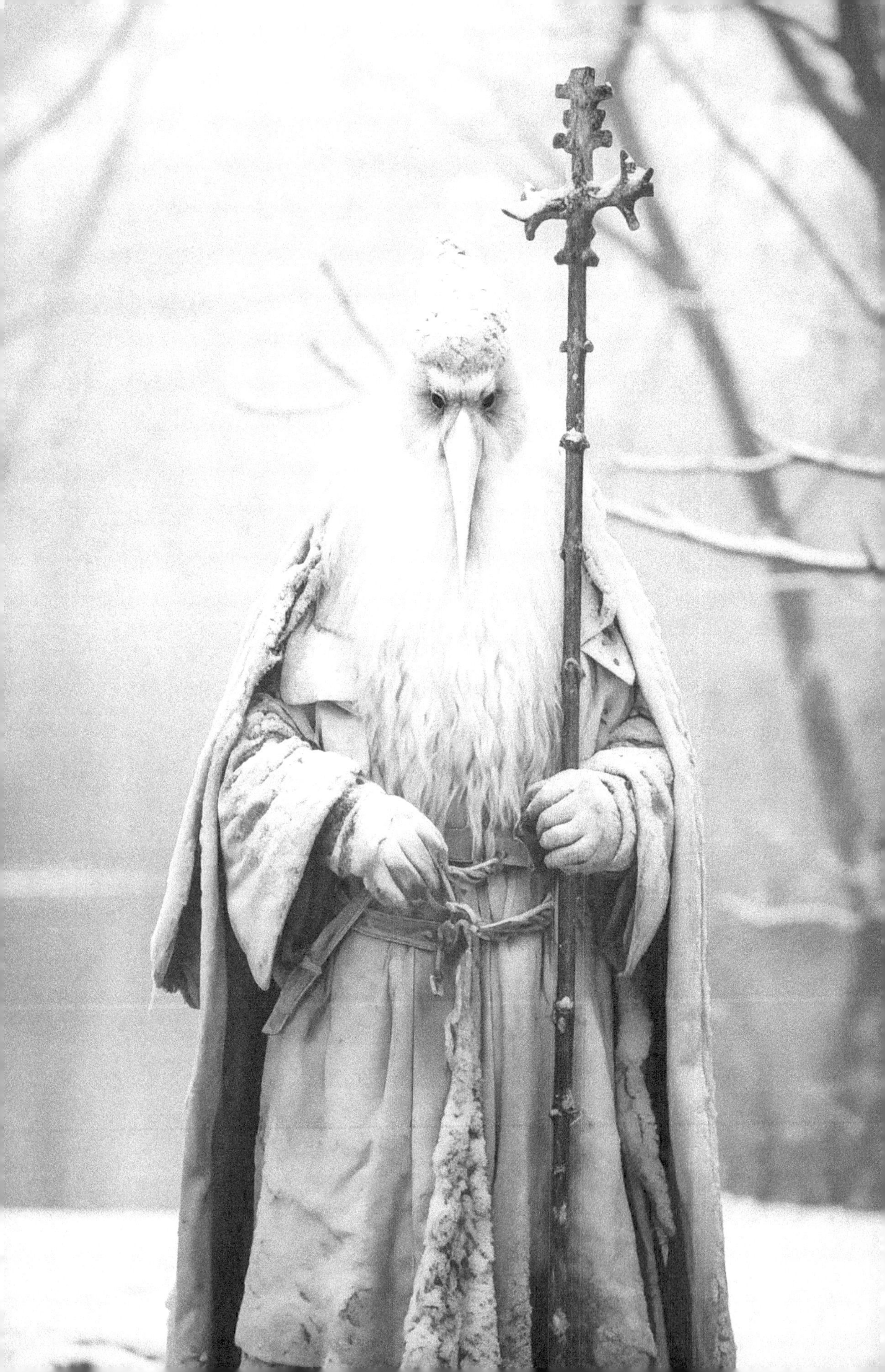

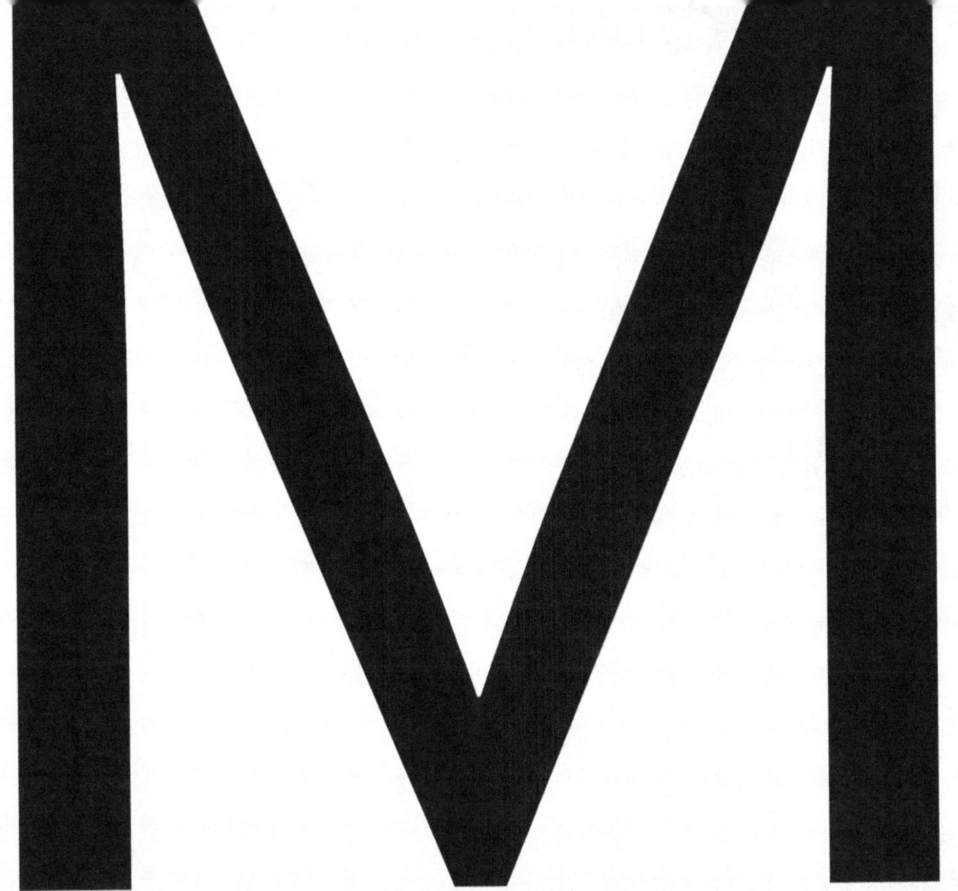

Maybe there is spirituality without religion?

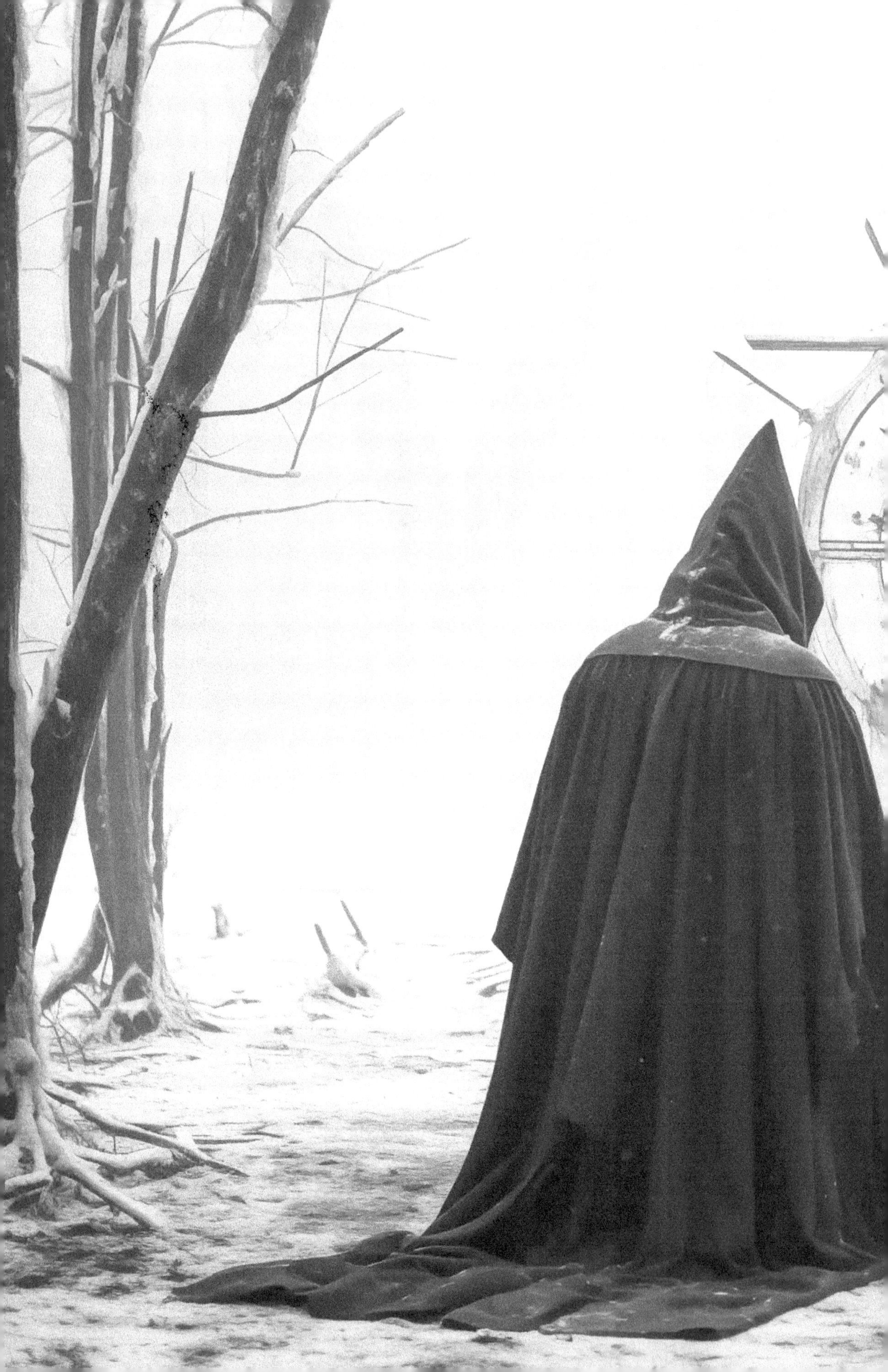

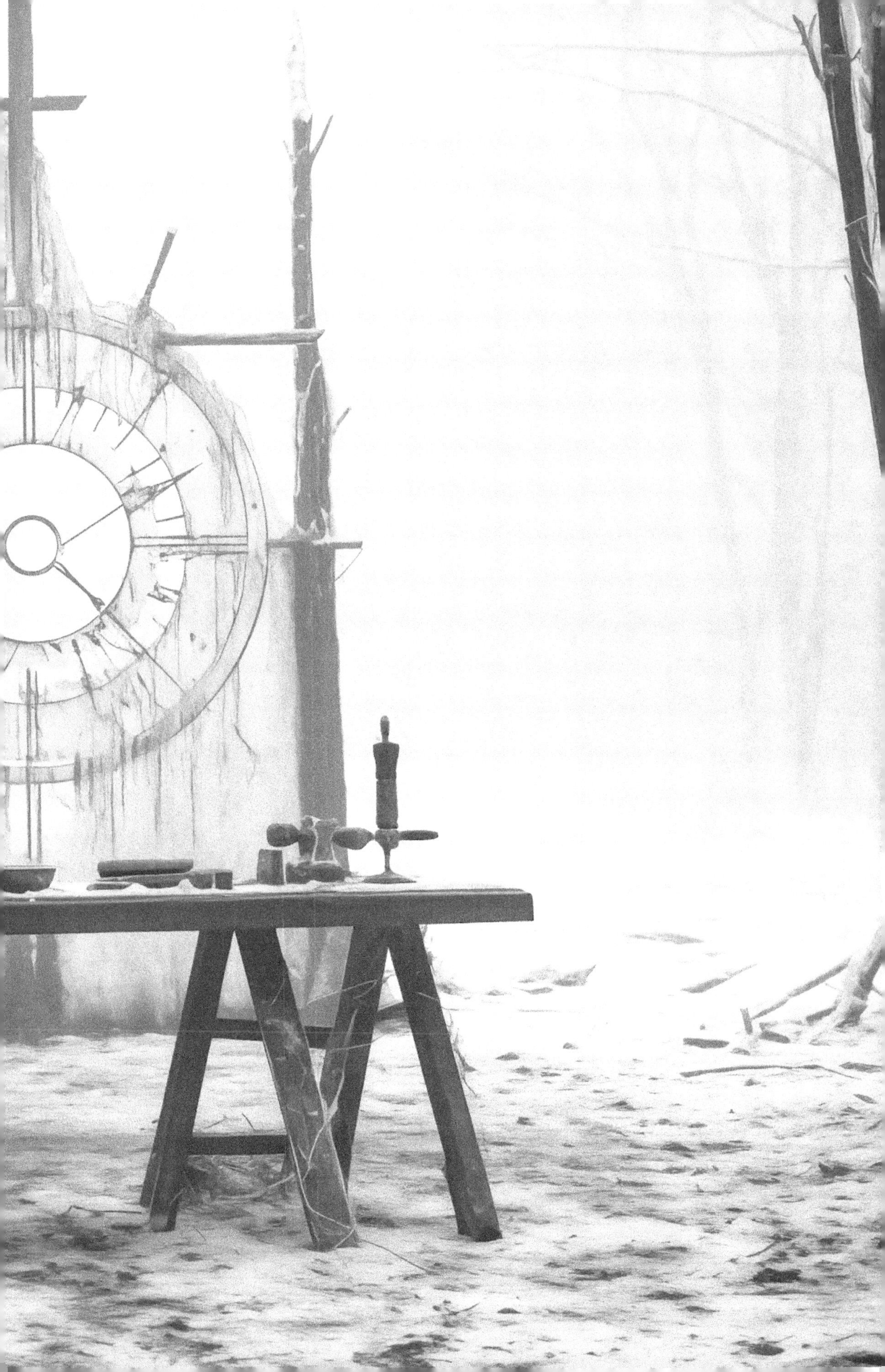

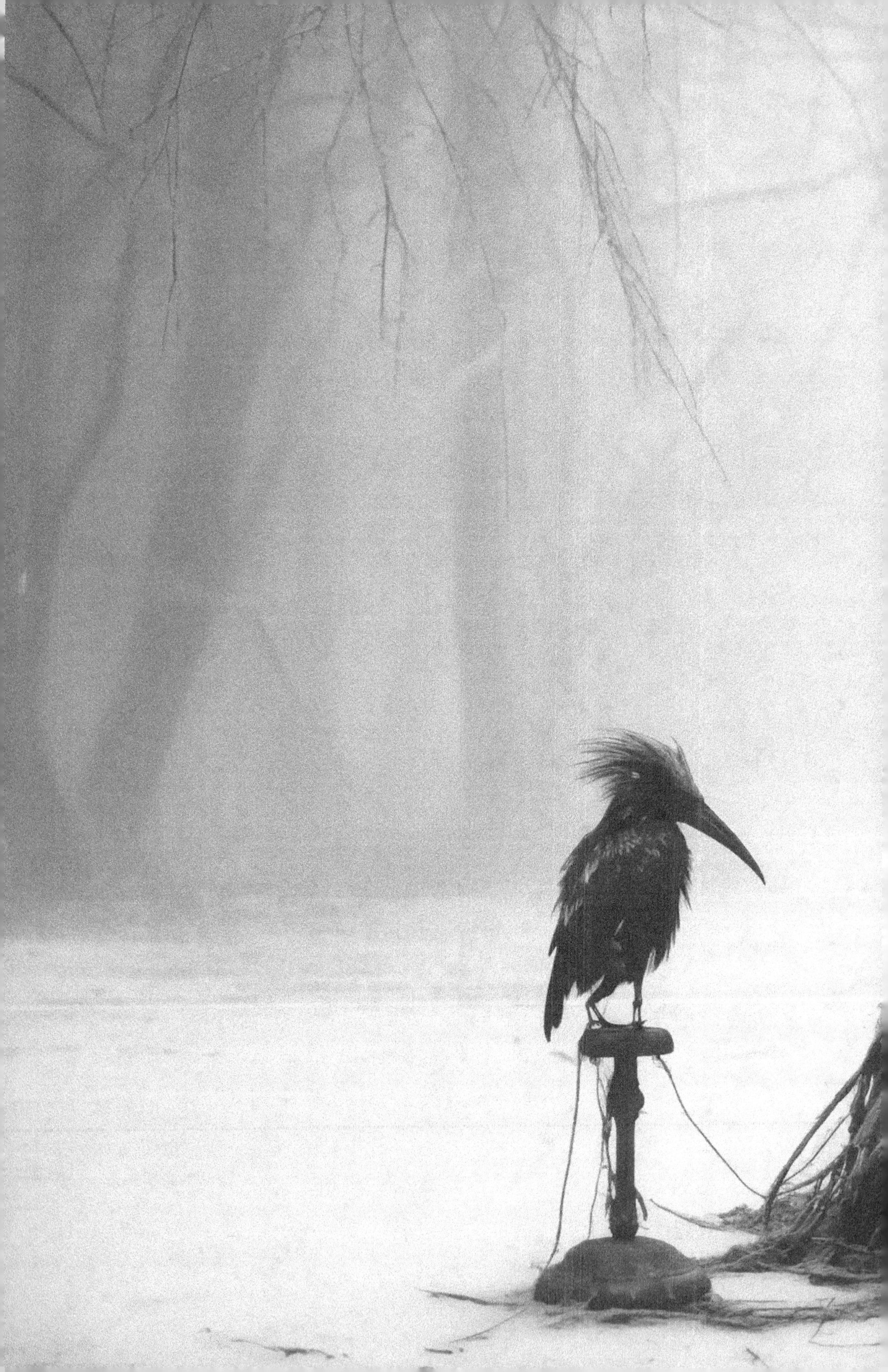

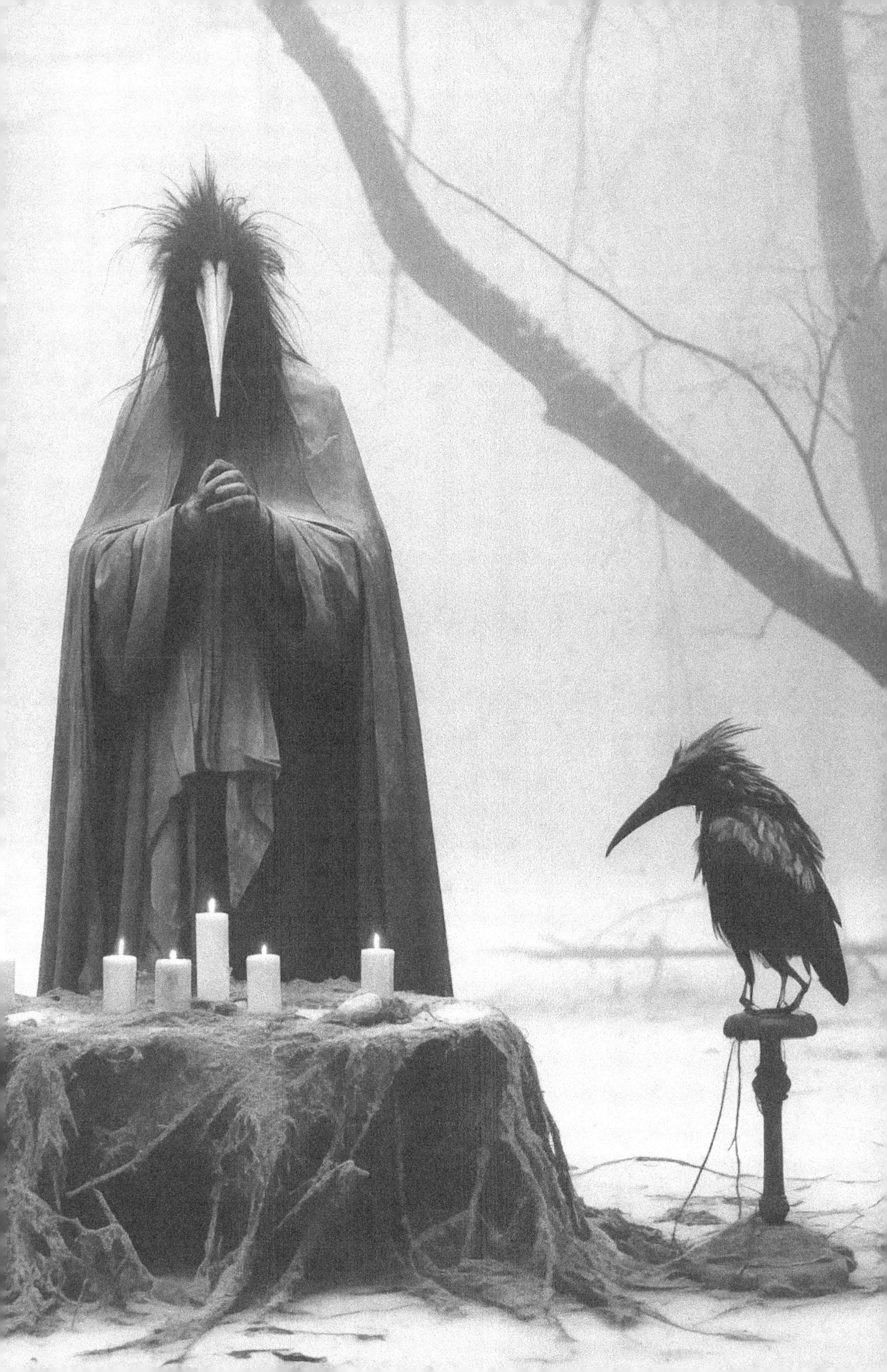

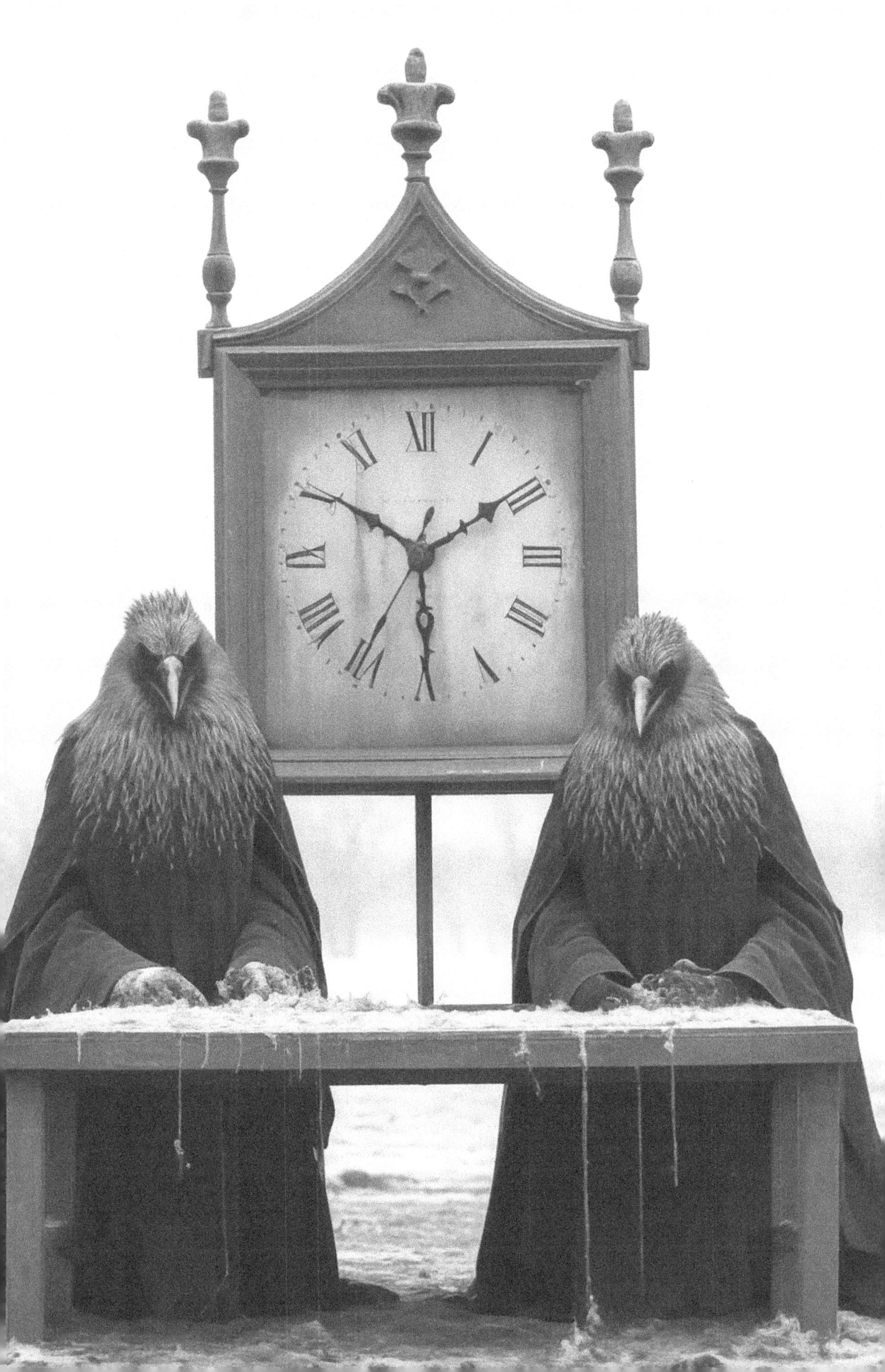

It's a shame
that nature has to
mistrust us.

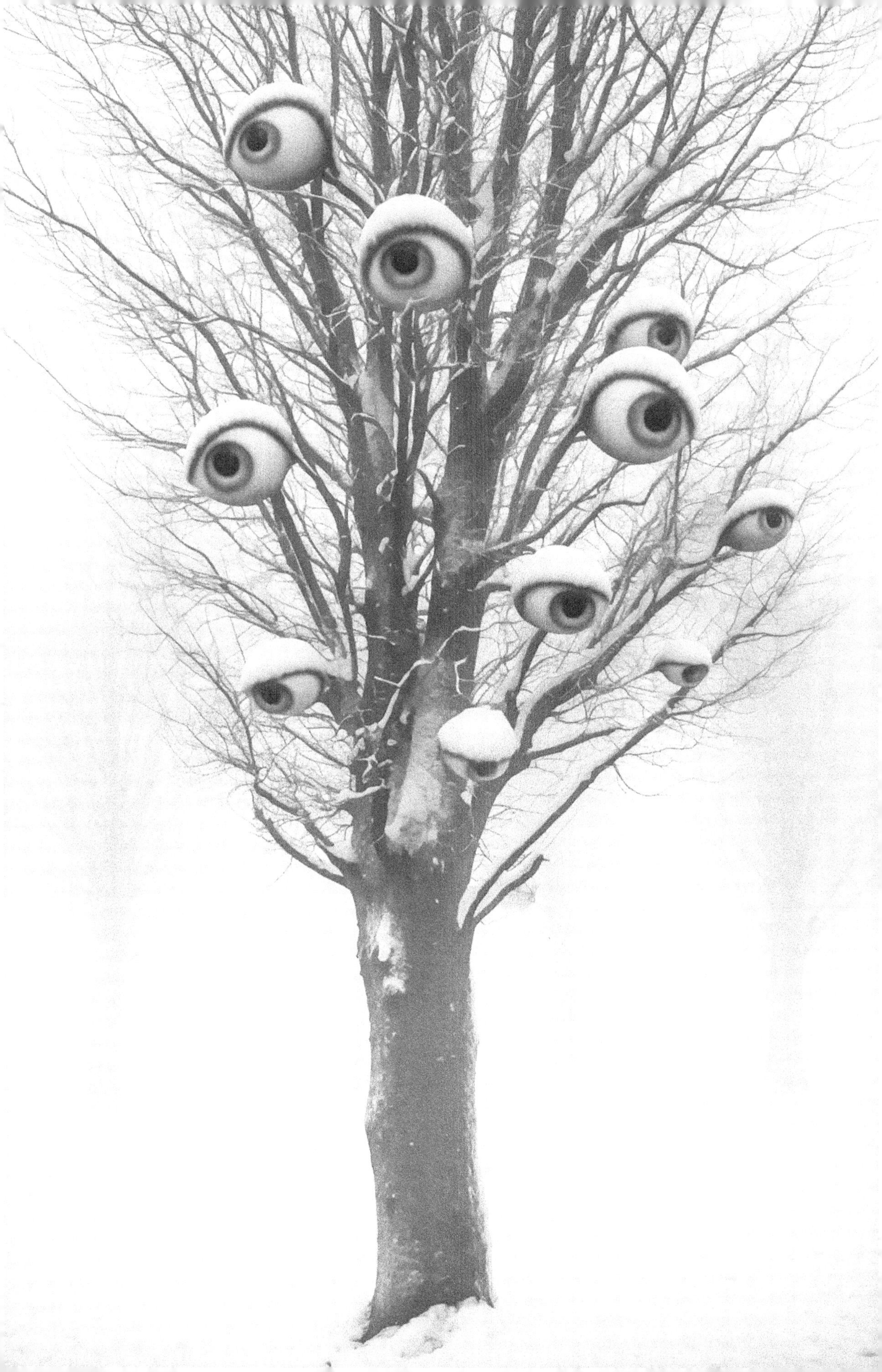

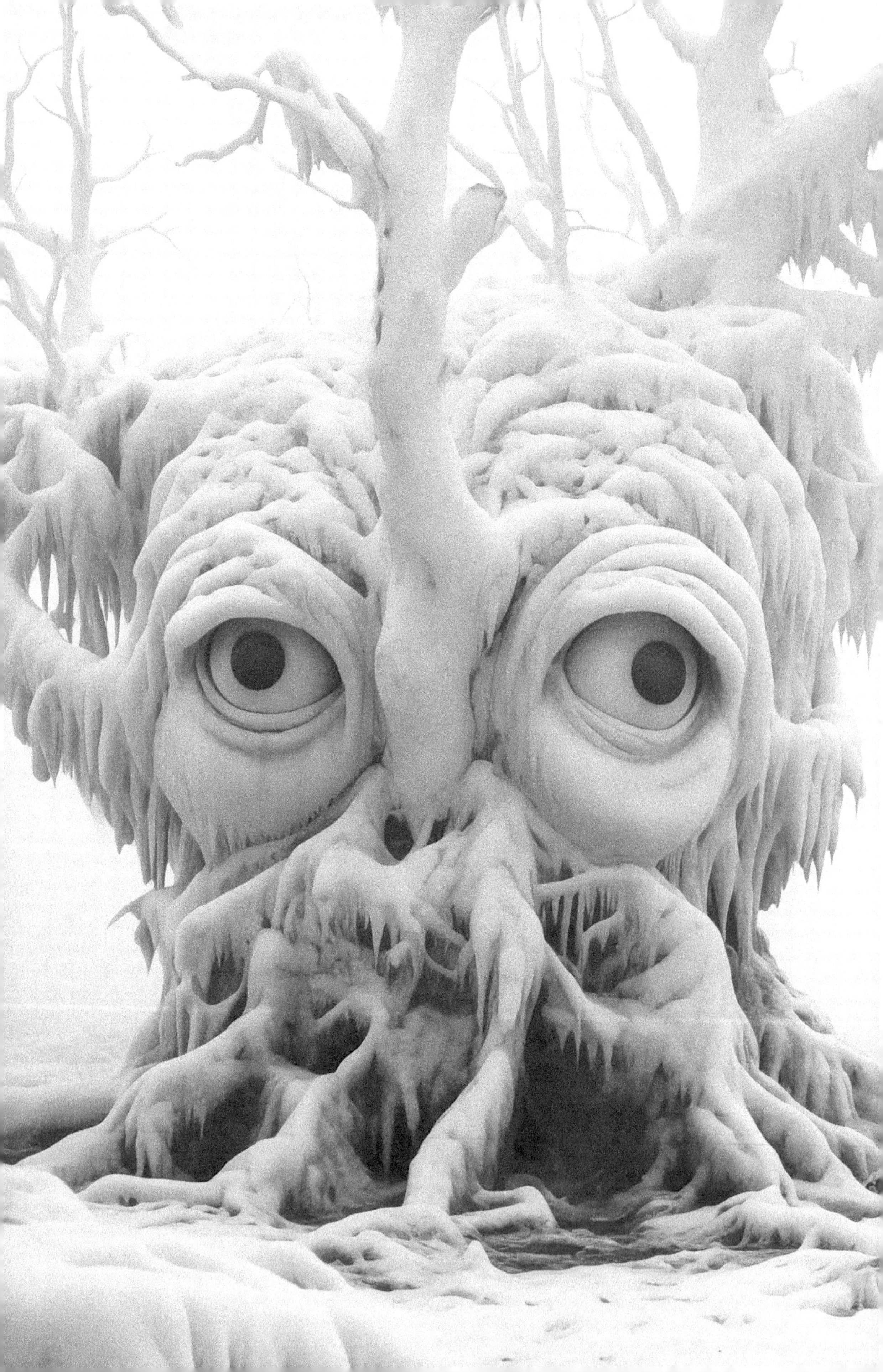

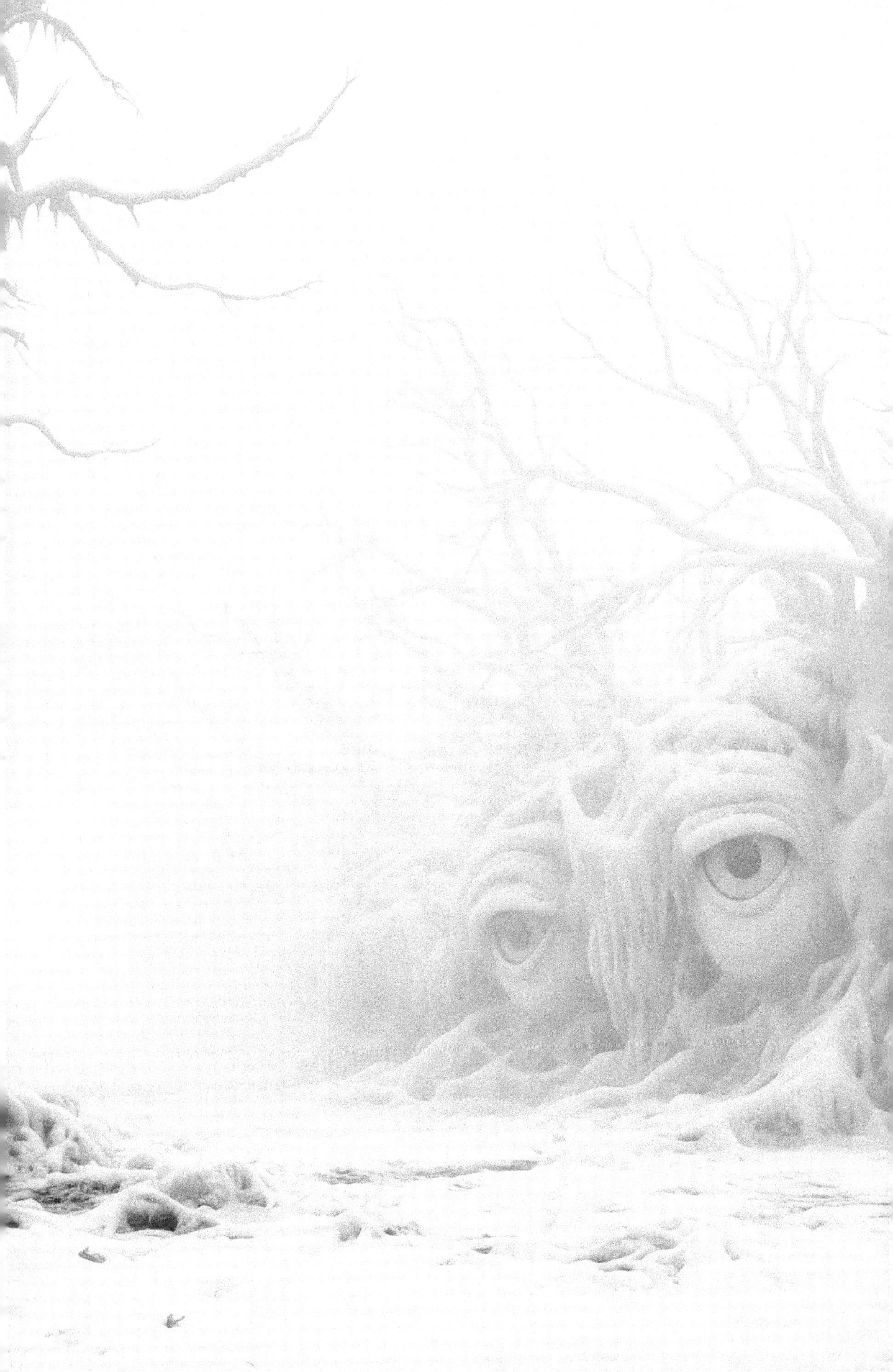

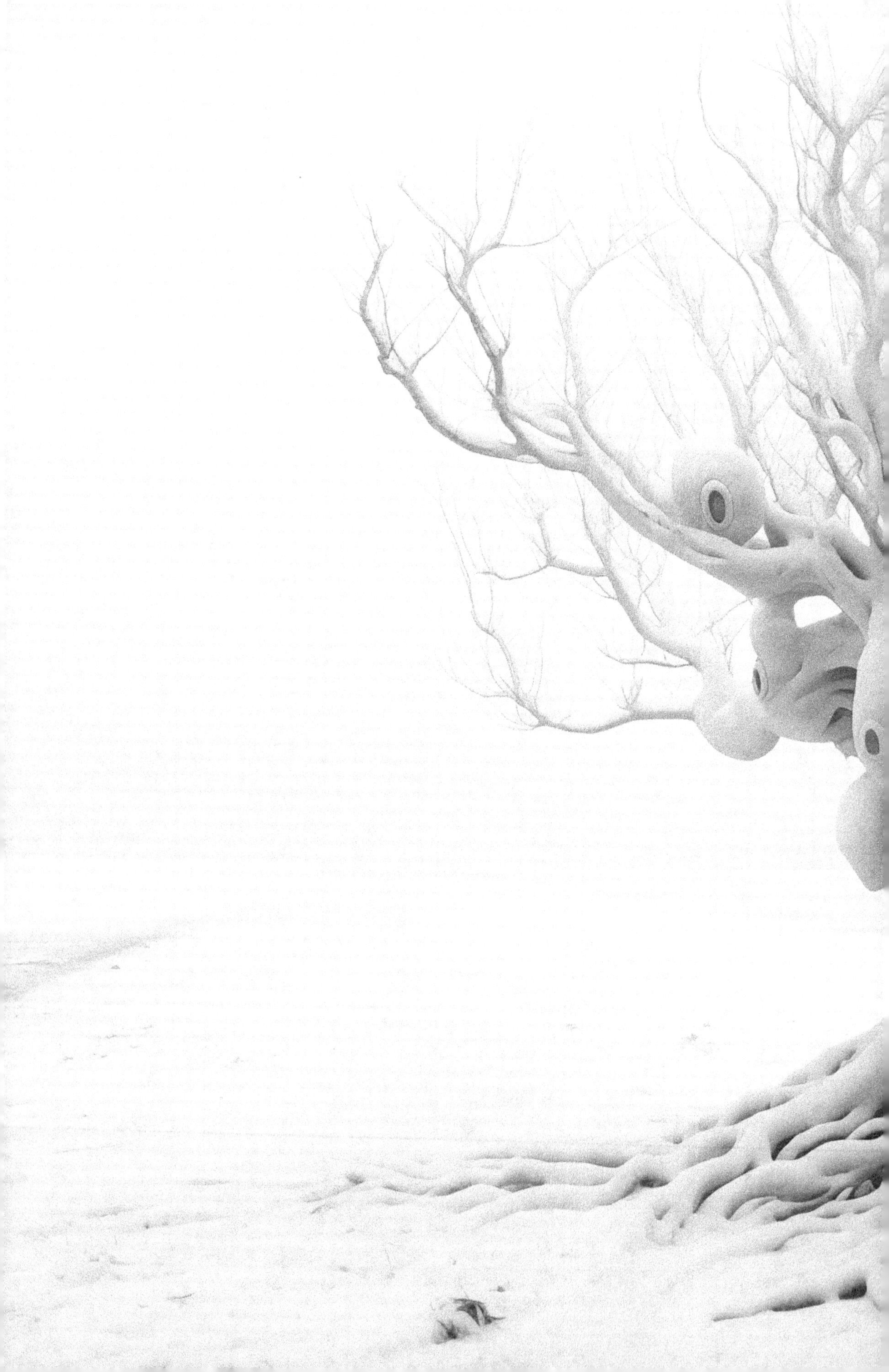

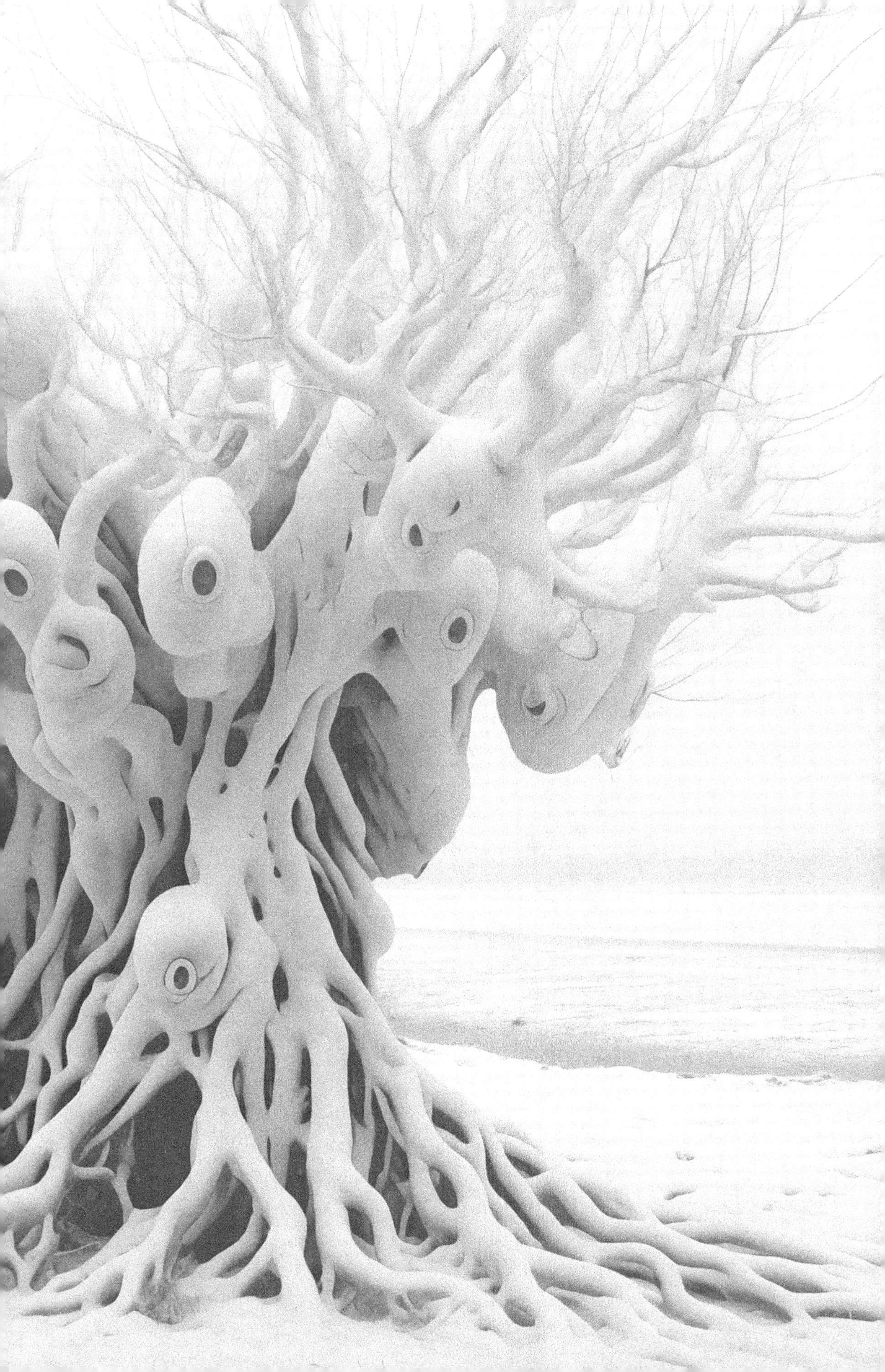

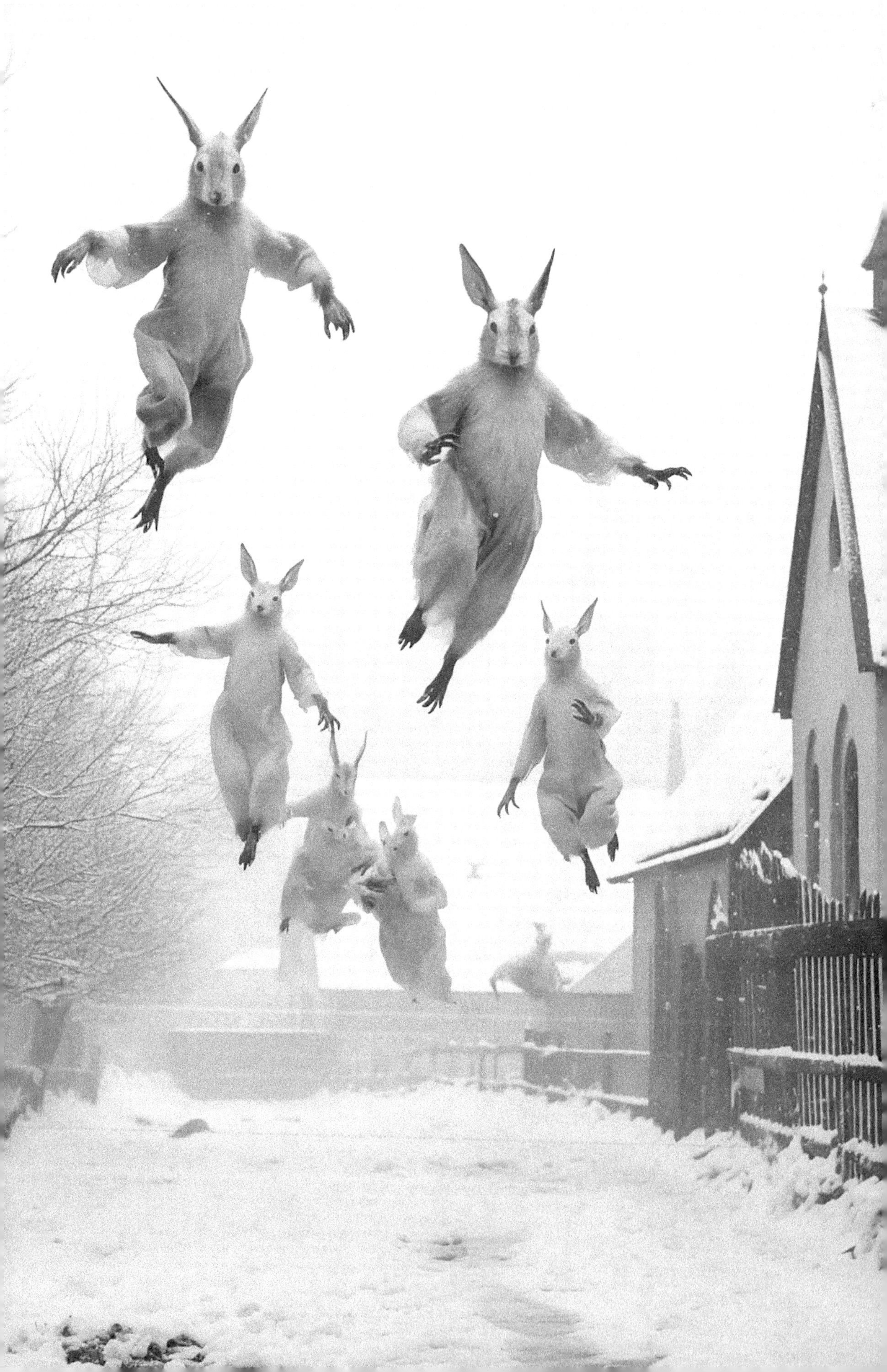

Jump
around!

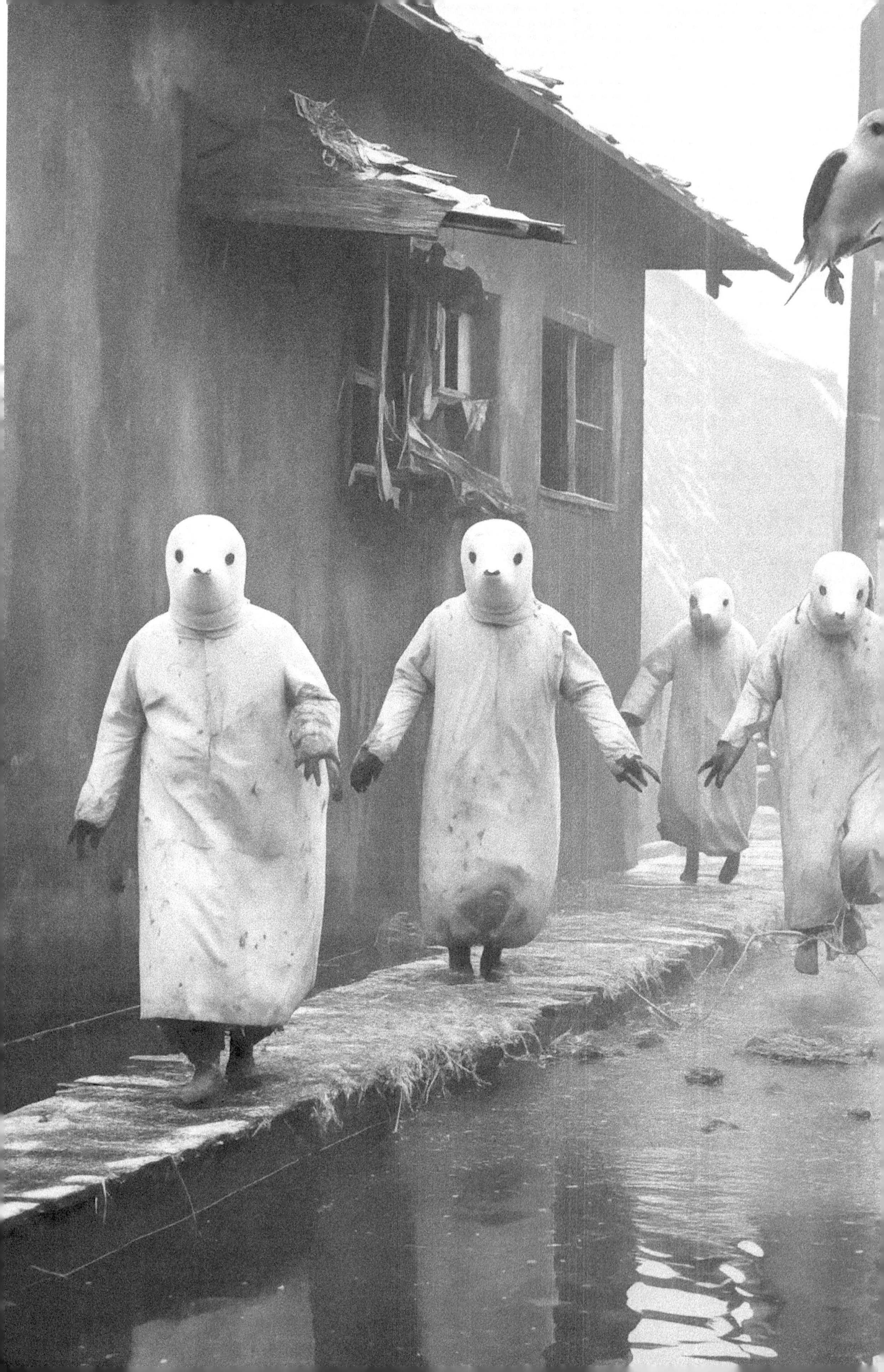

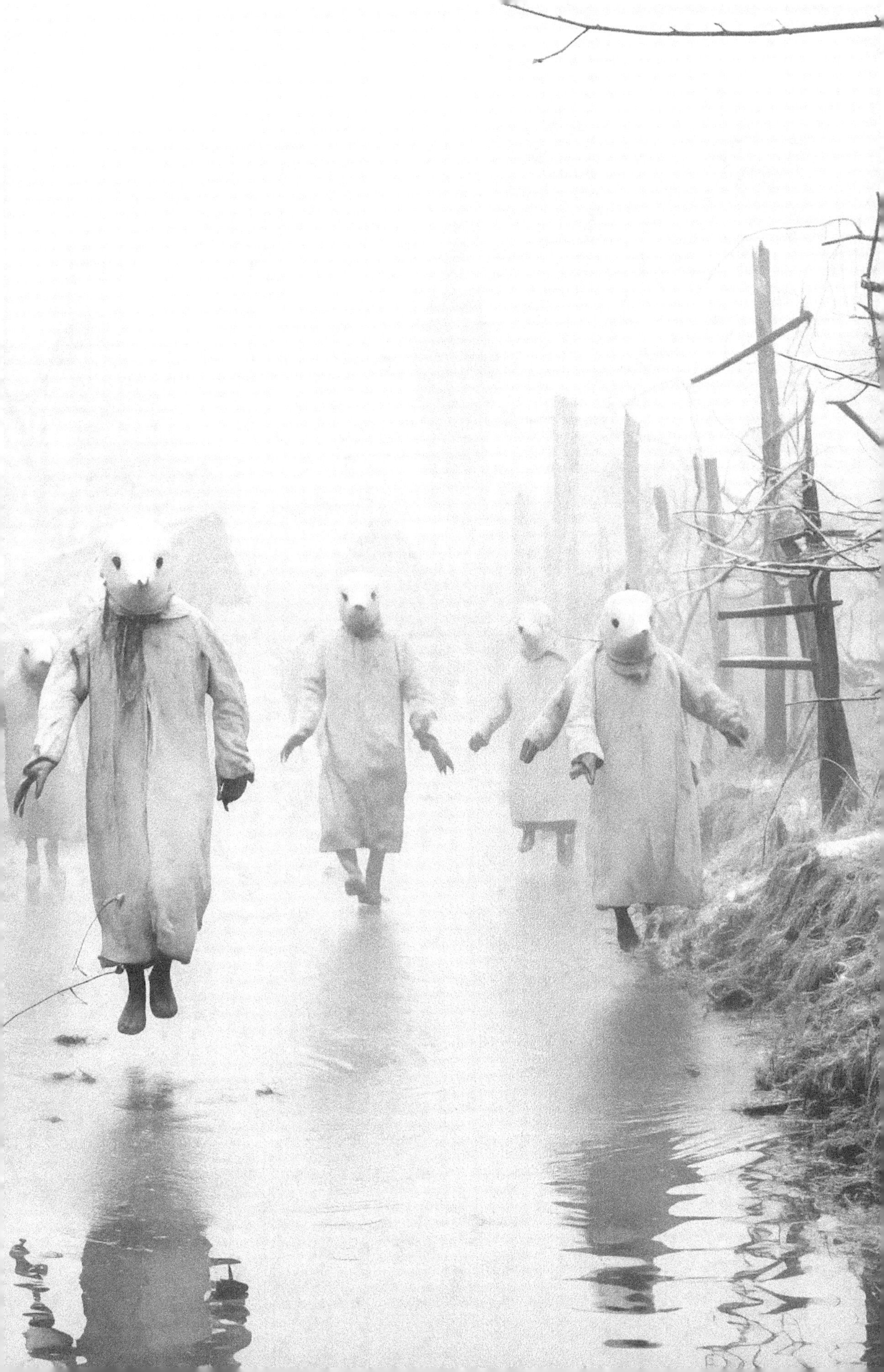

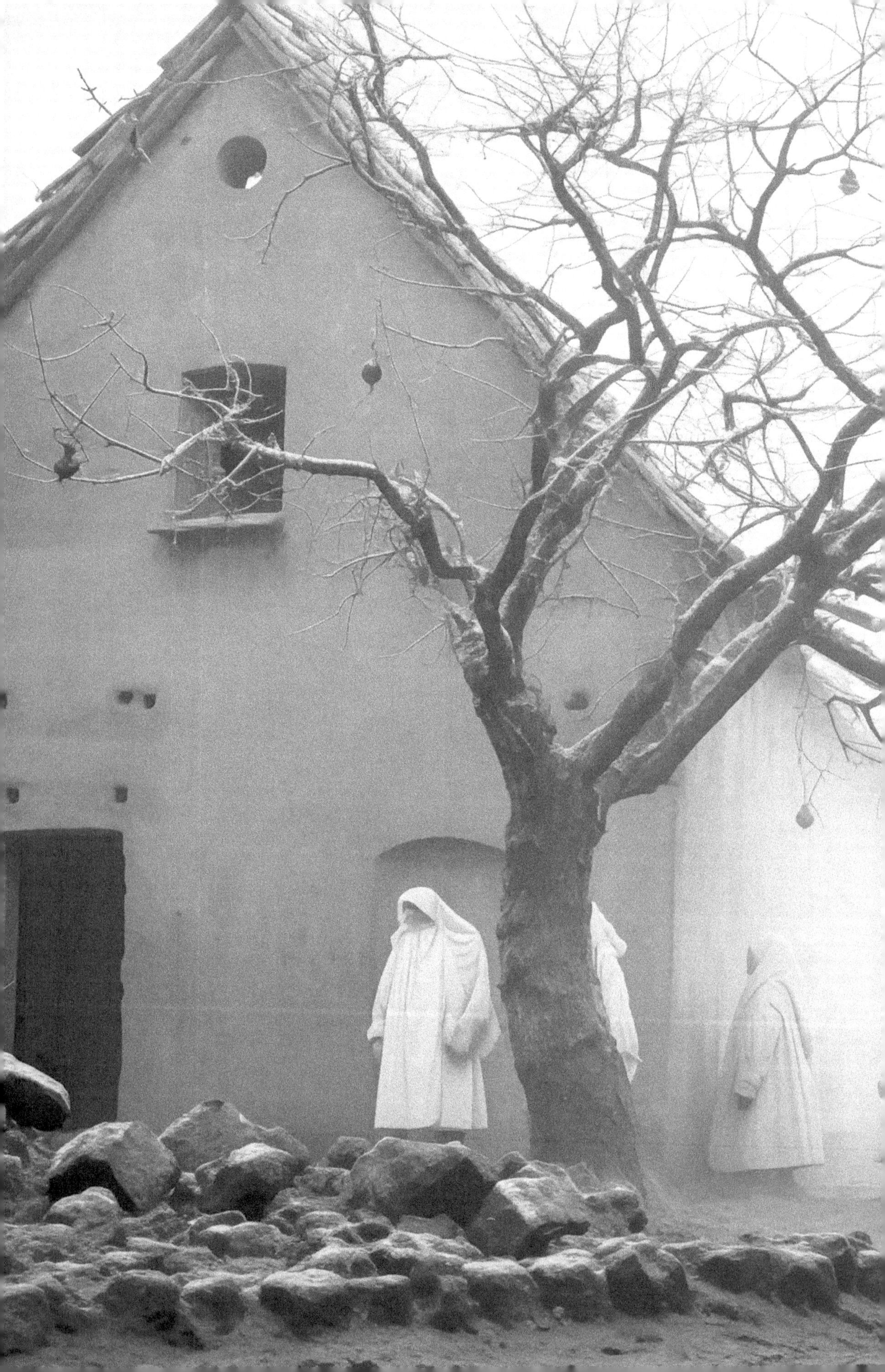

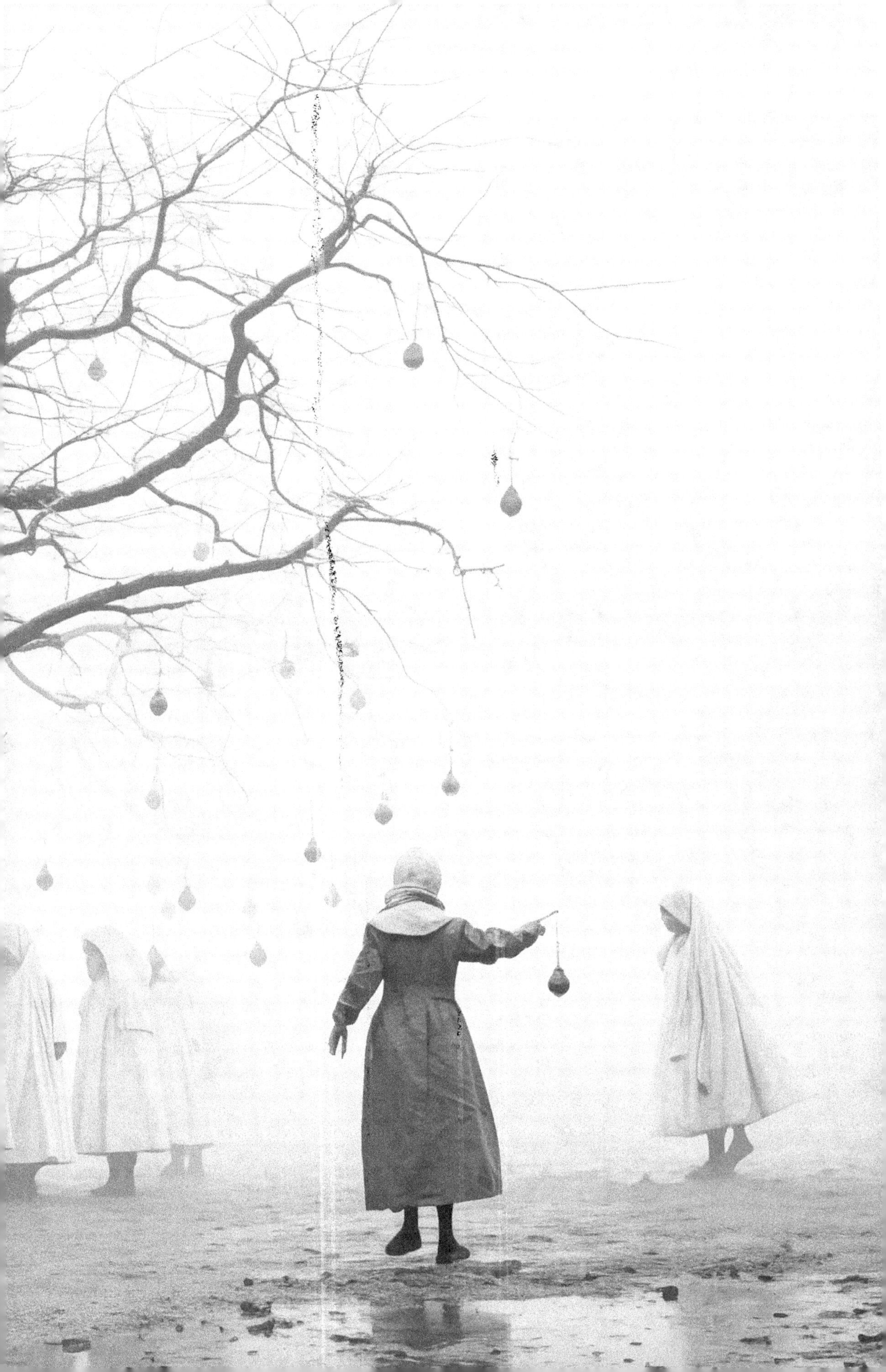

We are many and yet will all perish.

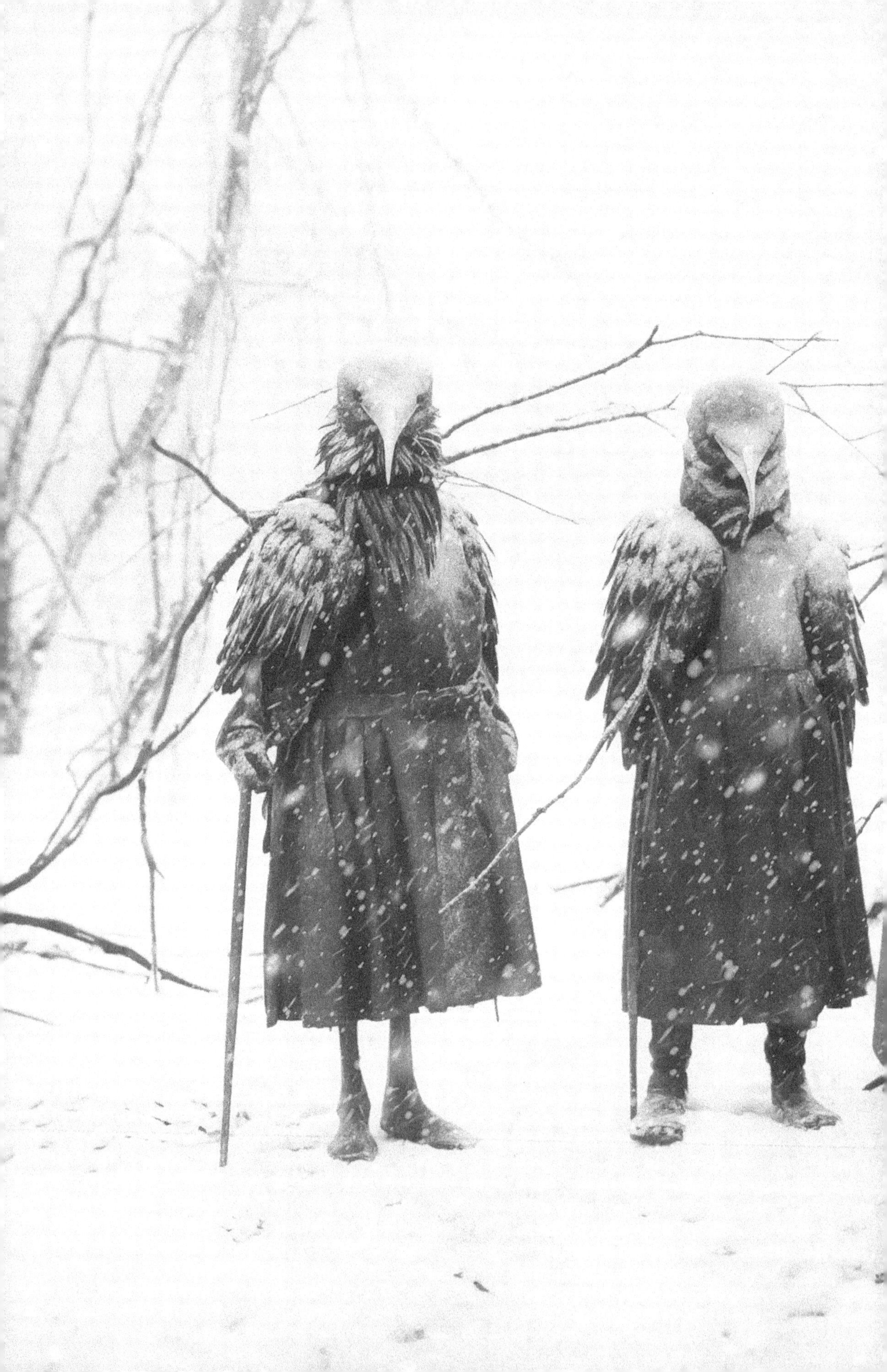

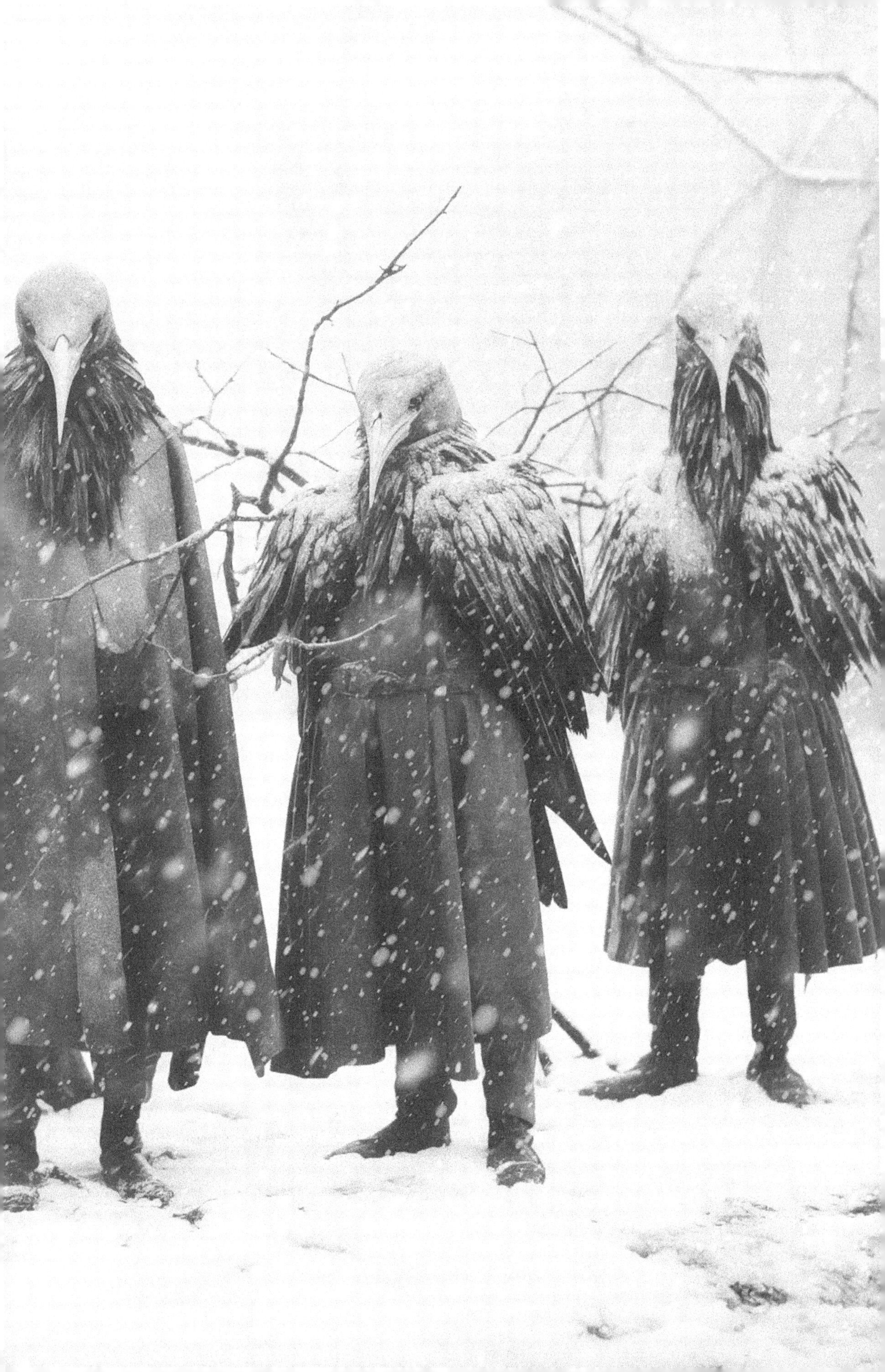

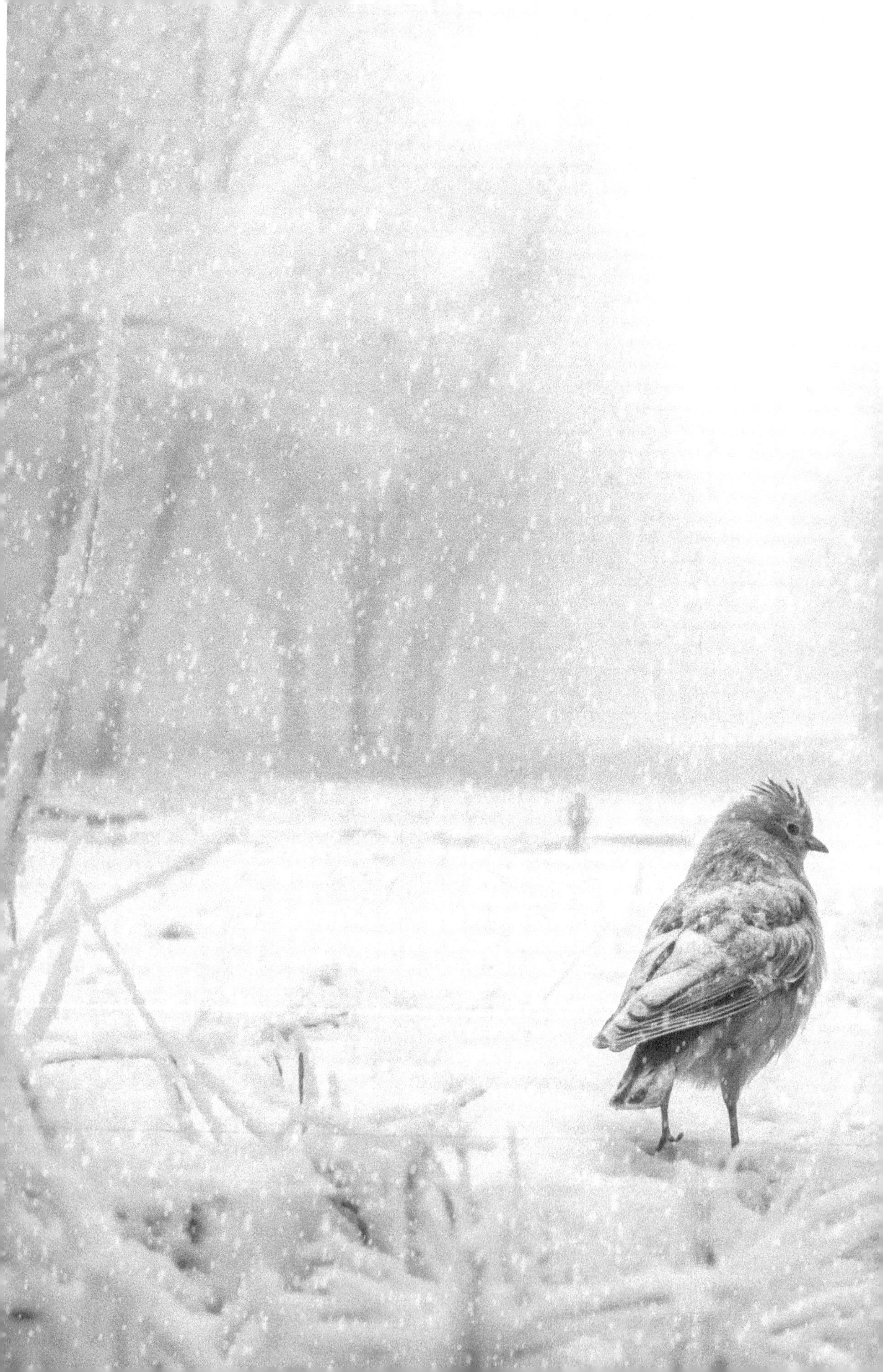

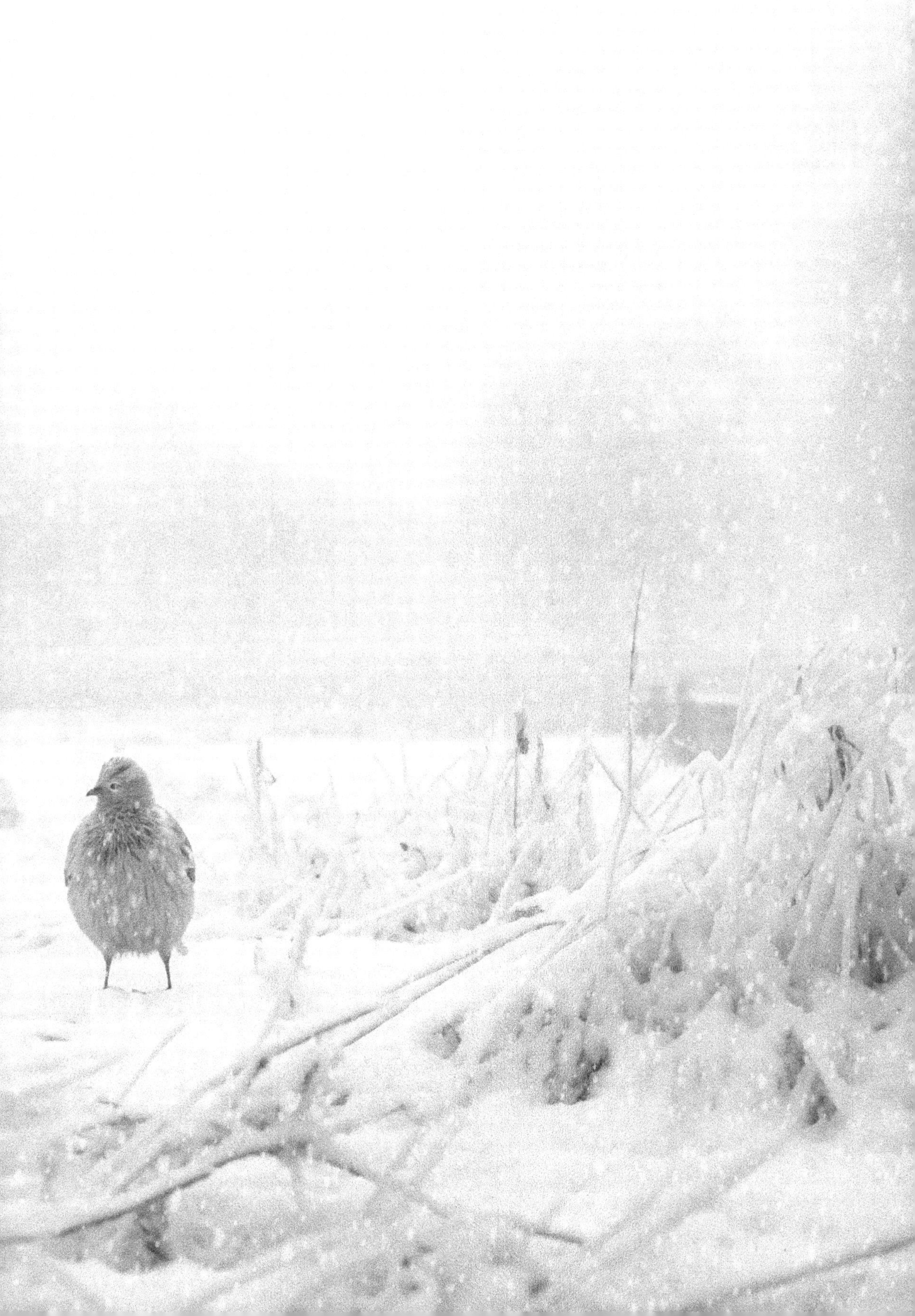

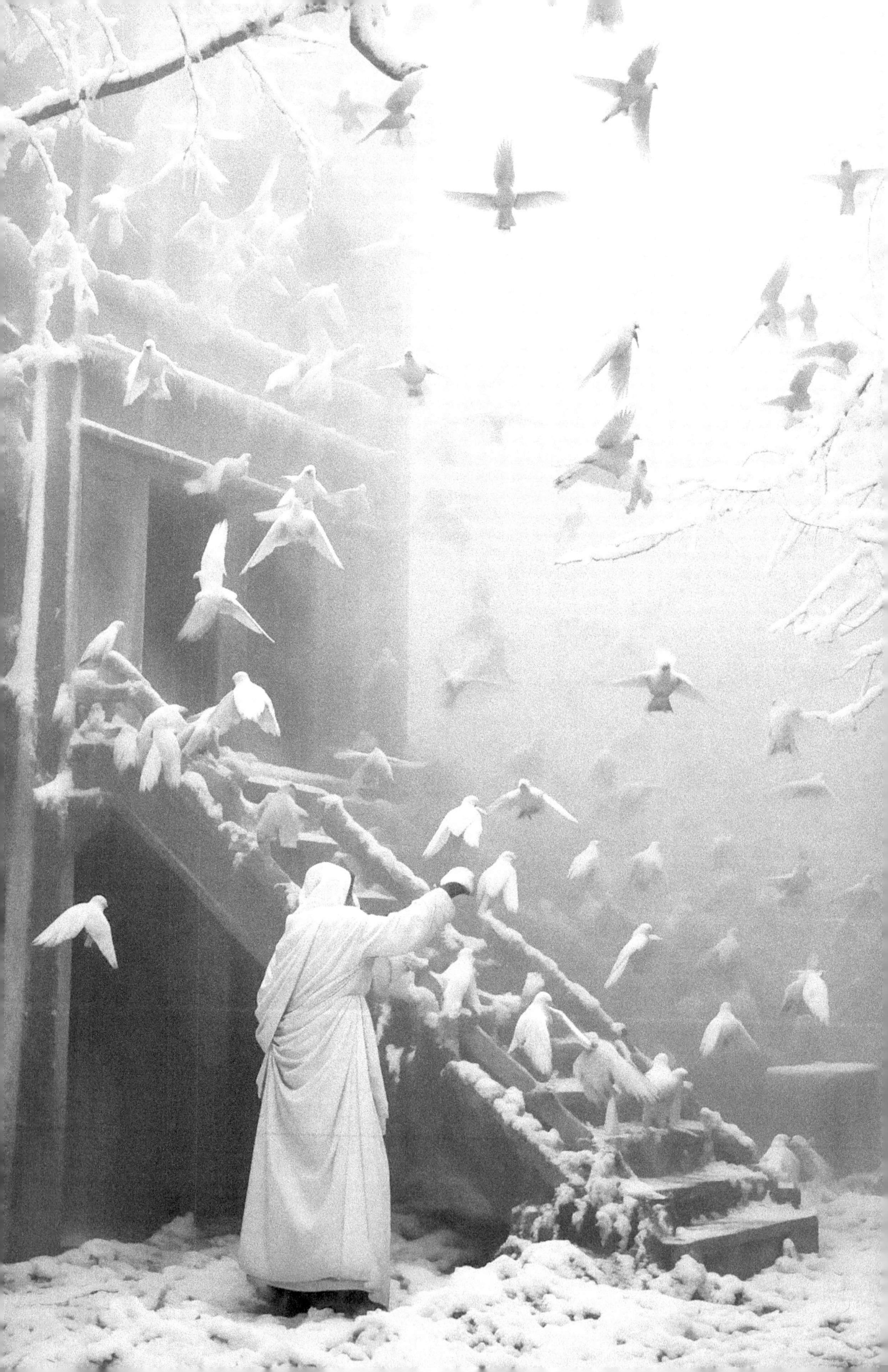

Thou shalt
treat all
creatures
with
kindness.

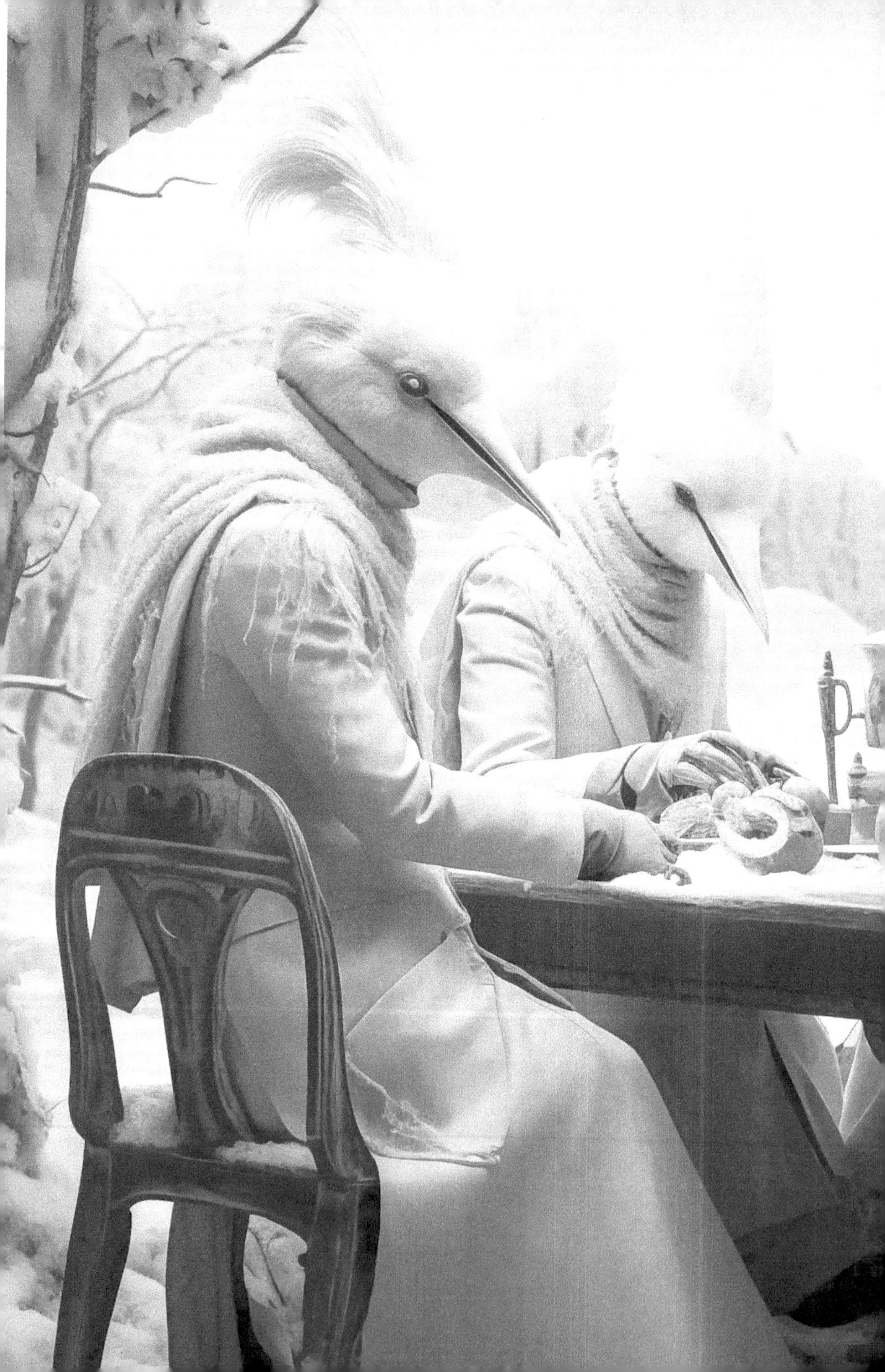

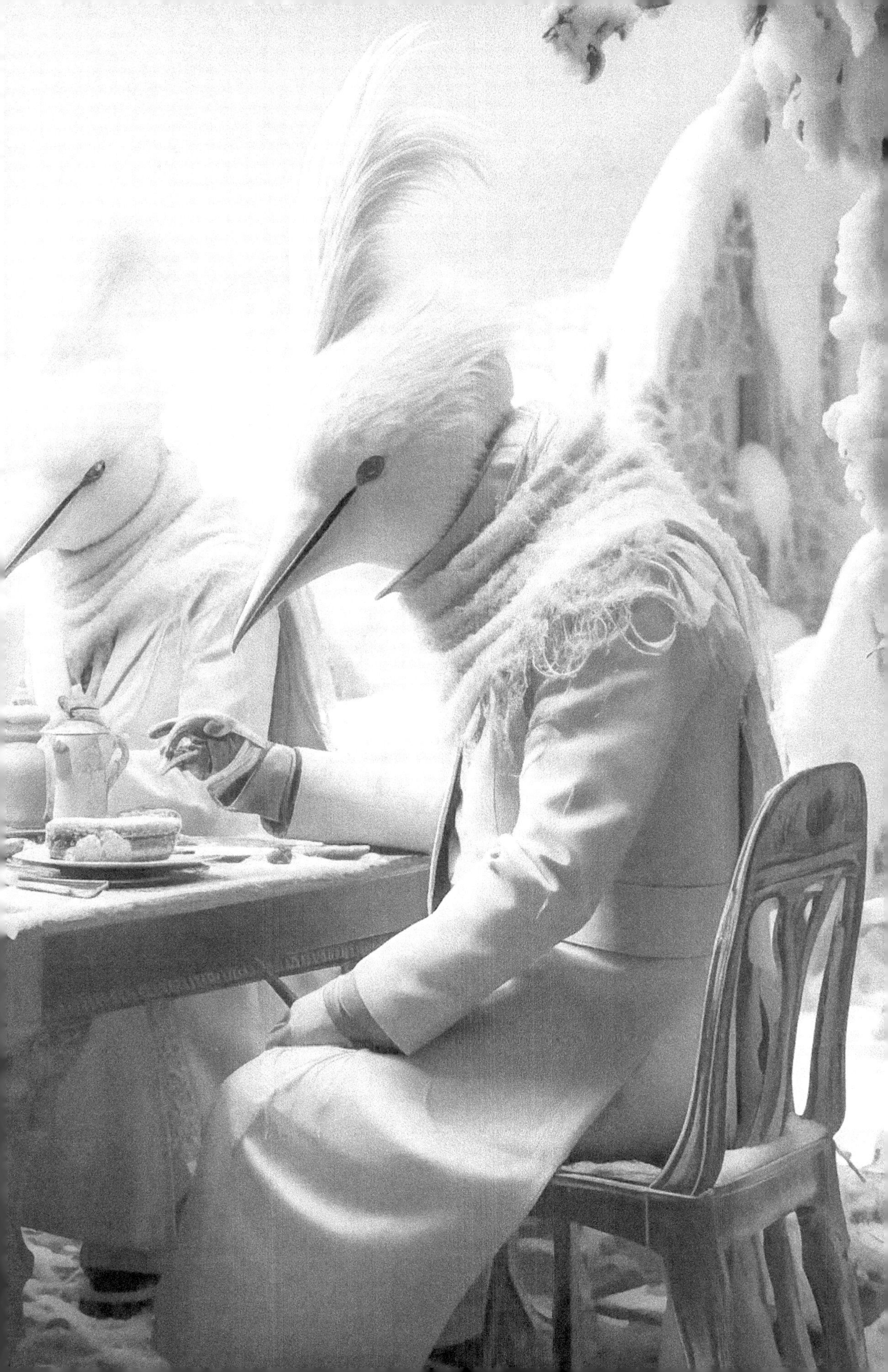

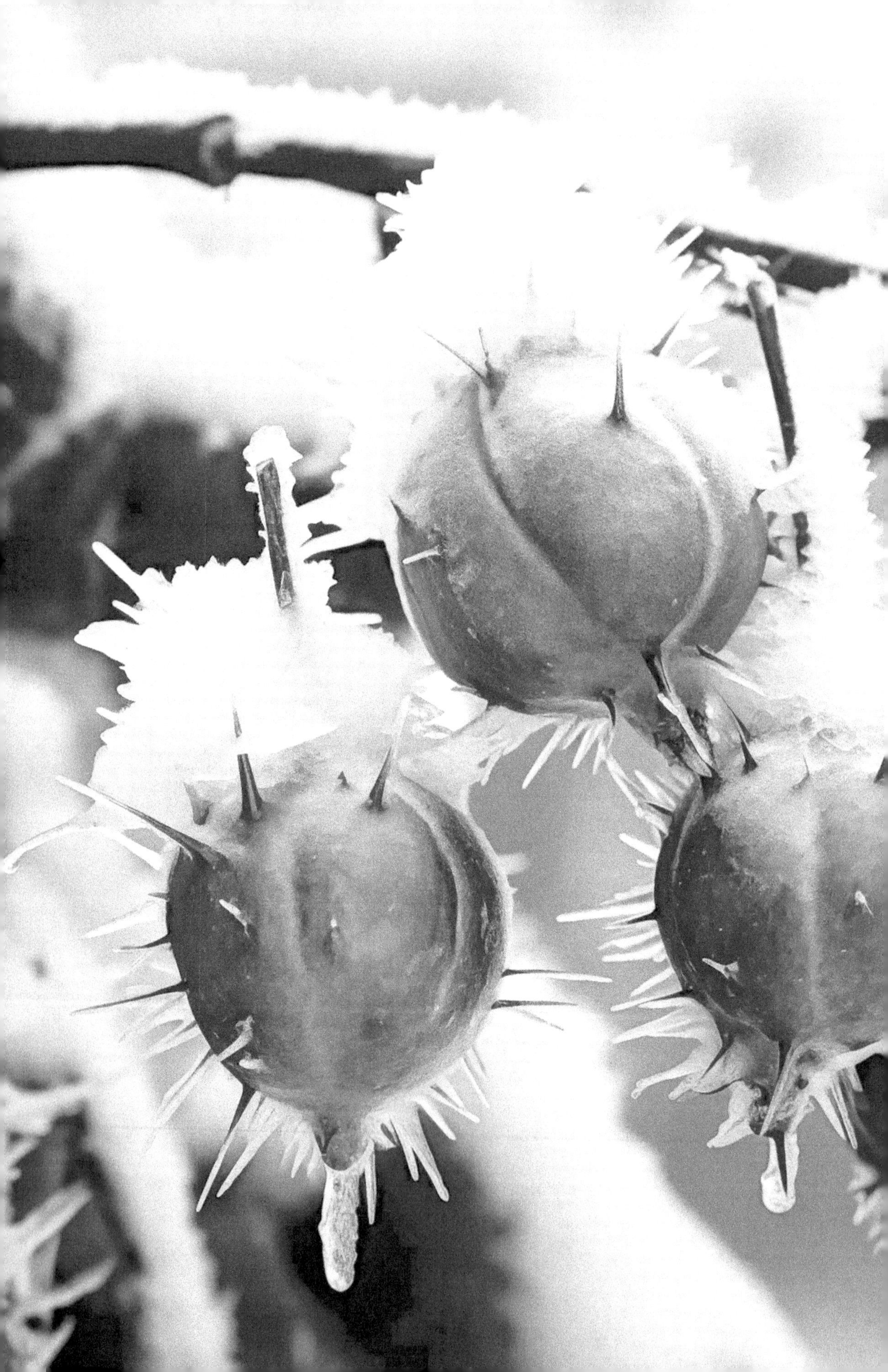

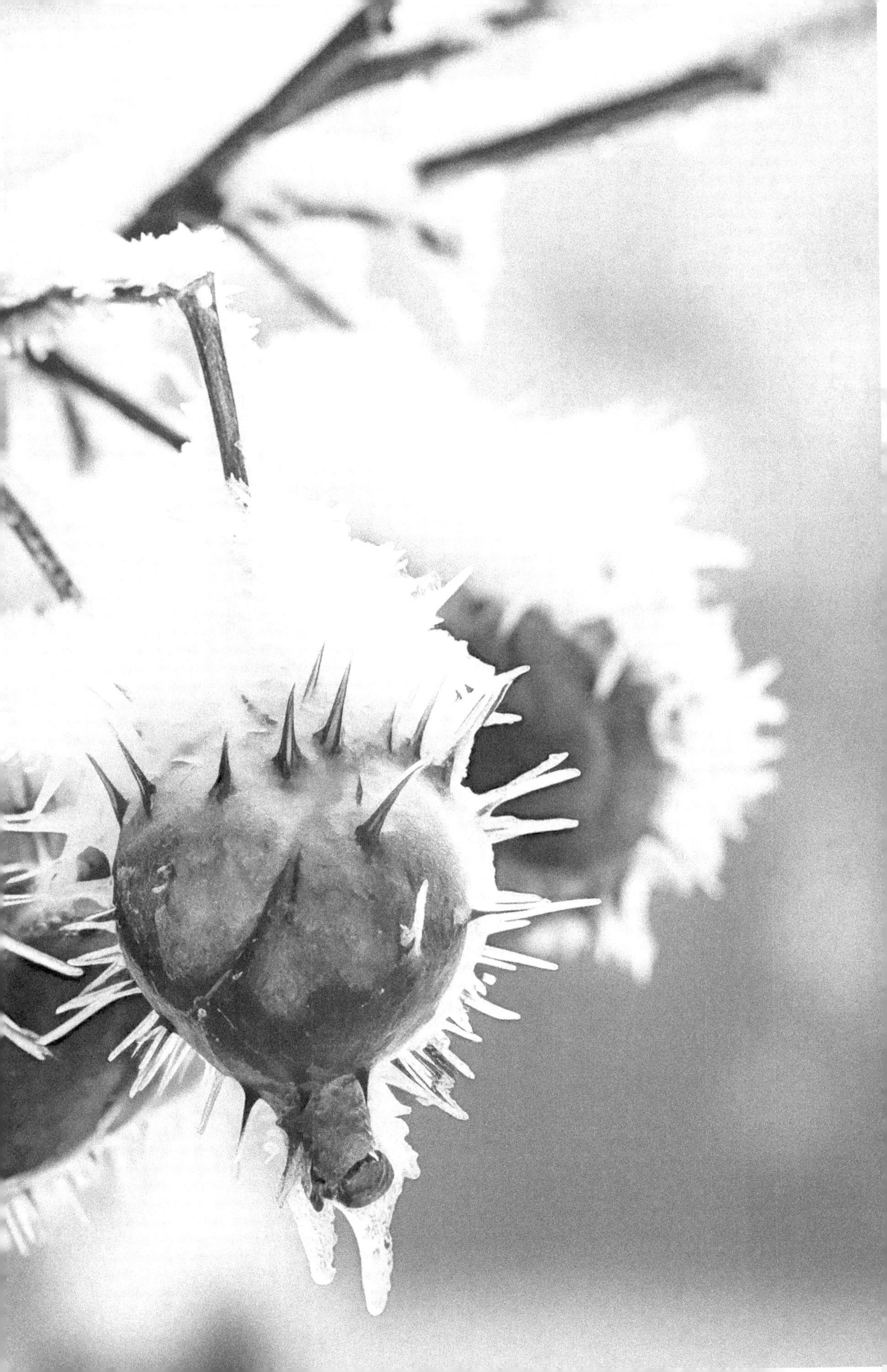

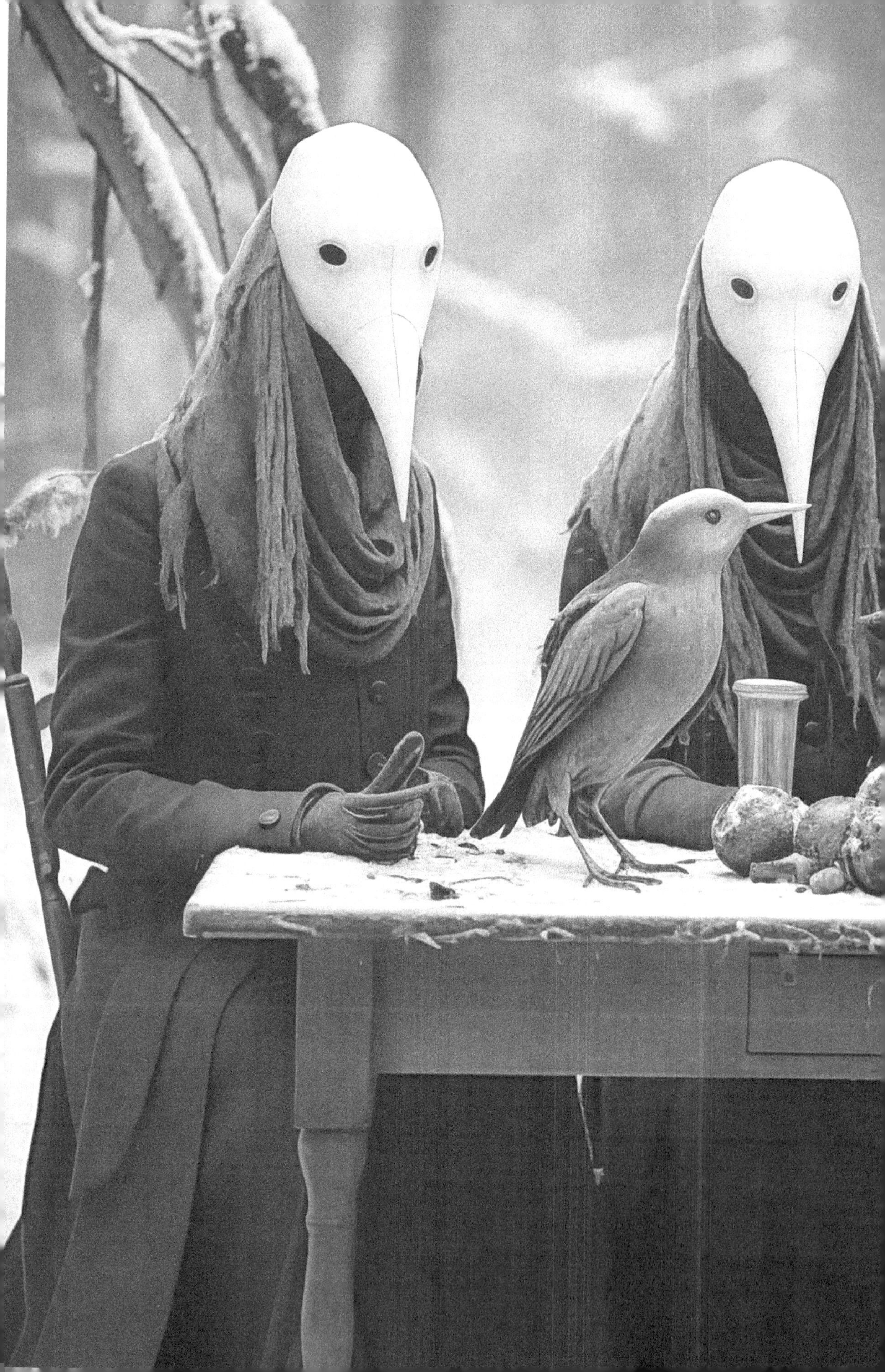

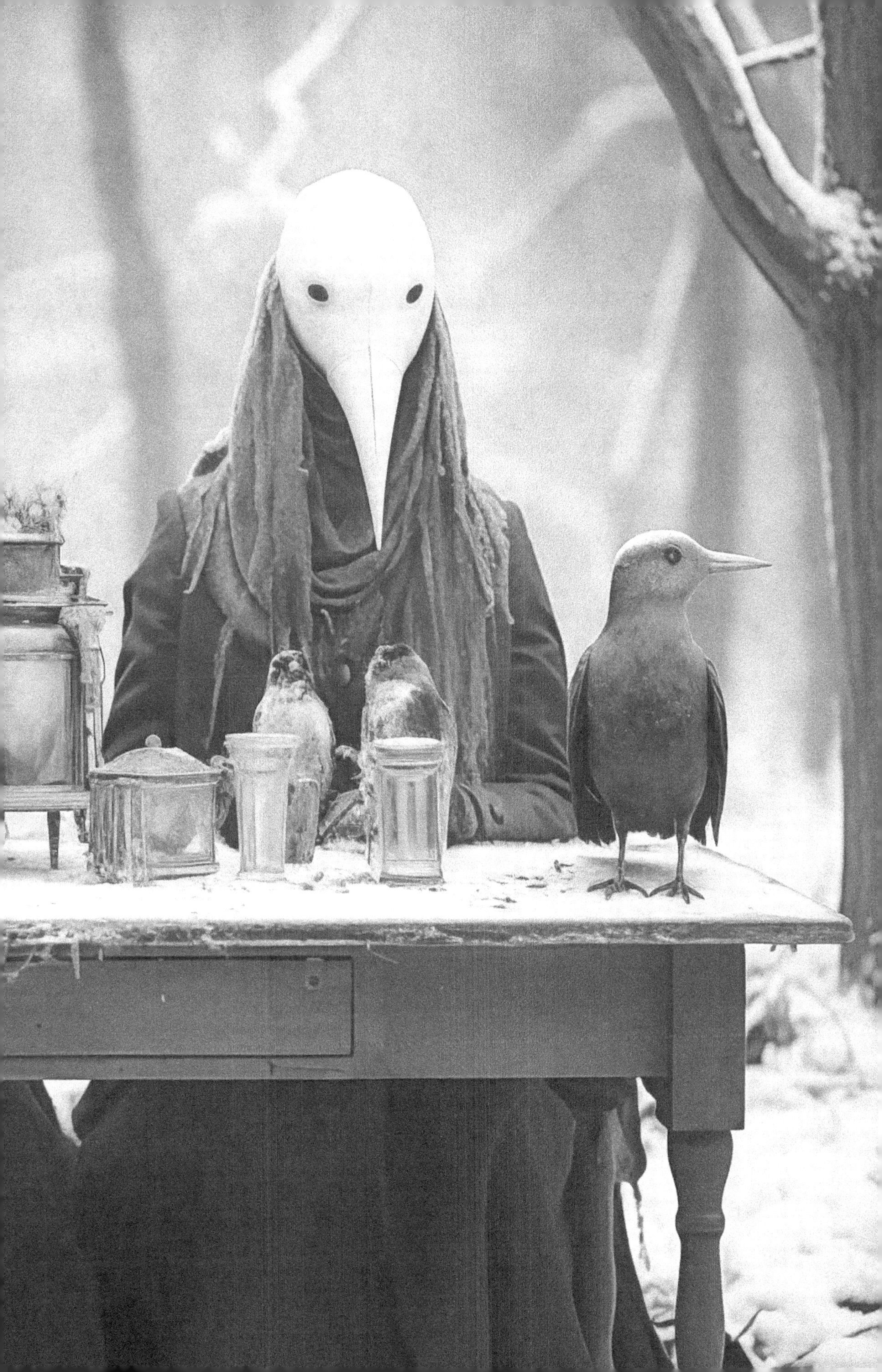

DARK FRUITS OF WINTER

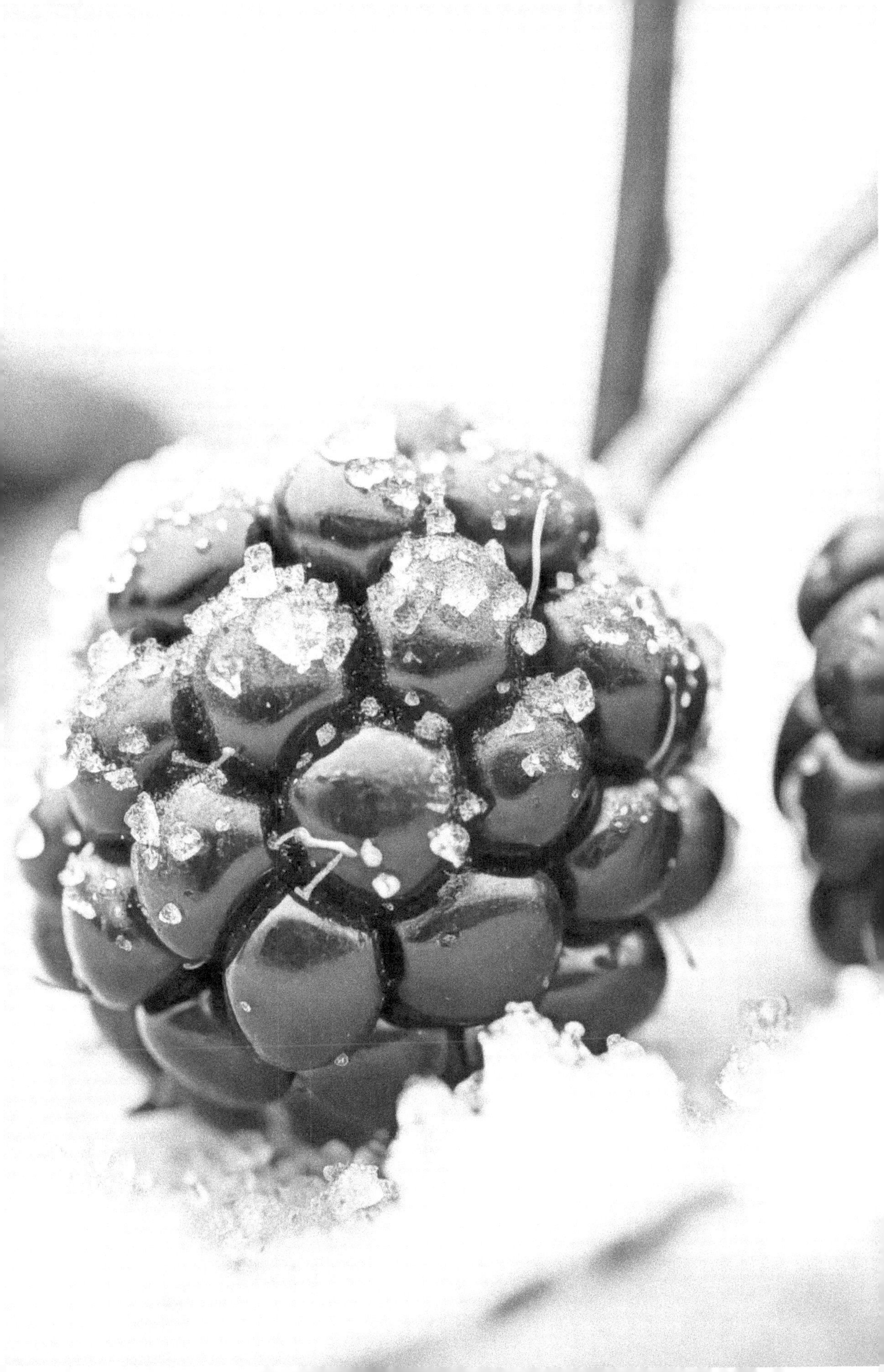

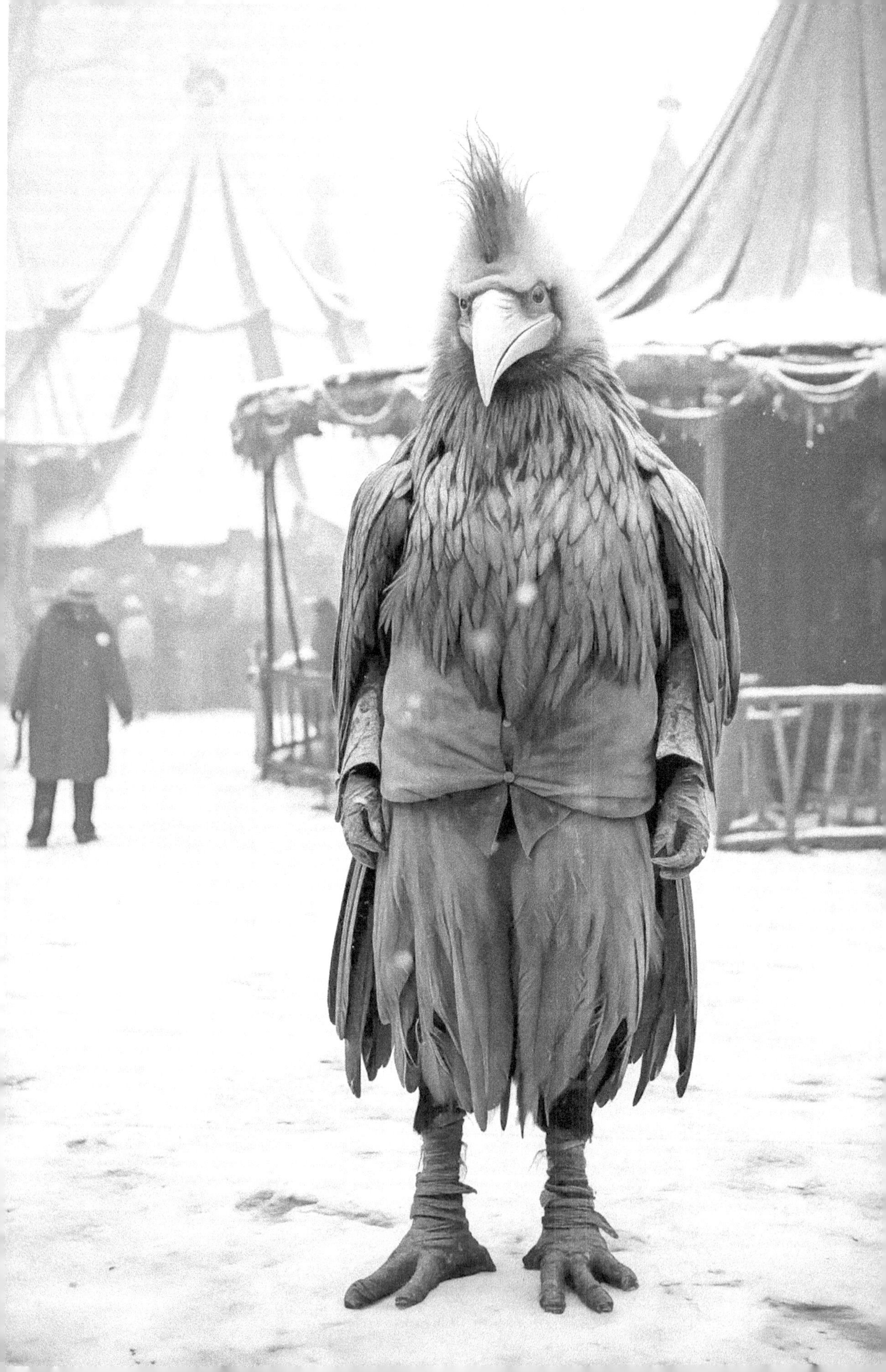

For the jugglers
and traveling folk.

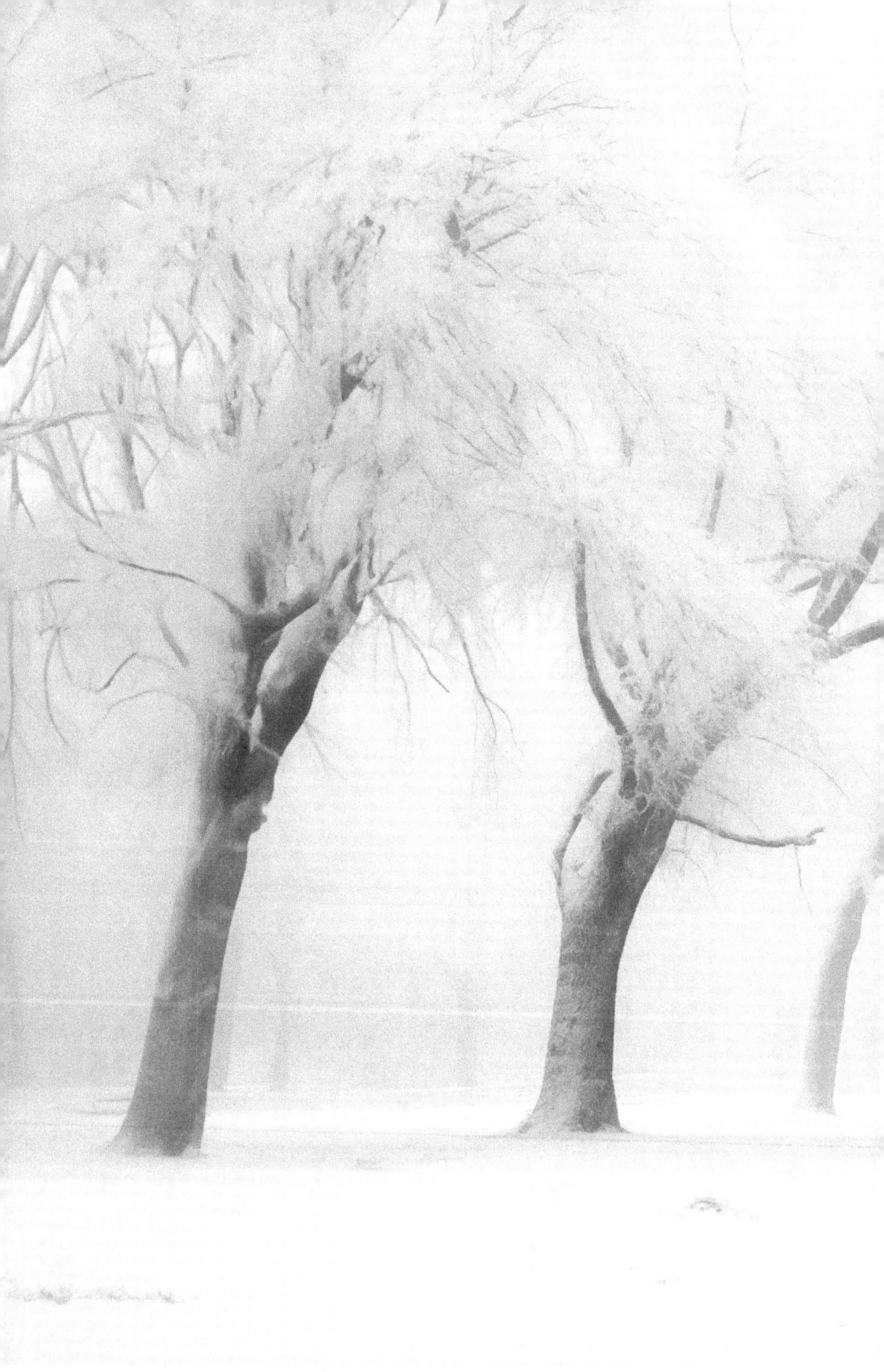

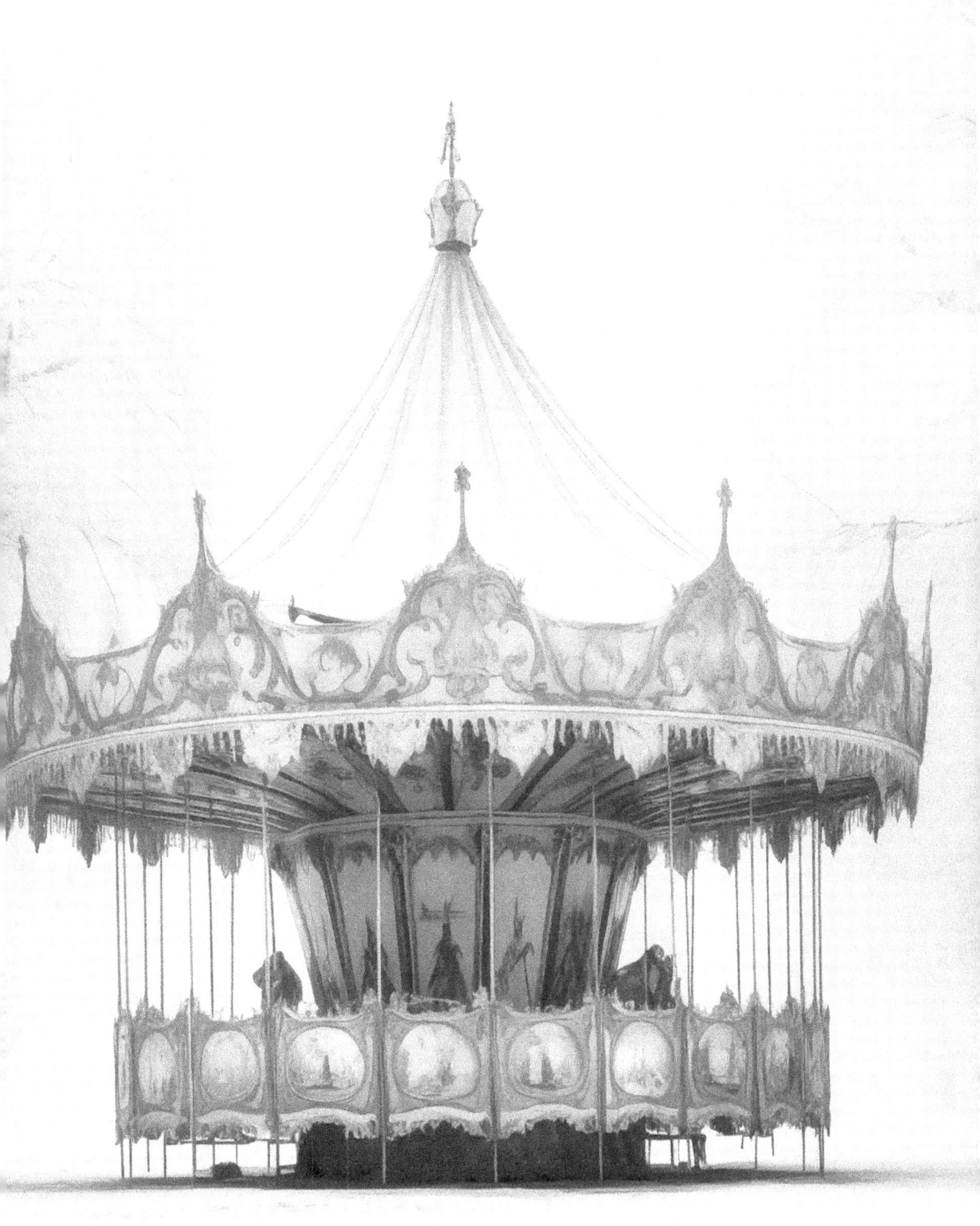

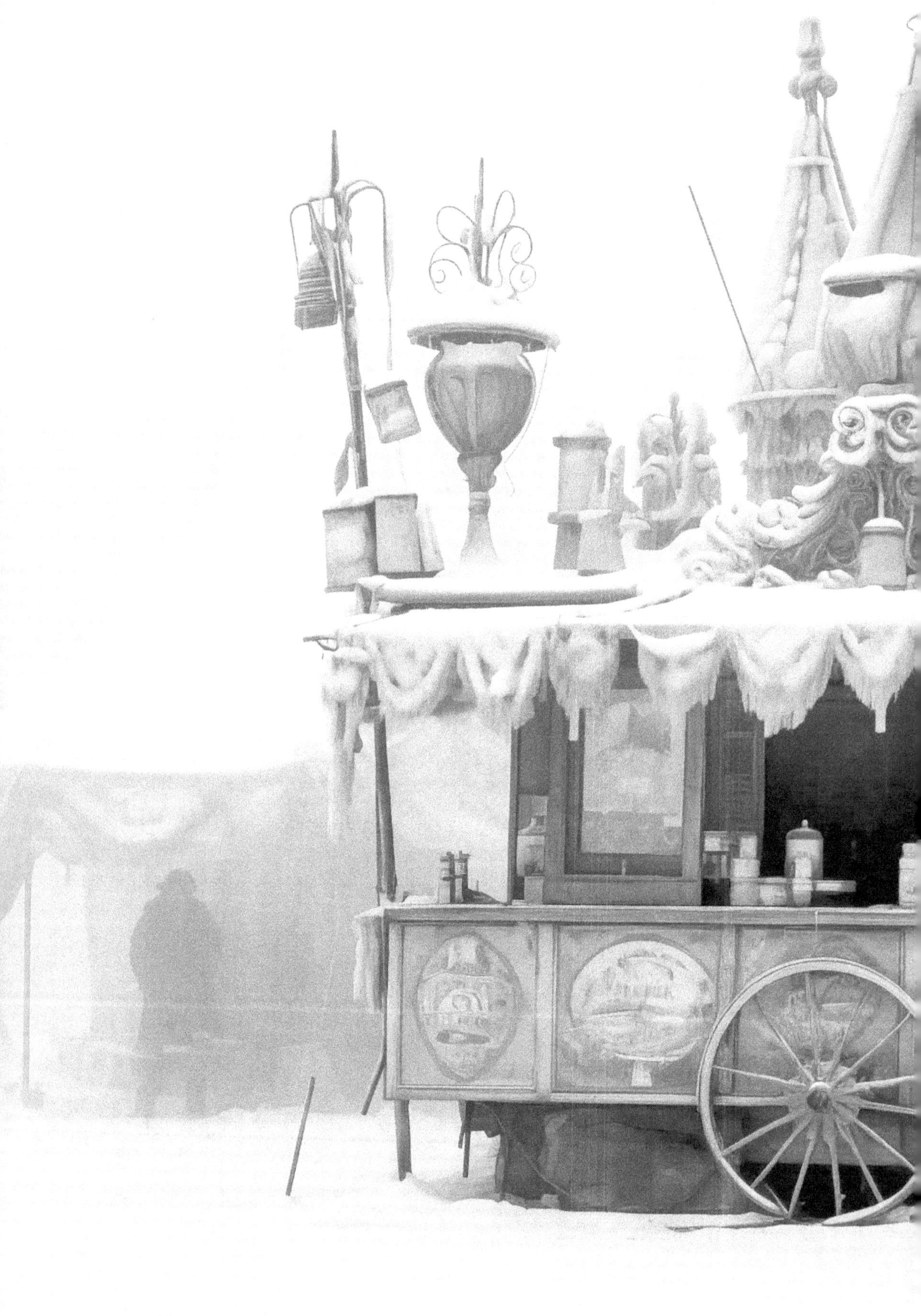

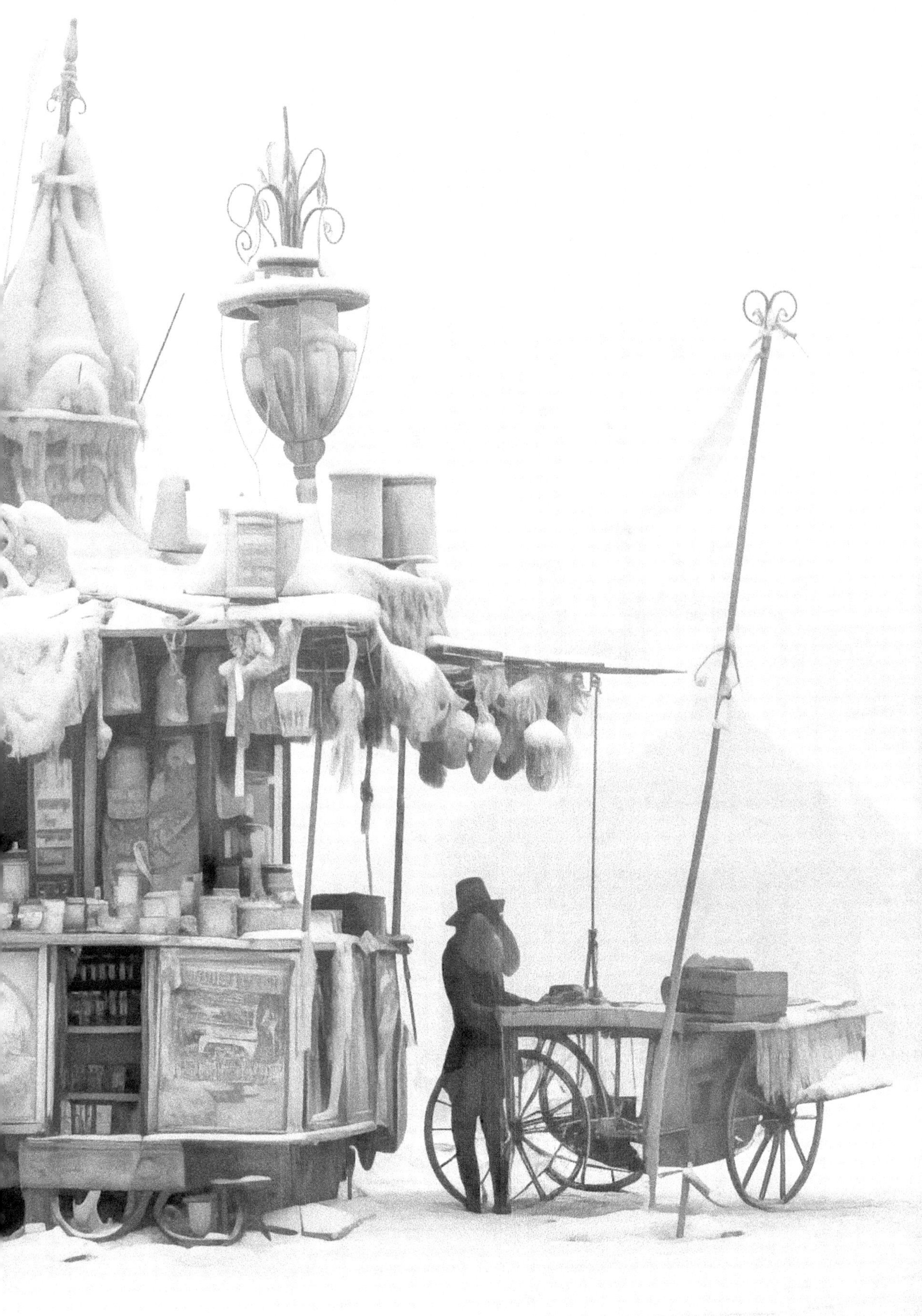

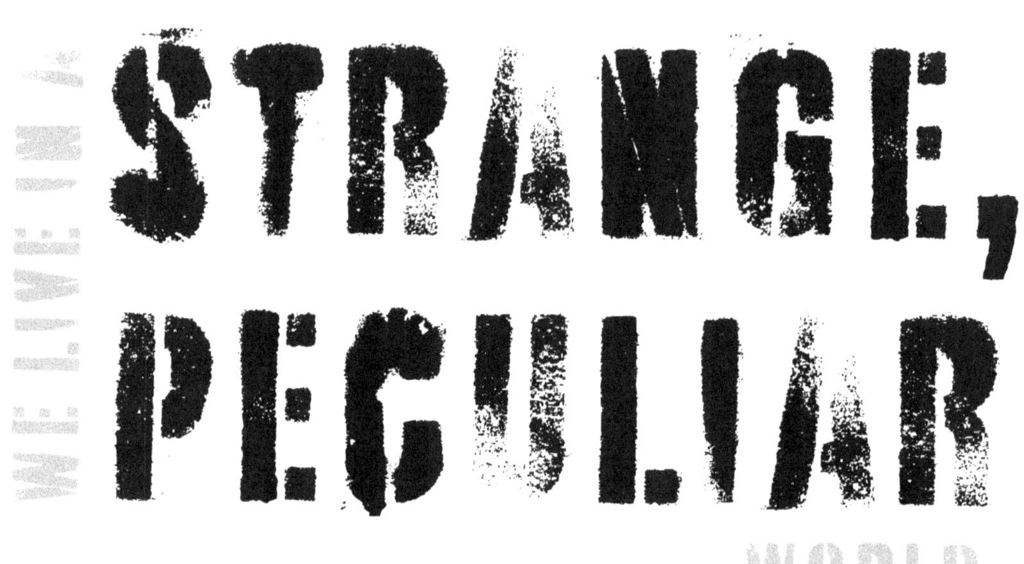

WE LIVE IN A
STRANGE,
PECULIAR
WORLD.

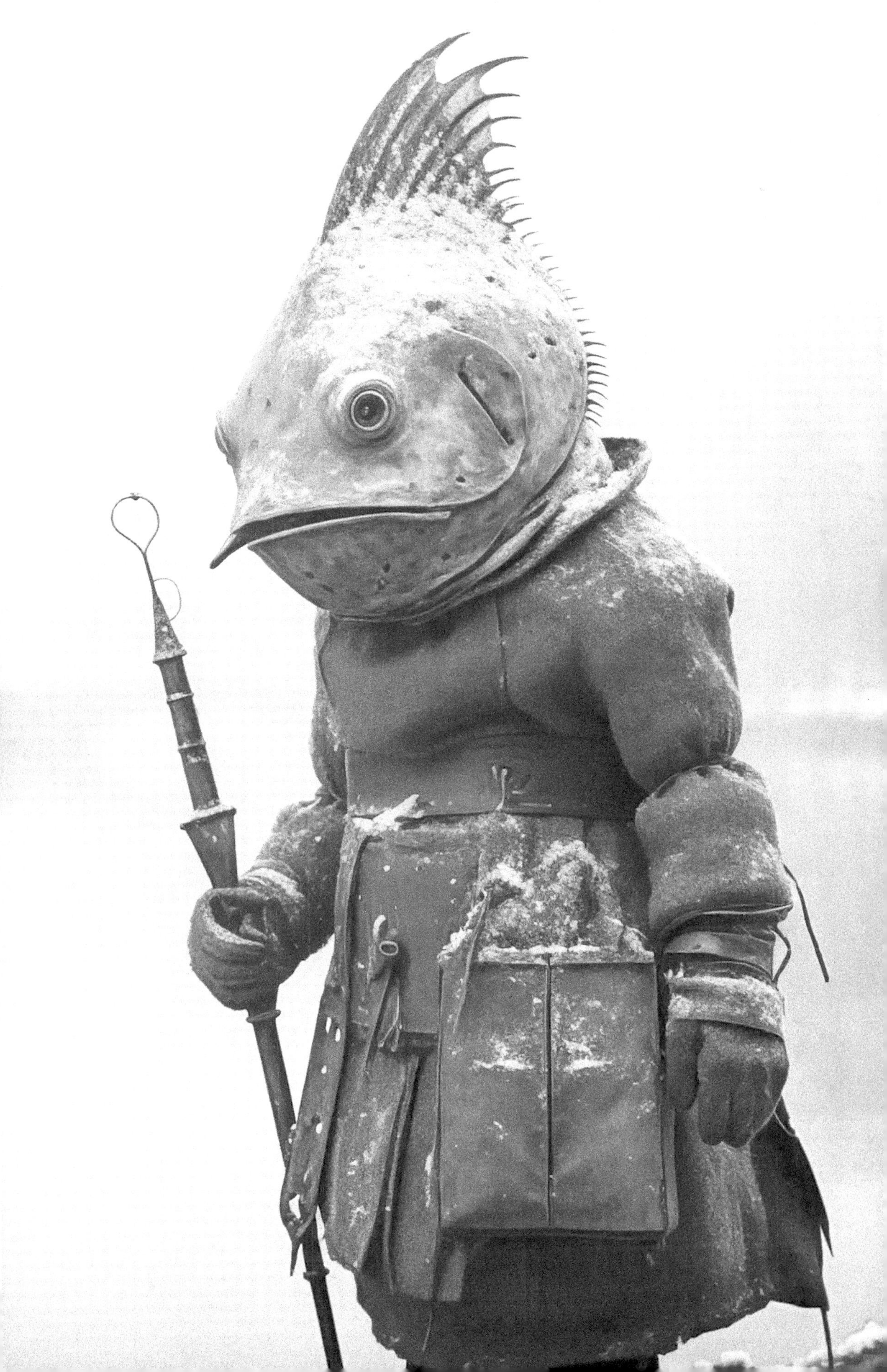

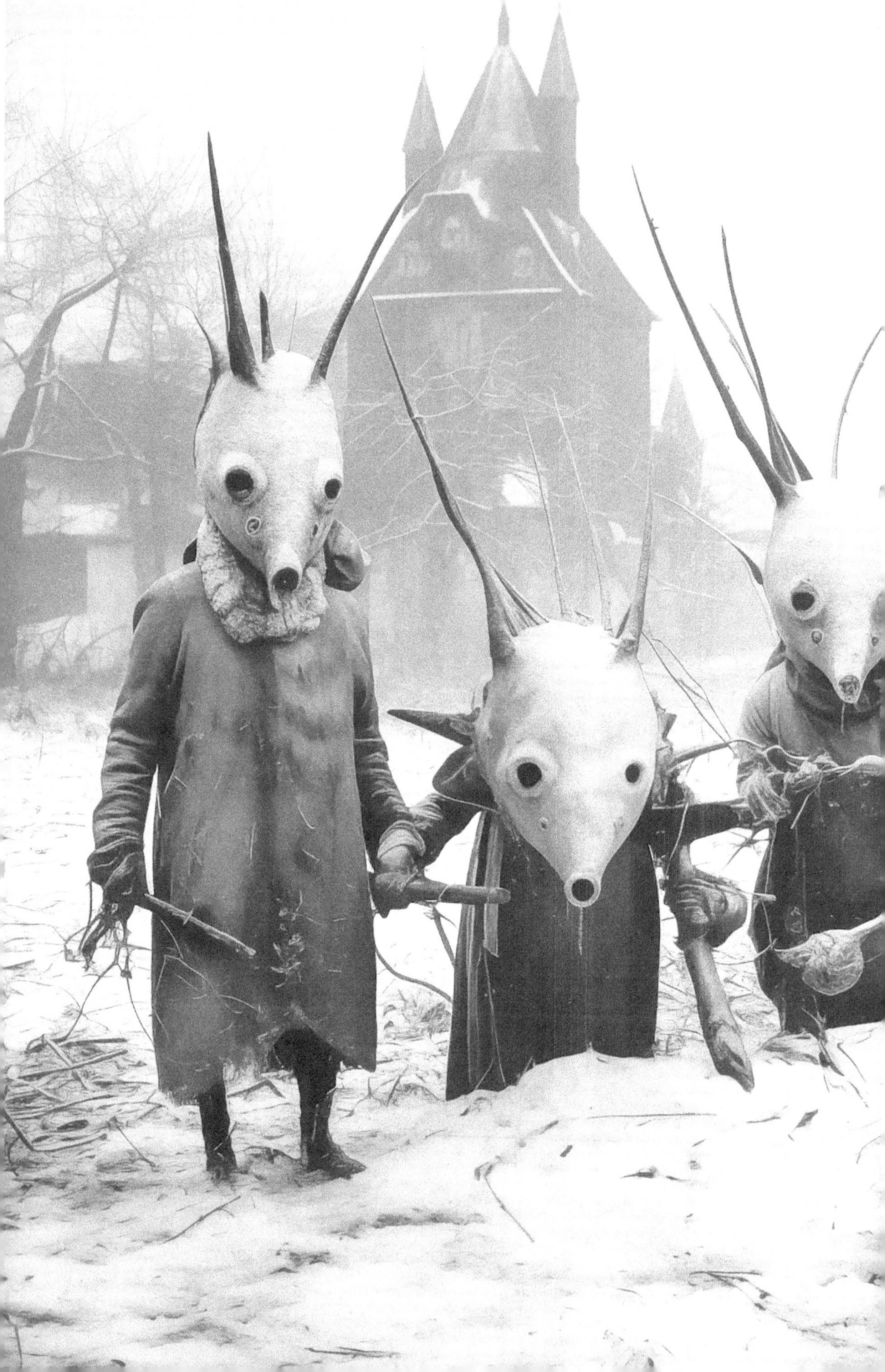

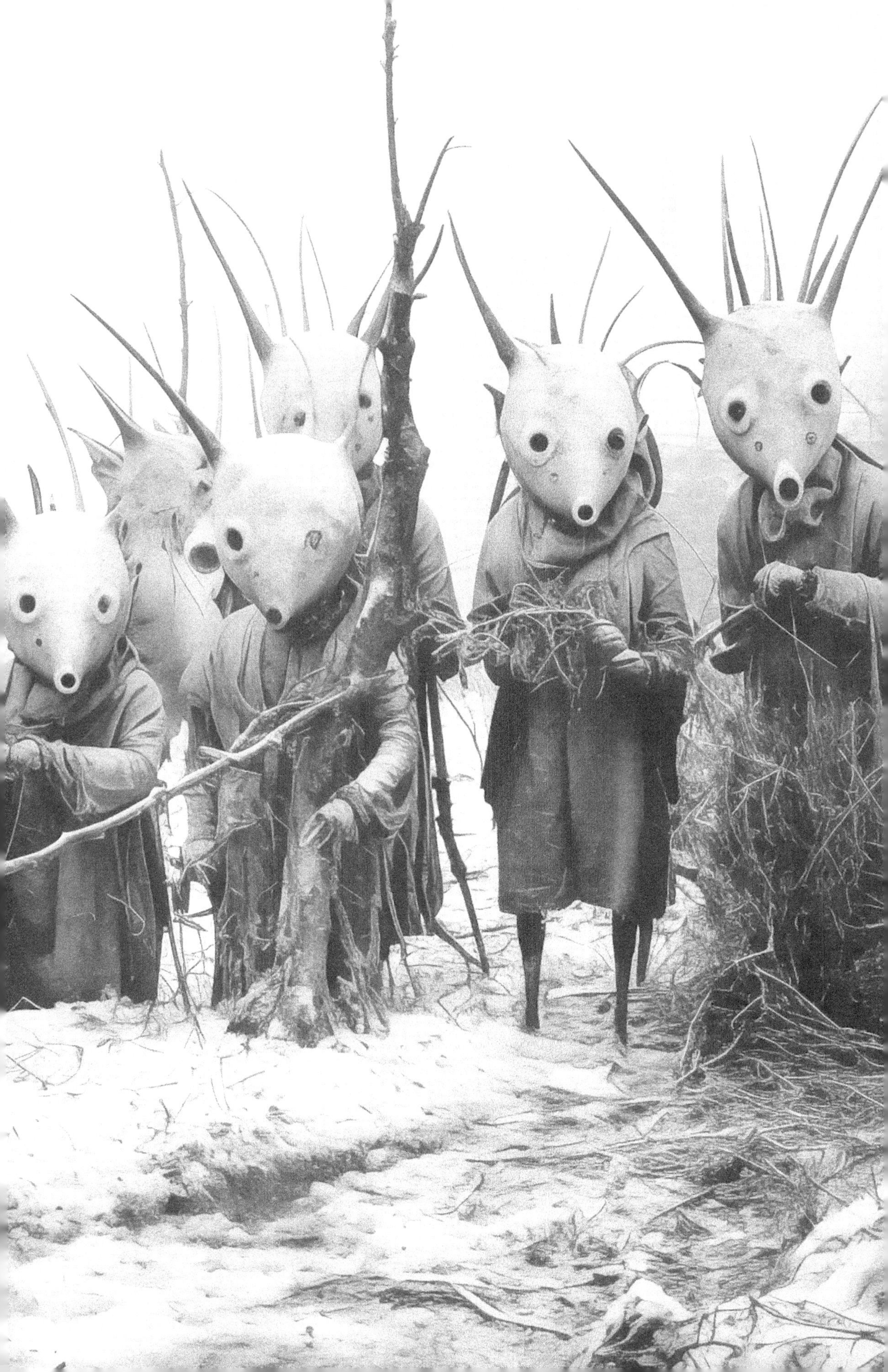

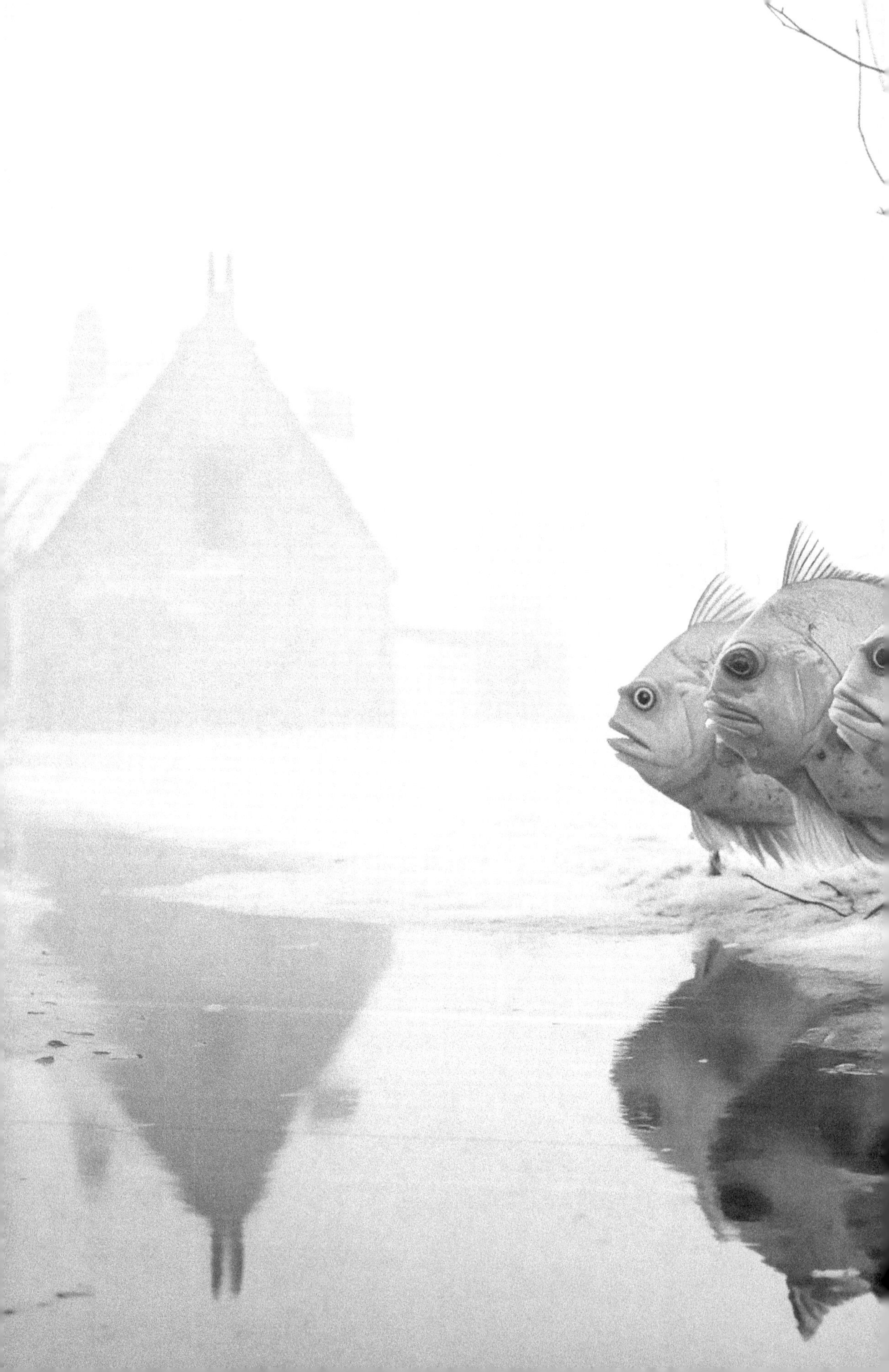

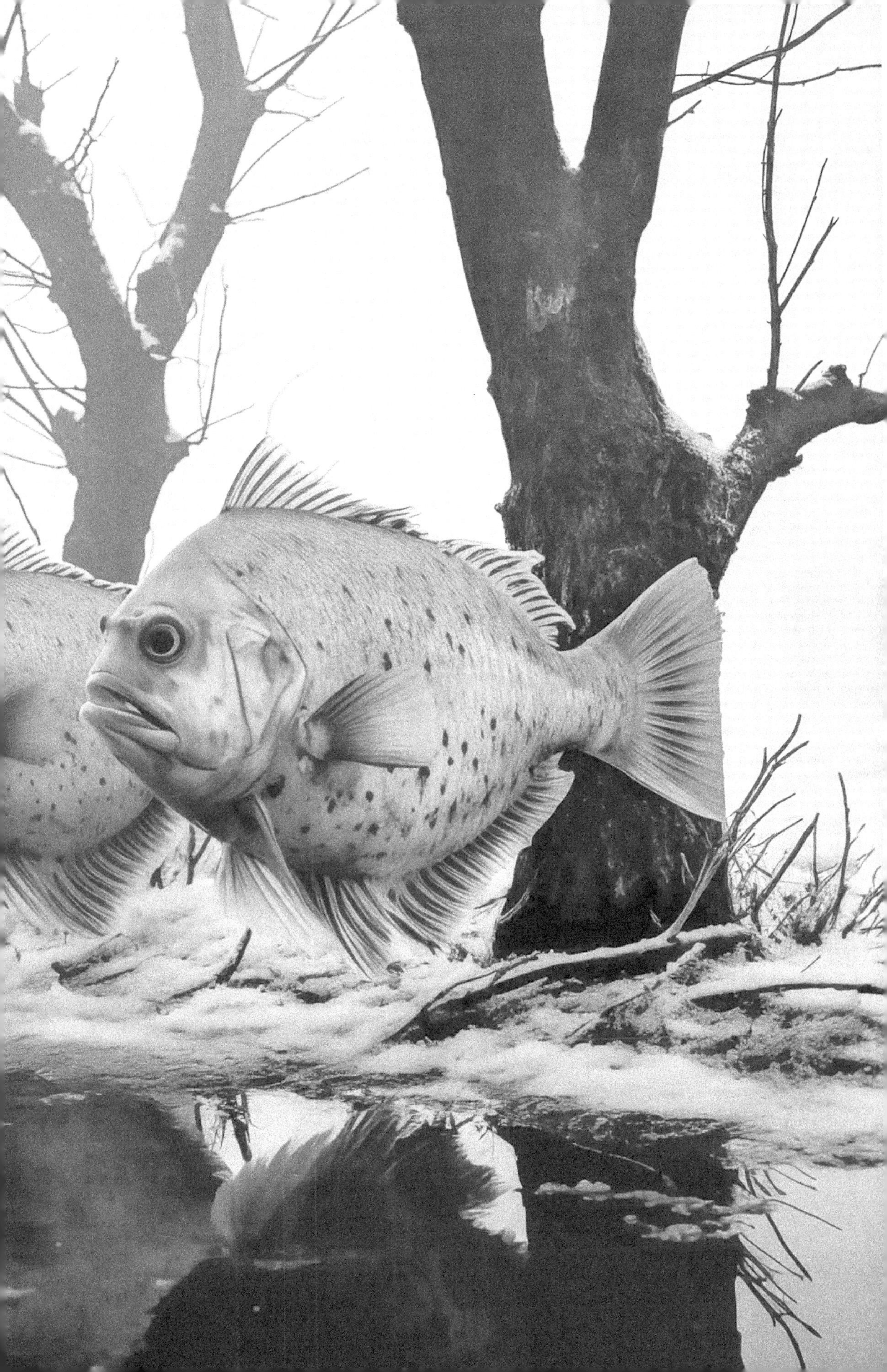

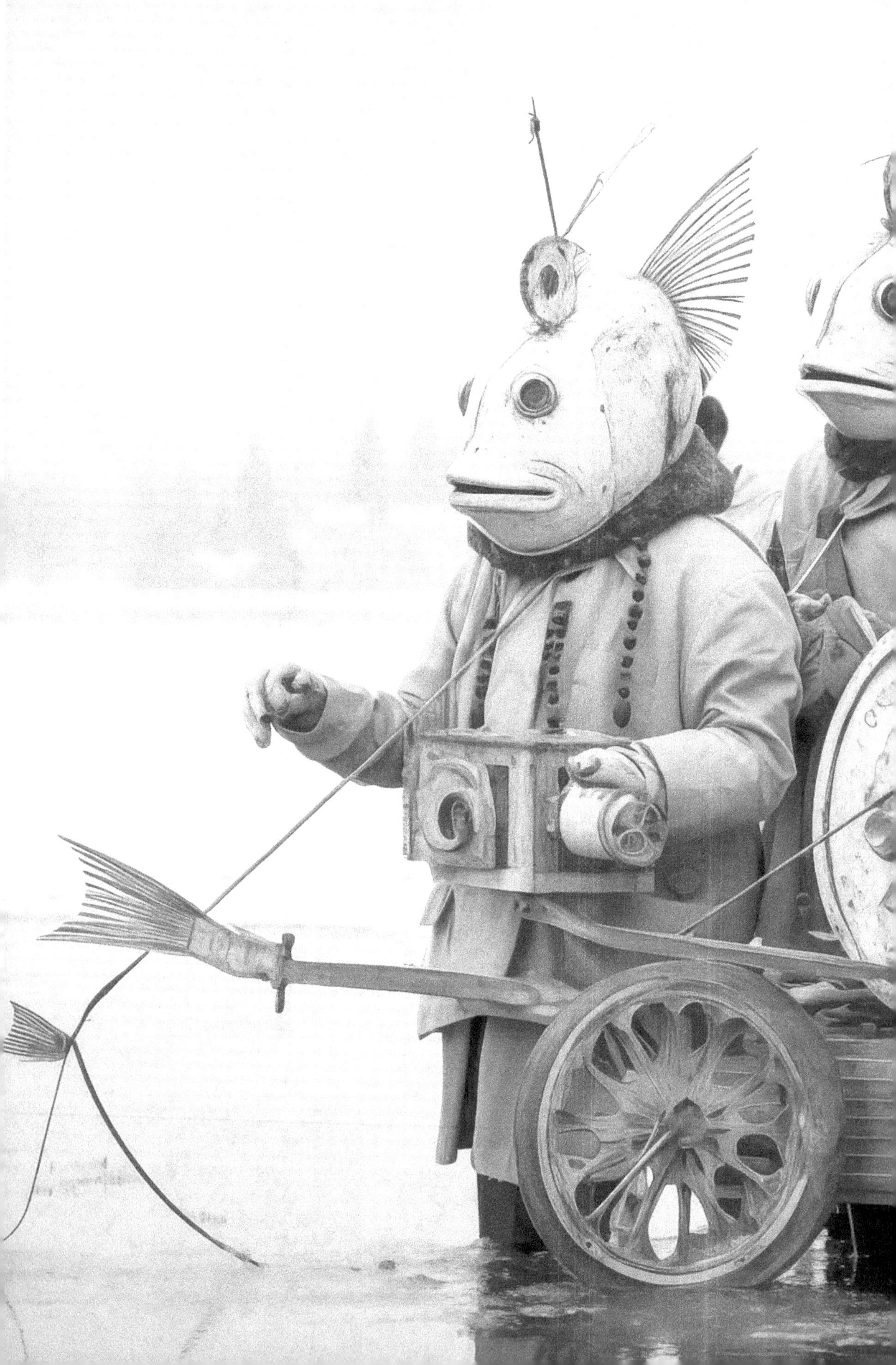

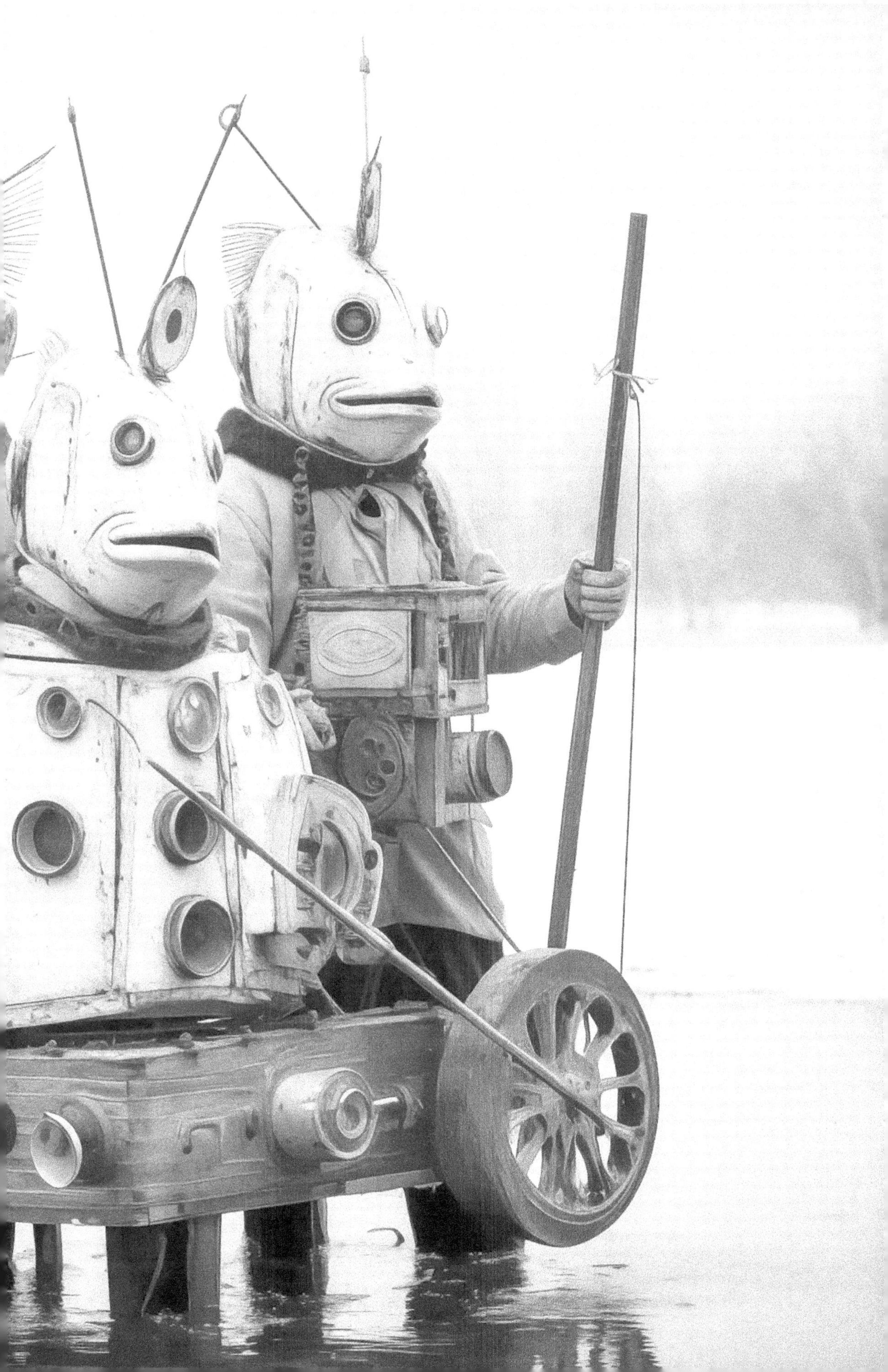

No one
to forgive our sins.

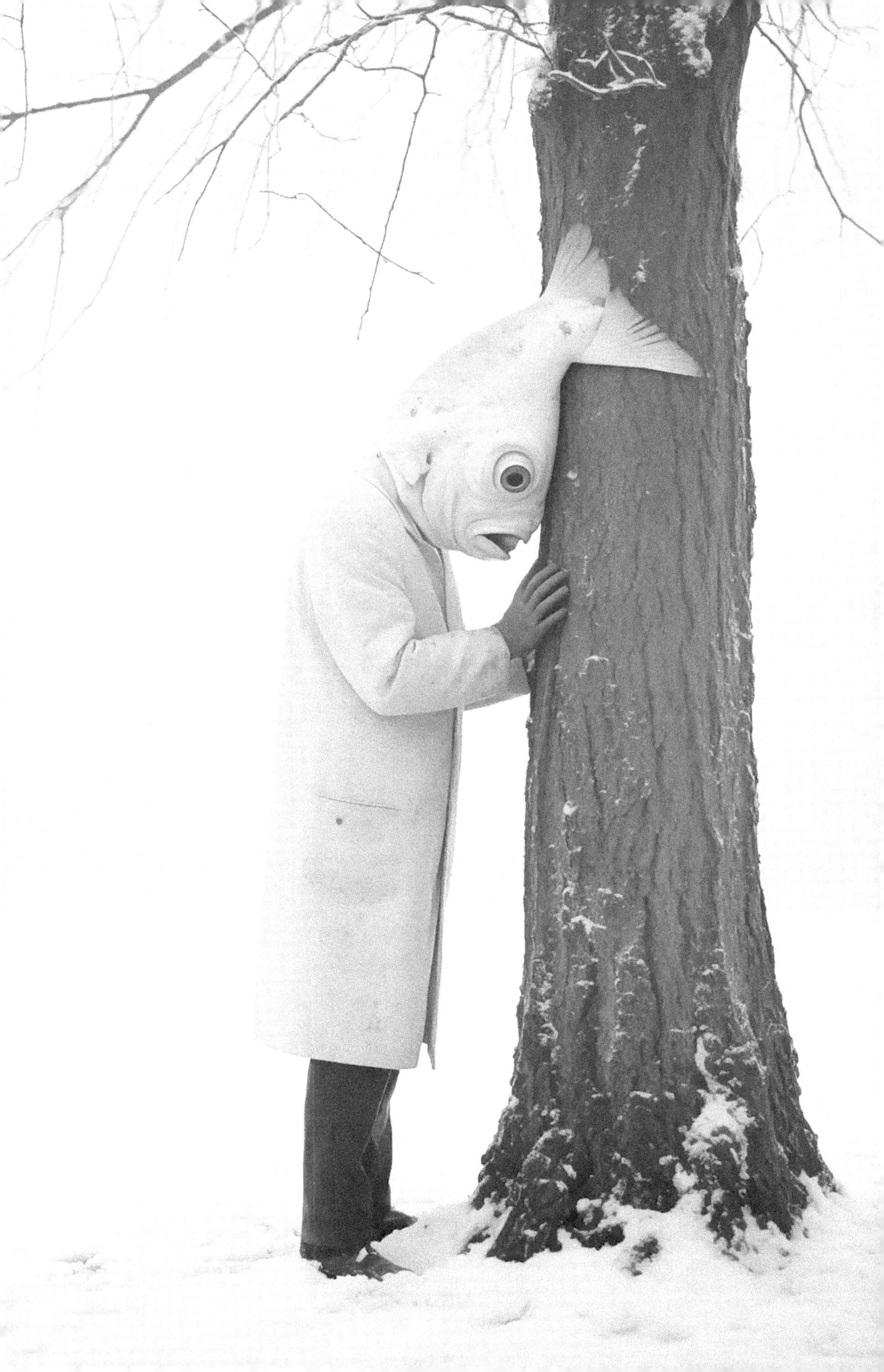

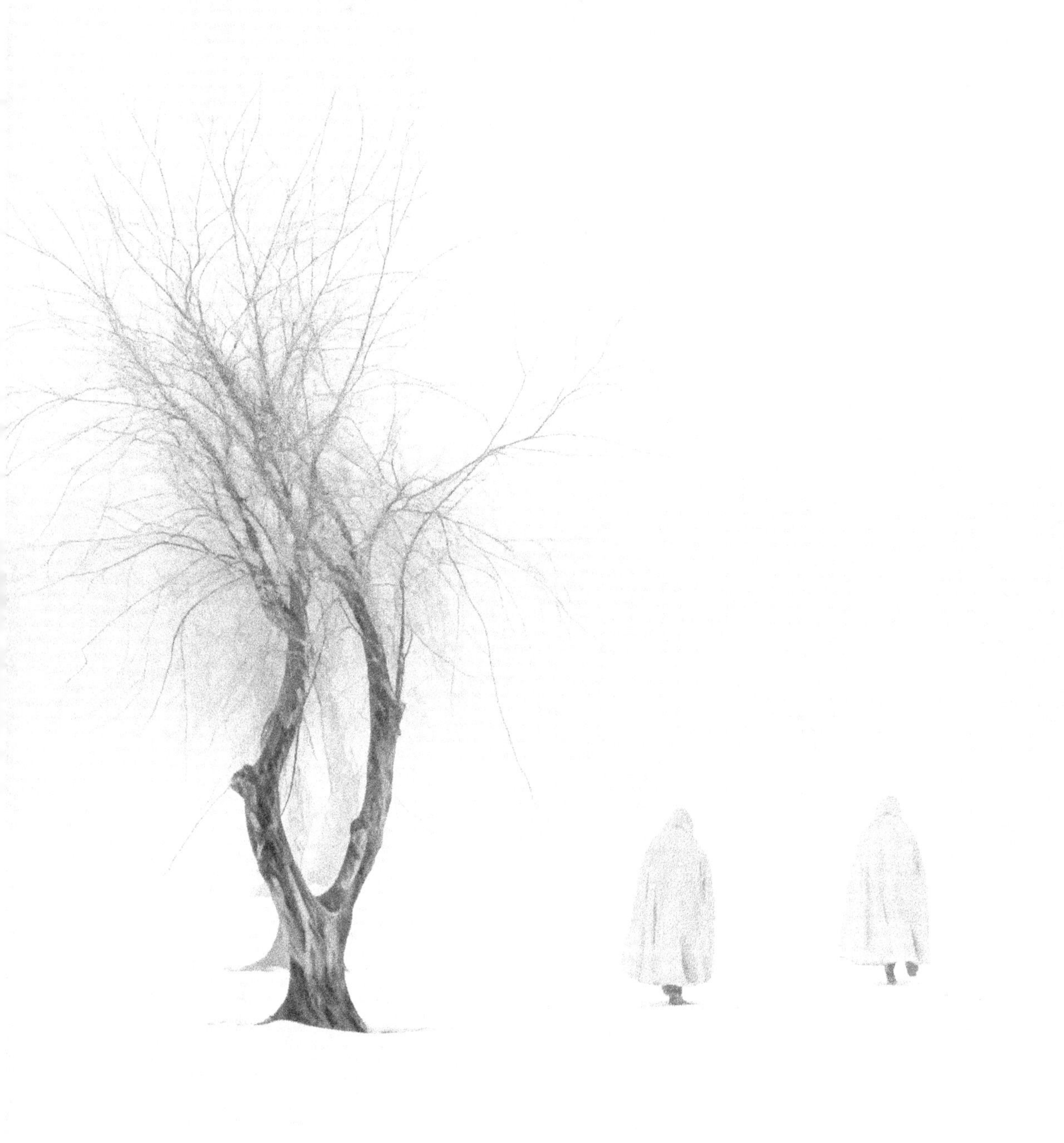

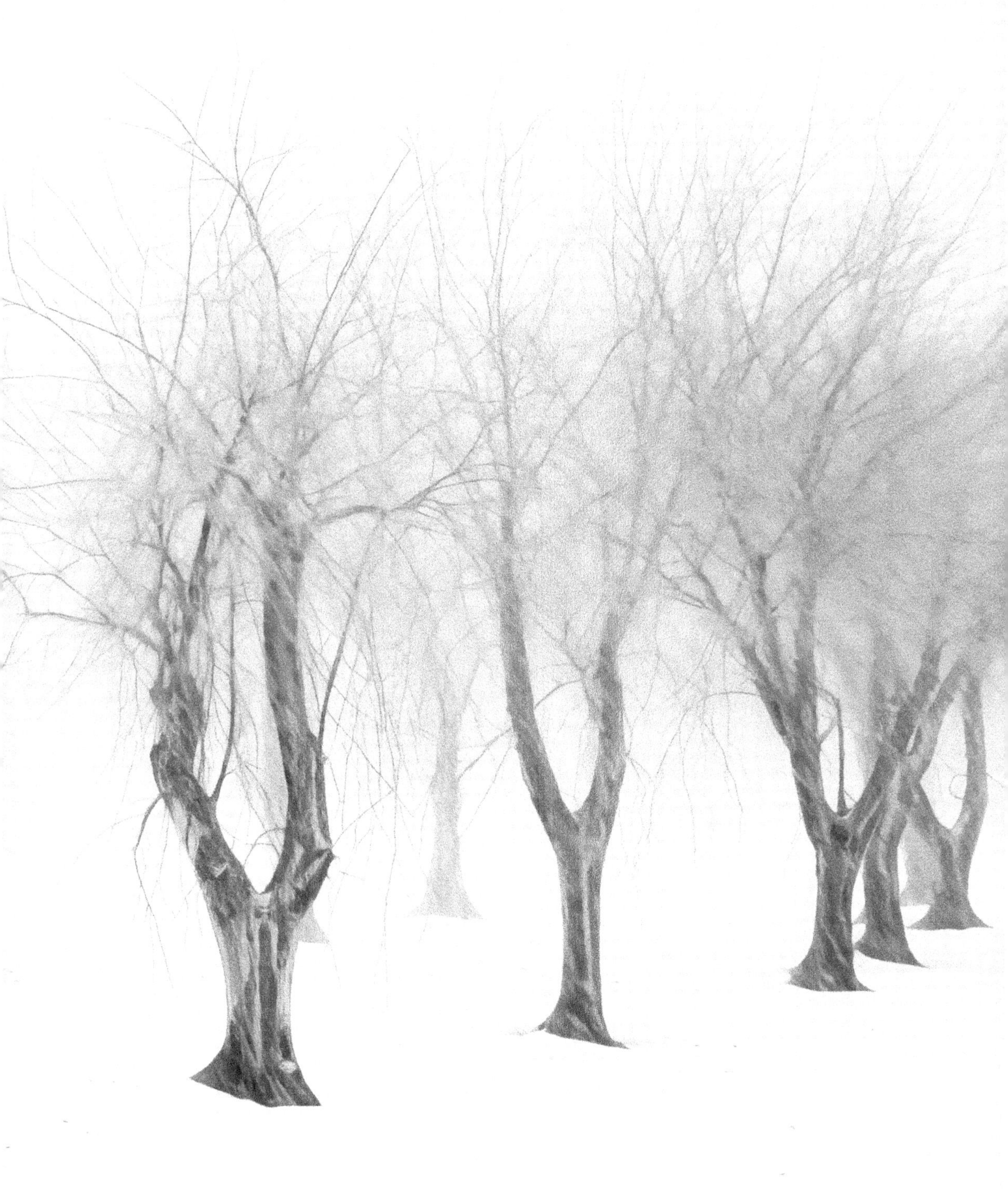

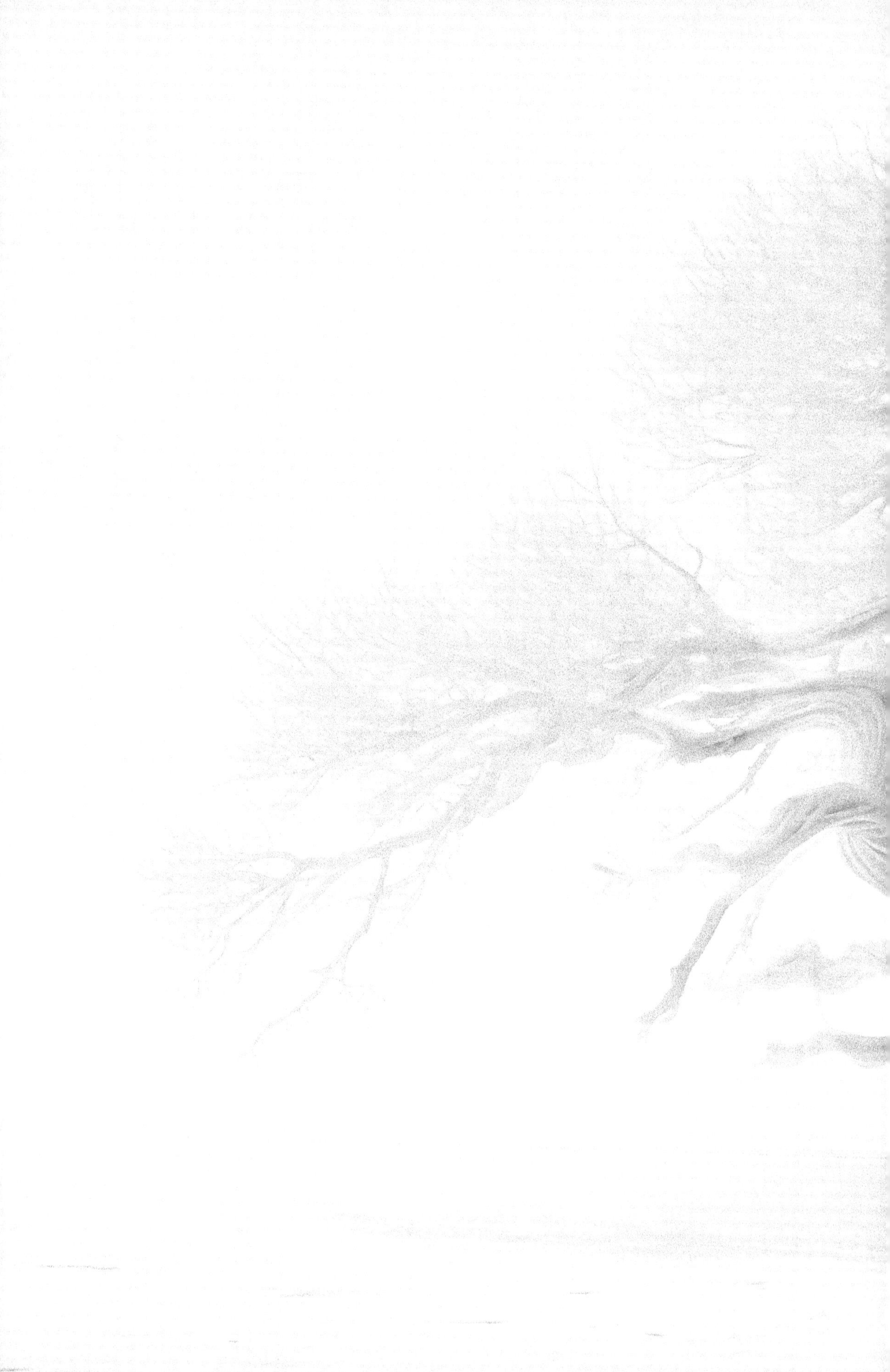

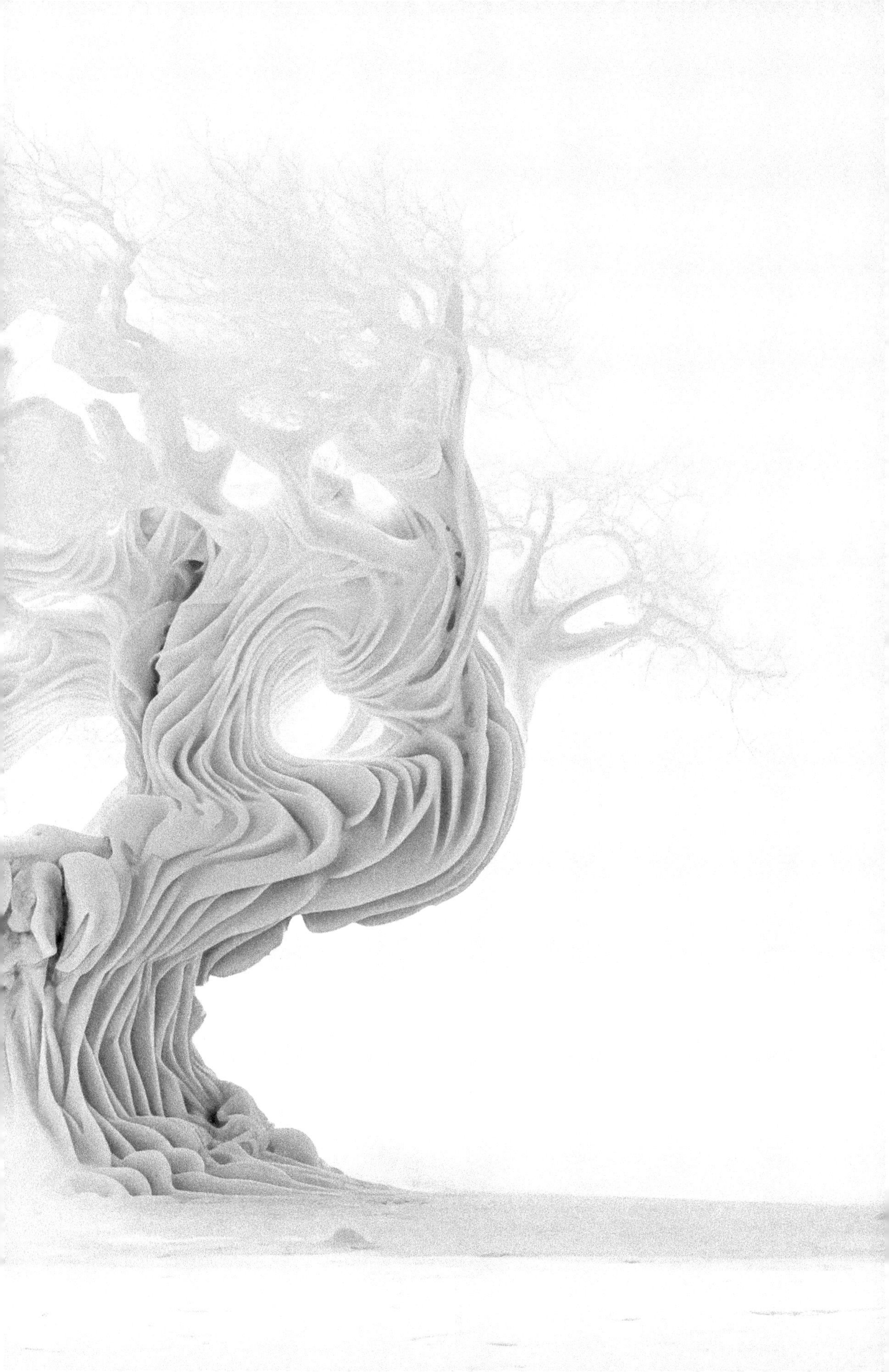

Time
to say
goodbye.

9 798871 331705